ALSO BY GABRIEL SHERMAN

*The Loudest Voice in the Room: How the Brilliant,
Bombastic Roger Ailes Built Fox News—and Divided a Country*

BONFIRE

OF THE

MURDOCHS

How the Epic Fight to Control the
Last Great Media Dynasty Broke a Family—and the World

GABRIEL SHERMAN

SIMON & SCHUSTER
New York   Amsterdam/Antwerp   London
Toronto   Sydney/Melbourne   New Delhi

Simon & Schuster
1230 Avenue of the Americas
New York, NY 10020

First Simon & Schuster hardcover edition February 2026

SIMON & SCHUSTER and colophon are registered trademarks of Simon & Schuster, LLC

Interior design by Wendy Blum

Manufactured in the United States of America

10   9   8   7   6   5   4   3   2   1

Library of Congress Control Number is available.

ISBN 978-1-9821-6741-7
ISBN 978-1-9821-6744-8 (ebook)

Let's stay in touch! Scan here to get book recommendations, exclusive offers, and more delivered to your inbox.

For Jennifer

For a son dishonors his father,
a daughter rises up against her mother,
a daughter-in-law against her mother-in-law—
a man's enemies are the members of his own household.

—Micah 7:6

CONTENTS

CONTENTS

BONFIRE

OF THE

MURDOCHS

PROLOGUE

O N THE MORNING OF SEPTEMBER 16, 2024, a convoy of black SUVs carrying the most powerful media dynasty in the world snaked through the Nevada high desert like a funeral procession, which in some ways it was. Rupert Murdoch had destroyed his family in pursuit of his life-long dream of anointing firstborn son, Lachlan, his successor. The final resting place was not a cemetery but the Washoe County Courthouse in Reno.

The reckoning had been nine months in the making. On December 6, 2023, Murdoch put forth a motion to amend the irrevocable family trust to cement Lachlan's control over a right-wing media empire that had shaped politics on three continents for the last half century. Murdoch's adult children from his first marriages—Prudence, Elisabeth, and James—united to stop him. The roots of the family war stretched back much further. From birth, Murdoch had pitted his children against one another in a Darwinian struggle to determine who would run News Corp, the global conglomerate Murdoch built out of a single Australian newspaper he inherited from his father. The rivalry played out in pull-up contests James and Lachlan did as children and in the competitive games of charades the family played at Christmas. This was much more than a boardroom battle: it was a blood feud to win a father's love.

Around 8:00 a.m., the first vehicle pulled to the curb and was surrounded by journalists: Prudence and her husband, Alasdair MacLeod, a longtime News Corp executive. At sixty-six, Prudence was dressed entirely in solemn black, which contrasted sharply with her shoulder-length platinum hair. Prue was the only child from Murdoch's first marriage to Australian flight attendant Patricia Booker. As the oldest sibling, Prue kept the greatest distance from the business and never entered the succession race. She settled into her outsider status after it caused deep pain. Years ago, Prue was devastated when Murdoch didn't mention her when he named his children in an interview about the succession. She called Murdoch screaming.

A moment later, Murdoch's second daughter, Liz, exited the SUV with her husband, the artist Keith Tyson. At fifty-six, Liz wore a beige suit with the poise of a businesswoman who spent decades fighting to be taken seriously. She was by many accounts the sharpest, but Murdoch subscribed to old-fashioned primogeniture and dismissed the child many considered to be the most worthy successor. Liz quit the family business in 2000 and launched her own phenomenally successful television production company. Despite this injustice, Liz didn't express bitterness. She tried to maintain close relationships with her dad and Lachlan. In the family geography, Liz thought of herself as Switzerland. The Nevada trust case forced her to finally choose a side.

Last came the person most responsible for this legal reckoning: James. He clasped his wife Kathryn's hand as they approached the domed courthouse steps. James, fifty-one, wore a dark suit and slim tie—a corporate look he once rejected. The family rebel, James was the moody kid with bleached hair, tattoos, and piercings who loved archeology and dropped out of Harvard to start a hip-hop music label. But Murdoch was the sun upon which this family orbited, and his gravitational pull was too powerful to escape. James returned to the business in the mid-1990s. He adopted a ruthless persona and ascended to become Murdoch's heir apparent. But James's centrist politics and desire to make News Corp respected in elite circles rankled Murdoch. In 2012, James presided over News Corp's London tabloids when journalists working for Murdoch's *News of the World* were caught illegally hacking the phones of thousands of people to land scoops. James denied knowing about the hacking, but nevertheless Rupert used the biggest scandal in the company's history to demote him and promote Lachlan.

In exile, James's resentments matured into a moral awakening. He and Kathryn, a climate activist, shared a conviction that Fox News was a threat to democracy. When Donald Trump supporters ransacked the Capitol on January 6, 2021, James declared publicly: "Those outlets that propagate lies to their audience have unleashed insidious and uncontrollable forces that will be with us for years." To understand his father, James turned to Roman history. He memorized passages from Marguerite Yourcenar's 1951 novel *Memoirs of Hadrian* about a dying legacy-obsessed ruler in search of an heir: "We were too different for him to find in me what most people who have wielded total authority seek desperately on their deathbeds, a docile successor pledged in advance to the same methods, and even to the same errors." James had come to Reno to ensure history didn't repeat itself.

Then came a gap—twenty minutes that spoke volumes about the family's fractured dynamics. The arrivals had been carefully choreographed by advance teams to avoid a tense curbside encounter. A white Audi SUV stopped, and Rupert Murdoch stiffly climbed out with his fifth wife, Elena Zhukova, trailed by a phalanx of security guards. At ninety-three, Murdoch walked gingerly in a dark suit paired incongruously with running shoes. This diminished appearance belied the vast power he still wielded through ownership of Fox News, *The Wall Street Journal*, the *Times* of London, HarperCollins, and dozens of tabloids including *The Sun* and the *New York Post*. Murdoch built something beyond a conservative news empire: a fourth branch of government. His propaganda machine monetized outrage, spread conspiracy theories, and shaped the minds of millions across three continents. More than anyone, Murdoch's media created the presidency of Donald J. Trump.

Behind Murdoch emerged Lachlan with his wife, Sarah, a former model and television host. At fifty-three, Lachlan was still boyishly handsome, though flecks of silver showed the passage of time. Commentators described the Murdoch family war as "Shakespearean." In this framework, Lachlan was Hamlet. In 2005, he quit the business after being abused by Murdoch's courtiers and returned to Australia to build his own media business. Only after a decade of his father's relentless courtship did Lachlan accept his chosen-son status. That morning, Lachlan walked into the courthouse fully committed to carrying forth the Murdoch legacy. When Liz made one final appeal to him last fall before the lawsuits flew, Lachlan's response had been resolute: Rewriting the trust was about "dad's wishes . . . It shouldn't be difficult or controversial."

The courtroom doors shut and the Murdochs disappeared from view. This was how Murdoch wanted it. He had incorporated his trust in Nevada because the state offered the most generous privacy rules. No reporters or cameras would be allowed inside. Even the existence of the court battle was supposed to be secret. The Washoe County docket referred to the case simply as "In the Matter of Doe 1 Trust." Murdoch amassed his fortune shaping narratives and was determined to control his own.

Once seated, the Murdochs waited for Washoe County Probate Commissioner Edmund Gorman to call the hearing to order. Family members exchanged furtive glances, noting the subtle passage of time on their faces. It had been two years since they gathered in one room. In that period, a family had disintegrated. But to understand how the most successful media mogul in history had engineered his own family's demise, the story begins almost a century earlier in Australia, when a lonely boy sought to win the affection of a domineering father in a place called Cruden Farm.

PART ONE

CONQUEST

CHAPTER ONE

THE BOY PUBLISHER

IT WAS INEVITABLE THAT RUPERT would see his family torn apart by a succession drama—his own father had imbued him with a sense of destiny seventy years earlier. Keith Arthur Murdoch was a brooding Scot with an anvil-shaped nose, furrowed brow, and deep-set eyes who understood that journalism shaped events every bit as much as politicians in the halls of power. The exploits that made him Australia's most infamous journalist would teach his only son two enduring lessons: rules are meant to be broken, and newspapers are power.

Keith suffered from a debilitating stutter as a child. It was sometimes so bad that he couldn't buy a train ticket and instead had to scribble his destination on a piece of paper and show it to the stationmaster. Perhaps because of this disability, he rejected a career behind the pulpit and set out to become a journalist. Keith gained fame during the First World War as a thirty-year-old foreign correspondent for the Melbourne *Age*. In 1915, the paper sent him to cover the British invasion of Turkey's Gallipoli peninsula. Keith was appalled to witness aristocratic British officers using Australian soldiers as cannon fodder in a hapless campaign to march on Constantinople. Keith evaded military censors and delivered an eight-thousand-word account of the "ghastly and costly fiasco" to Australia's prime minister. This dispatch would become known as Keith's "Gallipoli letter." His writing style crackled with righteous outrage, life-and-death stakes, swooping egos, and starkly defined heroes and villains—essential tabloid ingredients. "It depicted a very idealized sense of the Australian soldier being sent to slaughter by the gin-and-tonic-swilling Brits three miles off the shore," Rupert later recalled. The sensationalized scoop spurred Britain's prime minister, Herbert Asquith, to withdraw ninety thousand troops, thereby saving countless Australian lives. "It may not have been fair, but it changed history," Rupert later said of his father's report.

For the rest of the war, Keith remained in London mastering the dark art of tabloid journalism from the reigning Godfather of Fleet Street: the round-faced press baron Alfred Harmsworth, better known as Lord Northcliffe. (His enemies dubbed him "Napoleon of Fleet Street." To his staff he was simply "The Chief.") The notorious publisher ran the *Daily Mail* and *Daily Mirror* on the belief that journalism was about profit, not public service. "A newspaper is to be made to pay . . . Let it give the public what it wants," Northcliffe declared. "The three things that are always news are health things, sex things and money things," he told his staff. To that end, Northcliffe filled his papers with lurid stories of crime, sex, and trivia. In 1905, Northcliffe scandalized the British establishment by buying the prestigious *Observer.* Three years later, he incited elite panic when he snapped up the money-losing *Times* of London.

By 1914, Northcliffe controlled 40 percent of the morning newspaper market and 45 percent of evening circulation, a concentration of press power never seen before or since. Northcliffe used his vast influence to whip up anti-German sentiment among the British public before the outbreak of the First World War. He was also a rabid anti-Semite and published headlines such as "Why Jews Don't Ride Bicycles." But Northcliffe's power was waning when Keith arrived at his knee. The press magnate was increasingly paranoid and erratic. He brandished a pistol in the newsroom and told people Germans were trying to murder him with poisoned ice cream. In 1922, Northcliffe died at the age of fifty-seven, perhaps from syphilis. By then,

Keith had returned to Australia and, with Northcliffe connections, assumed the editorship of the *Melbourne Herald*.

Keith revitalized the struggling evening broadsheet with the Northcliffe formula: short articles, sharper headlines, and contests. Melbourne society dubbed Keith "Lord Southcliffe." But readers approved: the *Herald*'s circulation jumped 40 percent within a year of Keith's takeover. The board promoted him to managing director. Keith bought rival papers, magazines, and radio stations across Australia to create the country's first national media conglomerate. As successful as Keith was, the board refused to grant him significant equity in the *Herald*, which was a point of resentment. So Keith quietly used his wealth to buy personal stakes in newspapers in Brisbane and Adelaide.

By the late 1920s, Keith was among the country's wealthiest businessmen. He lived in a twenty-room Georgian manor that he decorated with antique Chinese porcelain. "I know you despise me for my love of money," he told an employee as he showed off the collection, "but how else do you think you could acquire such beautiful things as these?" The one thing Keith did not yet have was a wife. In 1927, at the age of forty-two, Keith noticed a photograph in a society magazine of an eighteen-year-old, almond-eyed debutante named Elisabeth Greene. A year later, they married. Keith purchased a ninety-acre property thirty miles south of Melbourne as a wedding gift. There, they built an antebellum-style mansion at the end of a long gravel drive lined with lemon-scented gum trees. Keith named his idyll Cruden Farm after the Aberdeenshire village of his Scottish clergyman father, Patrick. At midnight on March 11, 1931, Elisabeth gave birth to a son: Keith Rupert Murdoch. Everyone called the boy Rupert.

BY MOST ACCOUNTS, RUPERT was a lonely child. He spent many friendless hours on the farm hunting rabbits, shoveling manure, and riding his Shetland pony named Joy Boy. Sir Keith—he was knighted in 1933—was an absentee father to Rupert and his three sisters, Helen, Anne, and Janet. When Sir Keith did return home, he was often morose and withdrawn.

"Keith had little patience with Rupert and perpetually gave the impression of being disappointed," a childhood acquaintance said. Rupert discovered one subject earned his father's approval: newspapers. Rupert began hanging around the *Herald*'s newsroom. The fresh-ink smell, clattering typewriters, and rumbling presses enchanted him. On weekends, Rupert lounged on his father's bed as Sir Keith edited articles with a pen. "The life of a publisher is about the best life in the whole world," Rupert later said.

Whereas Sir Keith was aloof, Elisabeth was overbearing. Rupert recalled that his mother taught him to swim by throwing him in the pool of a cruise ship during a voyage to England. "I had to dog-paddle to the side, and I was screaming," he said. Another time, Elisabeth made Rupert sleep in a hut on the farm to "toughen him up." "Maybe they thought I was an old monster in those days," Elisabeth conceded. At other moments, though, Elisabeth indulged her son. She encouraged Rupert to spend time with her rakish father, Rupert "Pop" Greene, a hard-drinking wool trader and gambler. "He was always gambling on horses and cards . . . and had no idea of responsibility," Elisabeth said. Pop spoiled Rupert with ice cream and let him drive his car before his feet could reach the pedals. Sir Keith despised his father-in-law's corrupting influence. "It was one of my father's nightmares that I'd turn out like my grandfather, which I probably did, a bit," Rupert said. But Elisabeth also had standards—she would later be horrified by Rupert's tabloid sensationalism.

When Rupert was ten, Elisabeth shipped him off to the prestigious Geelong Grammar boarding school, Australia's analog to Eton. Rupert despised it. He was pudgy at a school that valorized competitive sports. Off the field, Rupert's wealthy classmates ostracized him. Rupert blamed the humiliation on his father's lowbrow newspapers. "I felt a loner at school, probably because of my father's position," Rupert recalled. Rupert also chafed under Geelong's strict military rules. He stashed a motorcycle off campus and snuck out to gamble on horses. Teachers flogged him with a cane when he got caught. "I can remember one particular Fascist type who let me have it with special brutal delight," Rupert said. The teacher's beating kindled in Rupert a general desire for retribution he later deployed against his media rivals.

Perhaps to fit in, Rupert rejected his father's conservatism and adopted the socialist politics in vogue among upper-class youth. Classmates mocked him as "Comrade Rupert." "Nobody took him seriously," said Richard Searby, a Geelong classmate who would spend decades working for Rupert. "It seemed incongruous that Sir Keith Murdoch's son could be a rampant socialist. It was, everyone agreed, just a boyhood aberration."

Rupert graduated in the spring of 1950. He wanted to skip college and work for the *Herald* immediately. Keith dismissed the plan and pulled strings to get Rupert into Oxford's Worcester College. Rupert was enraged. "My only palpable goal at that time was to change the world. And avoid going to Oxford," Rupert said. Rupert continued his left-wing rebellion there. He famously displayed a bust of Lenin on his dorm room mantelpiece, earning the nickname "Red Rupe." In letters to his father, Rupert lauded Lenin as "The Great Thinker." Once, Rupert found himself locked out of his Oxford dorm after attending a *Daily Worker* rally in London, so he slept in the local Communist Party office. A worker with a red-star cap entered and greeted Rupert: "morning, Comrade."

Rupert may have mastered *Das Kapital*, but he devoted little time to actual coursework in his chosen major of politics and economics. "I was impatient by then to get back home and start doing newspaper work," he recalled. At the end of his freshman year, Keith threatened to drag him back to Australia in disgrace.

Keith relented only when Elisabeth insisted he give Rupert a second chance. She warned her son he would lose her "last shred of respect" if he didn't shape up.

By this point, Keith had suffered two heart attacks and prostate cancer. He expressed fear that his callow only son wouldn't be ready to inherit three newspapers—the Brisbane *Courier-Mail,* and the Adelaide *News* and *Sunday Mail*—that Keith acquired through a holding company called Cruden Investments. "I can't afford to die. I've got to see my son established, not leave him like a lamb to be destroyed," Keith confided in a friend. In January 1948, Sir Keith dictated his last will and testament: "I desire that my said son Keith Rupert Murdoch should have the great opportunity of spending a useful altruistic and full life in newspaper and broadcasting activities and of ultimately occupying a position of high responsibility in that field with the support of my trustees if they consider him worthy of that support."

What Keith needed was a regent to groom his young prince. The job fell to the *Herald*'s London correspondent, Rohan Rivett. A ginger-haired and lanky journalist, Rivett was in his early thirties, but already a legend back home. He wrote an acclaimed memoir about his harrowing experience as a Japanese prisoner in the Burmese jungle during the Second World War. Rupert idolized Rivett like a surrogate older brother. He spent weekends with Rivett and his wife, Nan, at their country home an hour from Oxford. In the spring of 1951, Rupert joined the couple on an 1,800-mile tour to Austria and Switzerland. Rivett kept Keith apprised of Rupert's progress. "He will make his first million with fantastic ease," Rivett wrote Keith.

It was welcome news because Keith's health was deteriorating. In the summer of 1951, Keith took Rupert on a tour of the United States. They met Harry Truman at the White House and *New York Times* publisher Arthur Sulzberger at Hillandale, the Sulzbergers' Connecticut estate. Keith beamed that Rupert was finally showing maturity. "I think he's got it," he told Elisabeth. One October night a year later, Sir Keith sat on his bed to undress. He unclasped his watch and placed it on the nightstand when he felt his body convulse. The heart attack killed him instantly. He was sixty-seven. "It was so wonderfully easy for Keith, but so very difficult for all of us," Dame Elisabeth later said. Rupert got the news thousands of miles away in England and couldn't make it home in time for the funeral. For the rest of his life, Rupert seemed driven to prove his father's doubts wrong. "Some people live forever in the shadow of their distinguished fathers," longtime *Sun* editor Larry Lamb said. "Whatever else, Rupert was always determined that he would cast the longer shadow."

————

RUPERT WANTED TO RETURN immediately to Australia to run his father's papers. But lawyers needed time to sort out his father's tangled estate. Elisabeth, perhaps remembering her husband's own Fleet Street education, sent Rupert to London to finish his newspaper training with Lord Beaverbrook at the *Daily Express*. Born William Maxwell Aitken in Canada, the paranoid and ruthless Beaverbrook had supplanted Northcliffe as Fleet Street's ruling press baron. Beaverbrook's publishing philosophy could be summed up as Northcliffe on steroids. "The Beaver," as he was known, unleashed his papers to viciously attack enemies and advance right-wing causes. Evelyn Waugh immortalized Beaverbrook as the fictional Lord Cooper in his famous novel *Scoop*.

Fleet Street thrilled Rupert. He lived out of the Savoy Hotel and spent his days at "the Beaverbrook brothel," as Rupert called the *Express* newsroom. Rupert studied how editors filled each day's paper with gossip, sex, crime, and right-wing politics—a recipe Rupert would replicate with his papers. Rupert was having such a grand time, in fact, that he wanted to stay in London. He cabled his mother: "I'm staying."

But trouble dragged him back home. Rivett, now in Australia, cabled Rupert with urgent news: Keith's former employer, the *Melbourne Herald* group, was launching a Sunday edition of its Adelaide *Advertiser* to put the Murdochs' *Sunday Mail* out of business. Rupert saw it as retaliation because his mother rebuffed the *Herald*'s offer to acquire the *News* and *Sunday Mail*. "It made me angry. I thought they were trying to take advantage of my mother," Rupert said.

On September 8, 1953, Rupert, aged twenty-two, returned to Australia with one goal: revenge. Within days, he went to Adelaide to launch his first newspaper war against his father's former company the Herald Times Group. It was an inauspicious beginning. When he pulled into the *Adelaide News*, an attendant didn't recognize him and barked, "Hey, Sonny! You can't park here." Murdoch was accustomed to being underestimated. While others would see him as an opportunistic predator, ready to lay waste to whatever fell under his gaze, Rupert saw himself as a moralist, the enemy of entrenched, arbitrary power. Rupert and Rivett ran a front-page article about the *Herald*'s campaign to pressure Dame Elisabeth to sell. Rupert slashed newsroom costs and fought a nasty circulation battle that bled the *Herald* as much as it bled him. Rupert's pain tolerance was greater. After two years of steep losses, the *Herald* waved the white flag and merged the Sunday *Advertiser* with Rupert's *Sunday Mail*. Rupert's victory burnished his reputation for risk-taking. People began calling him "The Boy Publisher."

"Expand or perish!" was Rupert's creed. In 1955, Rupert leveraged the cash flow of his Adelaide papers to purchase a Melbourne-based magazine publisher and *The Sunday Times* in Perth. Then he snapped up newspapers in Darwin, Alice Springs, and the Northern Territory. In 1957, Rupert won a license to operate a television station in Adelaide. He began spending months in New York and Los Angeles to acquire the rights to broadcast American shows in Australia.

Rupert's personal life expanded, too. In 1954, Rupert met a blond flight attendant and part-time model named Patricia Booker. They were an unlikely match. Booker was four years older and came from a modest family. "I didn't know who Rupert Murdoch was, and I didn't really like him very much at all," she later said. She rejected his first request for a date, but his persistence won her over. They married in 1956, much to Dame Elisabeth's dismay. A daughter, Prudence, was born two years later. Unfortunately for the relationship, Rupert was an absentee father just like Keith had been. "I was totally involved in the business—probably very inconsiderate," Rupert said. Within a couple of years, it was evident the marriage was doomed. Rupert justified his parental failing as the price of conquest. He was about to move into the country's biggest and most competitive newspaper city.

IN THE LATE 1950S, two rival clans—the Fairfaxes and Packers—dominated Sydney's cutthroat newspaper market. Neither took Rupert from Adelaide seriously. Which was why the Fairfaxes sold Rupert the Sydney

Mirror tabloid in 1960. "I was amazed they agreed," Rupert said. "They were pretty sure . . . I'd collapse."

Rupert took command of the *Mirror* newsroom with a zeal bordering on messianism. He pushed his editors to out-shock the competition. "GANG RAPES GIRL 10," "PROWLER STRIPS WOMAN NAKED," "NUDE TOP IN BUS" screamed headlines. Editors even made up news whole cloth. When the *Mirror*'s foreign correspondent failed to file his dispatch from the civil war in Dutch New Guinea, the paper published a fictitious account under his byline riddled with racist clichés including descriptions of shrunken heads and cannibals. Rupert's anything-goes publishing philosophy horrified his status-conscious mother, Elisabeth. "Rupert, you must do something to rescue our name," she told him. In response, Rupert launched *The Australian*, the country's first national broadsheet.

Sydney life intoxicated Rupert. "In those days, I was doing everything to excess. Drinking, smoking, gambling, whoring, you name it," he recalled. In 1962, he fell for a nineteen-year-old *Mirror* reporter named Anna Torv. A steely blonde—half Estonian, half Scottish—Anna caught Rupert's attention when she interviewed him for the *Mirror*'s employee newspaper. "He was like a whirlwind coming into the room. It was very seductive," she recalled. Soon, they were a couple.

Rupert was racing forward at breakneck speed. In 1967, he divorced Patricia so he could marry Anna. It was a sad and bitter split. Patricia had a brief and tumultuous second marriage to a heavy-drinking Adelaide hairdresser named Freddie Maeder. The upheaval was hardest on their eight-year-old daughter, Prue, who felt neglected by her stepfather's fast lifestyle. "You'd get up and get ready for school and they'd say, 'No! Let's all go to the races!'" Prue recalled years later. "All children like to know where they are. If you get up and put on your school uniform, you want to go to school." Maeder burned through Patricia's divorce settlement by investing in a Spanish orange juice company. When the marriage ended, Patricia fell into a depression and spent the rest of her life supported by Rupert in a modest Adelaide flat.

Rivett would become another casualty of Rupert's unchecked ambition.

When Rupert arrived at the Adelaide *News* a decade earlier, he promised not to act "like a cocky bastard." Rivett returned his loyalty by making Rupert the godfather of his third child. For Rupert, though, promises were like inconvenient facts: fungible when they got in the way of profit. Rupert meddled in editorial decisions almost from the beginning, undermining Rivett's authority and causing staff to complain about "Rupertorial interruptions." After Rivett denied Rupert's request to put advertising on the paper's back page that was reserved for sports, Rupert simply waited for Rivett to go on an extended vacation and instituted the change himself. Rupert also watered down Rivett's coverage of a local murder trial because it undermined Rupert's effort to curry favor with government officials who approved lucrative television licenses.

In the summer of 1960, Rivett opened a typewritten letter from Rupert marked "personal and confidential." "After much long and tortuous consideration, I have come to the unhappy conclusion that you will have to step down from the Editor-in-Chief's Chair. Doubtless you would not agree with my reasons, which are many, so it is better not to go into them at this stage," Rupert wrote. As he reeled, Rivett noticed a glib handwritten note tucked into the envelope. "In coming to this decision to 'close your innings' as editor of The News I have not lost sight of all your achievements and our long personal friendship makes the whole thing impossibly hard. But here it is!" Rivett was blindsided by Rupert's betrayal. Rupert, though, expressed little emotion. He had already developed a spooky ability to cut off relationships that no longer served his corporate needs.

After Rivett's departure, Rupert shed what remained of his Oxford leftism. He developed an antipathy to unions and turned socially conservative. Rupert banned his editors from wearing collared shirts or suede shoes because he said they were only worn by "poofters," an Australian slur for gay men. Having survived Sydney's newspaper wars, Rupert was growing into a budding mogul. He bought a yacht named *Ilina* and a twenty-four-thousand-acre sheep farm in Cavan, about an hour's drive north from the capital, Canberra. "I had to admit it. I was a bloody capitalist," Rupert said. Toys were signifiers of success, but Rupert craved power above all. And to acquire it, he needed to leave Australia.

CHAPTER TWO

PERSONA NON GRATA

POLITICAL VIOLENCE CONVULSED THE WORLD in 1968. In twelve
tumultuous months, Martin Luther King and Bobby Kennedy were
murdered; American cities burned with racial strife; and nearly seventeen
thousand soldiers came home from Vietnam in body bags. Paris streets
flooded with student protests that seemed to augur another revolution. The
1960s had begun with such promise, but like Rupert, voters were moving
rightward. It was the perfect moment for a conservative media empire to be
born.

One night in mid-October 1968, Rupert was working late in his Sydney
office when a London investment banker named Stephen Catto called with
a life-changing opportunity: the *News of the World* was for sale. Founded in
1843, the weekly tabloid published lurid articles about prostitutes, criminals,
and scandals, earning the sobriquet "News of the Screws." The paper's voice
was an amalgam of voyeurism and Victorian outrage ("as British as roast
beef and Yorkshire pudding," its editor Stafford Somerfield declared). In the
1950s, circulation hit nine million, making it the most-read newspaper in
the world and its aristocratic owners, the Carr family, spectacularly rich. But
by the time Catto had called Rupert, circulation had declined by nearly three
million. The *News of the World*'s fifty-six-year-old chairman, Sir William

Carr, ignored the sinking profits and instead spent afternoons at the Savoy Grill working on a two-bottle-a-day scotch habit.

Catto told Rupert that Sir William's absentee ownership had ignited a civil war inside the Carr family. Derek Jackson, a disaffected cousin living in Paris, wanted to sell his 25 percent stake. Sir William couldn't afford to buy Jackson out, so Jackson offered his shares to the notorious left-wing publisher Robert Maxwell. Sir William was desperate to block Maxwell, a Jewish Czech immigrant and socialist member of Parliament. "This is a British newspaper run by British people. Let's keep it that way," declared a *News of the World* editorial, which noted incorrectly that Maxwell's birth name was "Jan Ludwig Hoch" (it was spelled Ludvik). Catto positioned Rupert as the Carrs' white knight who would prevent Maxwell from storming the gates. Rupert would buy 10.5 percent of *News of the World* stock and combine his share with the Carrs' 40 percent stake. Rupert jumped on a plane for London.

A few days later, Rupert and Catto sat in Sir William's town house pitching the partnership. The meeting took place in the morning, because after 10:30 a.m. Carr was usually drunk. Carr seemed amenable to Rupert's offer until Rupert, jetlagged and irritable after the twenty-five-hour flight, demanded Carr resign as CEO. Carr balked at a thirty-seven-year-old Australian dictating terms to a Fleet Street eminence. "Let Maxwell get it," Rupert said, and stood to leave. Carr's banker panicked and pressed Rupert to reconsider while he discussed the deal with Carr. Rupert waited in an adjoining room with a telephone, where he called Australian Prime Minister John Gorton to make sure he could legally take several million dollars out of Australia on a moment's notice.

The brinkmanship worked. Carr agreed to make Rupert a co-CEO. In return, Rupert promised that he wouldn't buy more stock, which would allow the Carrs to retain majority control. Sir William's wife, Lady Carr, invited Rupert to lunch at Coq d'Or in Mayfair to celebrate the pact. The meal was supposed to be Rupert's entry into London society, but it quickly went sideways. Rupert seemed impatient and lit a cigar before the first course arrived. Lady Carr left lunch worried about the Australian newcomer they let into the business.

Her fears proved prescient. Over the next few weeks, Rupert shredded every promise he made to the Carrs. He told Sir William he would stop Maxwell only if Carr named Rupert sole CEO. Rupert then secretly bought Jackson's shares to become majority owner. In March 1969, Rupert drove to Sir William's Sussex estate where he was recovering from heart surgery. Rupert told him he was no longer chairman. Carr was devastated. The *News of the World* had been in his family since 1891. Rupert had snatched it from him in just four months. "Yes, you hurt some feelings along the way," Rupert later explained, "but you do what you must do." Sir William died a broken man a few years later. Rupert offered to pay for a memorial service. Lady Carr refused.

RUPERT DIDN'T HAVE TIME to celebrate his victory. He inherited a struggling paper with a bloated and complacent staff. "It was an unbelievable mess. We would have gone broke with all the bits and pieces of rubbish they had," Rupert recalled. The biggest obstacle was *News of the World*'s imperious editor, Somerfield. "A pompous ass who sucked up to the aristocracy," Rupert said. Rupert wanted to fire Somerfield immediately, but that would require Rupert to pay out a huge severance. So instead, Rupert undermined Somerfield in the hope that he would resign and forfeit his golden parachute. Rupert replaced many of Somerfield's columnists, cut the paper's travel budget, and tore up a marketing campaign. Then, while Somerfield was vacationing in Spain, Rupert redesigned the paper's layout. Somerfield fired off an angry letter to the paper's board. "As Editor I am responsible for the newspaper and its contents," he wrote. Rupert responded with an ultimatum: "I didn't come all the way from Australia not to interfere. You can accept it or quit!" Much to Rupert's frustration, Somerfield didn't.

Even more troubling, *News of the World*'s circulation remained flat. On Fleet Street, single-copy sales determined a paper's profitability. Tabloids competed feverishly for exclusives so busy Londoners would buy them off newsstands. Rupert needed a scoop that would juice *News of the World* sales. In July 1969, Somerfield told Rupert he had a blockbuster. A down-on-her-luck former call girl named Christine Keeler was shopping a salacious memoir about her starring role in Britain's biggest Cold War sex scandal: the so-called "Profumo Affair." Several years earlier, British War Minister John Profumo had resigned in disgrace after the press revealed that he slept with then nineteen-year-old Keeler. At the same time, Keeler was *also* having an affair with a Russian spy. The story had it all: infidelity, sex, Cold War intrigue, and a government cover-up. Somerfield told Rupert *News of the World* should excerpt Keeler's memoir.

There was one problem: Keeler's book wasn't news. She had already published a memoir in 1964—*News of the World* even excerpted it. But in keeping with Rupert's philosophy that newspapers exist to make a profit, Rupert felt there was no shame in "telling a story twice," especially one filled with erotic details that would titillate readers. Rupert paid Keeler $50,000—five times the amount he ever spent on a story—for the exclusive publishing rights. He planned to publish Keeler's story in eight installments beginning in September 1969 right after Londoners returned from their summer holidays.

The whole thing blew up in Rupert's face. Politicians and journalists howled that Rupert was "cashing in on pornography." They blamed Rupert for needlessly humiliating a repentant Profumo, who had earned the public's admiration by doing social work in the slums of East London. "Jack Profumo has reclaimed his reputation so totally," a former leader of the House of Lords told a reporter. "It is quite revolting that some stale old stories are being published."

The blowback hit Rupert's bottom line. London's main private television station refused to air *News of the World* commercials. The Press Council, the newspaper industry watchdog, censured Rupert for "disservice to both the public welfare and to the press." Rupert remained defiant and blamed the criticism on jealous rivals. "People can sneer as much as they like, but I'll take the 150,000 extra copies we're going to sell any day," he said. The huge sales generated by the Keeler controversy proved readers shared Rupert's publishing philosophy.

But privately, Rupert was recalibrating. The Keeler debacle had taught him that Britain's establishment would never accept him—but it had also shown him something more valuable. The very fury of their reaction proved he had power. Every denunciation in Parliament, every sneer from the gentlemen's clubs, every letter of protest, was really an admission that he could make them lose their composure. And there was money to be made by making his working-class readers feel like the elites were trying to dictate what they could read. "Keeler—YOUR right to decide—vote now," read one *News of the World* headline.

The lesson wasn't to retreat—it was to be more strategic about when and how to provoke. If he was going to be an outsider forever, he might as well be the most successful outsider in Fleet Street history. And for that, he needed more than a struggling weekly. He needed a daily platform to wage his war on the British establishment.

THE CONTROVERSY SPILLED INTO Rupert's marriage. Anna, a practicing Catholic, was repulsed by the Keeler series. She also found life in London isolating. Rupert worked all the time, leaving Anna on her own to look after their infant daughter, Elisabeth. Anna and Prue had a fractious relationship. During a vacation at Rupert's sheep farm, eight-year-old Prue begged to come back to London with them, which Anna reluctantly agreed to. "Anna is a very ordered person," Prue said. "Everything was as it should be. You had to behave yourself."

Rupert's reputation made it virtually impossible for Anna to make friends in society circles. What could have been a grand adventure was turning into a private hell. Anna turned to writing as an outlet for her emotions. She dreamed of one day publishing a novel. But Rupert extinguished her nascent literary ambition when she asked him to read a short story. "What he said was so mortifying that I couldn't touch it again," she told a friend.

Still, she loved her husband and wanted people to see the man she had married, not the venal publisher that the press portrayed. In October 1969, Rupert's PR agent John Addey booked him on David Frost's television program to defend the Keeler series. "Be yourself. They'll love you," Addey told him. Anna also encouraged Rupert to go on, thinking that Frost would be a friendly interlocutor. Instead, she and Addey watched in horror as Frost skewered Rupert's self-serving rationale for publishing Keeler's recycled memoir. Rupert's temper flared. "This easy glib talk that the *News of the World* is a dirty newspaper is downright libel and it is not true and I resist it completely," he shot back. The nadir came when Addey jumped up and clapped at one of Rupert's attempted ripostes. "Your PR man is the only person who's applauded. You must give him a raise," Frost deadpanned. The audience laughed uproariously. Afterward, Frost sauntered backstage to invite Anna and Rupert for a drink. Anna seethed: "We've had enough of your hospitality."

Anna wanted Rupert to drive her straight to the airport so they could fly back to Australia. But Rupert wasn't one to cut and run. He would get revenge by buying the company that produced Frost's program and firing him. But before that, he looked for someone to blame. A few months after the Keeler debacle, Rupert fired Somerfield. "The son of a bitch led me down the primrose path," Rupert said. "I had no way of knowing what a stink publishing Keeler would create. I was too new to the scene." Having absolved himself of responsibility, Rupert cast himself as the victim. He complained Profumo's friends attacked him because Rupert dared to call attention to Profumo's sexual escapades that had jeopardized England's national security. The establishment was ginning up anti-Rupert hysteria to protect one of their own. It was corruption, pure and simple.

Rupert didn't wallow in self-pity for long. The ability to never look back was one of his superpowers. If he couldn't earn the establishment's approval, then he would win their respect by making himself the most powerful publisher on Fleet Street. The *News of the World*'s giant printing presses sat idle six days a week. Rupert had the capacity to publish a daily newspaper. Now he just needed to find one to buy.

IN 1964, THE INTERNATIONAL Publishing Corporation launched *The Sun*, an upscale, left-leaning broadsheet aimed at sophisticated young professionals who thought *The Times* was too stodgy. Its slogan was "born of the age we live in." But the experiment flopped. *The Sun*'s circulation started at 1.5 million and fell to 800,000 by 1969. After losing $30 million in five years, IPC was preparing to shut it down. Rupert found his takeover target.

In Rupert's analysis, *The Sun*'s failure was symbolic of everything that was dysfunctional with British journalism in the 1960s. Fleet Street had become too professionalized. Gone were the showmanship and mischief that thrived in the Northcliffe and Beaverbrook heydays. Rupert told anyone who would listen that British papers were "dull," "trite," "long-winded," and "edited for the benefit of each other instead of the public." Even the *Daily Mirror*, Fleet Street's reigning tabloid, introduced an "ideas" section. "If you think we're going to have any of that upmarket shit in our paper, you're very much mistaken," Rupert told a reporter. Rupert said newspapers needed to be "lively," "trenchant," "breezy," and "entertaining." Translation: sleazy and sensational. Just look at the *News of the World*, he argued.

Rupert knew he could make *The Sun* a success by transforming the broadsheet into a raucous tabloid. One day, while Rupert visited IPC's headquarters to meet its editorial director, Hugh Cudlipp, Rupert noticed a chart ranking the circulations of IPC's titles. The *Daily Mirror* outpaced *The Sun* by millions. Rupert walked over and flipped the cards to put the *The Sun* on top. It was a sign, not that any was needed by this point, of his ambition to make *The Sun* the most-read newspaper in the English-speaking world.

Unfortunately, Cudlipp had already made a deal to sell *The Sun* to Rupert's rival Robert Maxwell. Rupert used speed and creativity to turn the situation to his advantage. As soon as Rupert learned about the Cudlipp-Maxwell pact, Rupert secretly told the head of *The Sun*'s printing union that Maxwell was preparing massive layoffs. Rupert promised the union he would invest in the paper and save jobs. With Rupert's assurance, the union spoke out against Maxwell's offer. Cudlipp feared that selling *The Sun* to Maxwell would incite labor unrest at IPC's other papers. So Cudlipp sold *The Sun* to Rupert for a fire-sale price of $1.5 million.

Rupert had the paper. Now he hunted for his editor. In the summer of 1969, Rupert asked around and compiled a short list of seven editors to meet. The first was Larry Lamb, who ran the *Daily Mail*'s Manchester bureau. Lamb was a hard-drinking blacksmith's son from Yorkshire who lacked a college degree and carried a substantial chip on his shoulder to prove it. Rupert invited him for a discreet dinner at Rules, London's oldest restaurant. Over a meal of lobsters and three bottles of Pouilly-Fumé white wine—Rupert drank two—Rupert and Lamb plotted a glorious future for *The Sun*. Afterward, Rupert dropped Lamb at his hotel around 2:00 a.m. Lamb's room phone rang a few minutes later. "Bugger the short list," Rupert said. Lamb got the job.

The next morning, Lamb went to Rupert's flat in Sussex Square to hammer out a contract. Lamb bumped into Anna and marveled at how fast her husband moved. "He doesn't waste much time, does he?" Lamb said.

"No, not much," Anna said, smiling.

Lamb inherited a staff of eighty-five journalists, which was a quarter of the size of the *Daily Mirror*'s newsroom. What *The Sun* lacked in resources it made up for in esprit de corps. Rupert and Lamb framed the mission as a David vs. Goliath battle against the elites. "When I got *The Sun*, I was pretty much persona non grata in Fleet Street. A lot of people were looking forward to my failing with it. So I determined not to fail," Rupert later said.

The first issue was slated to appear on November 17, 1969. Rupert invited advertisers, journalists, and politicians to a launch party at *The Sun*'s Bouverie Street office. Virtually no one attended because Cudlipp hosted a rival party at the *Mirror*. Rupert's night took another turn for the worse when Anna pressed the ceremonial button to start the presses and nothing happened. When the first copies finally rolled off the presses three hours later at midnight, they were "visually crude, sloppily presented and virtually uncorrected," Lamb recalled. Cudlipp got a look at one copy delivered to the *Mir-*

ror party. "We've got nothing to worry about!" he declared. Cudlipp would regret his boast.

The inaugural issue was rough and riddled with typos, but its coverage reflected what readers *actually* cared about: sex, sports, and television. The first edition serialized Jacqueline Susann's erotic novel *The Love Machine*. Later issues ran articles like "Do Men Still Want to Marry a Virgin?" and "Men are better lovers in the morning—official." On the first anniversary of the relaunch, *The Sun* dropped the subtext and published a photo of a topless model on page 3. There was no grand strategy behind the decision. A *Sun* photographer had snapped pictures at a topless beach in the south of France and editors thought it would be fun to publish them. When Rupert saw the massive sales numbers for the issue, he told Lamb to do it again. Thus was born the infamous Rupertian institution known as "Page 3 girls."

The establishment struck back with venom. *The New Statesman* branded it "Rupert's shit sheet." The satirical weekly *Private Eye* gave him a nickname that would stick forever: "The Dirty Digger." In Parliament, MPs called for his prosecution. Local councils banned the paper from libraries.

Rupert derided what he saw as hypocritical elites. "If it's so objectionable, why are so many more people buying *The Sun*, tens of thousands of women included?" By the end of 1971, *The Sun*'s circulation doubled to 2.5 million. Within a few years, it surpassed the *Mirror* to become the best-selling tabloid on Fleet Street. Rupert wielded the success as a cudgel to hammer his publishing philosophy into British society. "I answer to no one but the public," he said. "They tell me what they want, and I give it to them." Rupert's war on the establishment was proving to be highly profitable. But it came with a price he hadn't anticipated: he was now a target.

IN DECEMBER 1969, RUPERT and Anna left London to spend Christmas in Australia, unaware they were in mortal danger. The trip was shattered when they got news that Muriel McKay, the wife of Rupert's deputy chairman, Alick McKay, was missing. London police soon arrested and charged Trinidad-born brothers Arthur and Nizamodeen Hosein for kidnapping and murdering Muriel.

Anna was terrified to discover that the brothers had intended to kidnap her. After seeing Rupert interviewed on David Frost's program, they hatched a macabre plot to abduct Anna and demand a £1 million ransom. The brothers followed Rupert's blue Rolls-Royce around London. Unbeknownst to them, the Murdochs allowed the McKays to use their car while they were in Australia. On December 29, 1969, the brothers dragged Muriel from her Wimbledon home thinking she was Anna. Muriel's body was never found. Police speculated the brothers fed her remains to pigs on a farm north of London.

Anna was horrified. Rupert, however, saw the kidnapping as an opportunity. He pushed *The Sun* to cover the story breathlessly ("MYSTERY OF PRESS CHIEF VANISHED WIFE" one headline screamed). *The Sun* became a character in its own reality show.

Anna wanted to leave England. Luckily, Rupert also wanted to quit London. He had proved his publishing philosophy worked, but Britain would never offer him anything more than profitable notoriety. There he'd always be "The Dirty Digger." In America, an outsider with enough audacity could rewrite the rules of power itself.

CHAPTER THREE

"I CAN'T LOSE"

WITH PROFITS POURING IN FROM *The Sun* and *News of the World*, Rupert enacted his battle plan to invade the United States. In the summer of 1973, he and Anna moved into a Fifth Avenue penthouse on Manhattan's Upper East Side in a building whose current and past residents included Laurence Rockefeller, Frank Jay Gould, and Elizabeth Arden. The Murdochs decorated the duplex with old-world elegance, filling eighteenth-century Chippendale bookcases with seventeenth-century china. Two brown velvet couches flanked the mantel. The twelve-room apartment had plenty of square footage for the growing family. Elisabeth and Prudence were joined by two brothers. Anna had given birth to Lachlan in September 1971 and James in December 1972. The chessboard for Rupert's dynastic game was set.

But the succession drama wouldn't play out for decades. In the early 1970s, Rupert was still focused on expanding his empire. Based on previous visits to New York, Rupert expressed confidence that the American media was ripe for disruption. He told friends that American newspapers were "elitist," "achingly dull," and a "waste of the reader's time." Furthermore, the industry was mired in a recession brought on by soaring newsprint costs, labor strife, and competition from television news. Dozens of dailies closed or were acquired by corporate chains such as Gannett and Knight Ridder.

Rupert briefly considered purchasing *The Washington Star*, the scrappy rival to *The Washington Post*, but balked at the *Star*'s $35 million asking price.

Around this time, the Australian tennis star John Newcombe, who was developing a resort near San Antonio, told Rupert that a local newspaper owner named Houston Harte wanted to sell a pair of dailies in San Antonio. To most people, America's fifteenth-largest city seemed like an inauspicious place to plant a flag. Rupert didn't think so. He had started his company in overlooked places like Adelaide, Perth, and Darwin. "You take what you can get," he once said. At a minimum, Rupert could use San Antonio as a laboratory to test Americans' appetite for his brand of tabloid journalism.

Rupert met Harte at the Continental Airlines ticket counter in the San Antonio airport one morning in the fall of 1973. He signed a contract to buy the morning *San Antonio Express* and evening *San Antonio News*, plus a combined Sunday edition, for $19.7 million. The *Express* generated a modest profit, so Rupert focused on transforming the *News*. San Antonians soon opened their papers to headlines like "AX ATTACKER KILLS SLEEPER." The largest school district canceled a program to distribute six thousand newspapers to students after teachers complained that articles were too graphic to be used as "classroom tools."

Rupert ignored the critics because circulation—the only feedback he cared about—shot up 25 percent. "The bottom line in this business is to make money," he said at the time. "If those who attacked me had their way, there would be no newspapers." Unfortunately, newspaper profits in the United States relied on advertising revenue, not single-copy sales, as was the case in Britain. San Antonio businesses didn't want to advertise alongside articles about misery and mayhem. The *News* actually lost *more* ad revenue under Rupert's ownership that year.

The struggles in San Antonio didn't slow Rupert's forward march. After failing to buy the *National Enquirer*, he launched his own supermarket tabloid, *The National Star*. In the run-up to the *Star*'s debut in the winter of 1974, Rupert descended on the paper's Manhattan newsroom staffed with

Australian and British tabloid veterans to mock up pages and rewrite headlines. His perpetual five o'clock shadow and lidded eyes gave him a swarthy, Nixonian air. Rupert spent $5 million on a television ad campaign for the *Star*, but it failed to generate profit. "We're not interested in the publishing judgment of Madison Avenue or professors of journalism," Rupert declared at a press conference. His bravado couldn't hide the fact that, two years in, his American incursion was failing.

RUPERT'S FORTUNES TURNED UPWARD in the winter of 1974. At a dinner party hosted by *Washington Post* publisher Katharine Graham, Rupert befriended Clay Felker, then the most influential editor in Manhattan. Felker founded *New York* magazine in 1968 with a masthead of star journalists including Tom Wolfe, Gloria Steinem, and Jimmy Breslin. Felker's weekly functioned more like an old-time Hollywood studio than a magazine. His ambitious writers constantly jockeyed for his attention. "Do you want to be a star?" Felker would ask a new writer he wanted to induct into his stable. It was an effective management tactic. *New York* writers churned out a remarkable number of zeitgeist-defining features that chronicled the triumphs, feuds, and flameouts of the city's ruling class. "Clay's real interest," Wolfe once said, "was status and how it operates in New York."

Like Rupert, Felker was an outsider, though from much humbler roots. Felker's parents, both journalists, raised him in Webster Groves, Missouri. Yet the forty-eight-year-old Felker positioned himself as the sophisticate in their relationship, treating the wealthy Australian as his eager pupil. "[Clay] explained Manhattan things to Rupert who he clearly saw as a bit of a rube," *New York* journalist Susan Braudy recalled after observing the two at a dinner.

Felker's tutorials were comprehensive: which writers the *Star* should hire, which restaurants Rupert and Anna should frequent, which Manhattan private schools the Murdoch children should attend. When Rupert wondered where New Yorkers spent the summer, Felker steered him toward the Hamptons.

Felker was generous with his guidance because he wanted something in return: lessons in the art of dealmaking. He had recently acquired *The Village Voice* and was planning to launch *New West*, a sophisticated California weekly. "The way to operate is with OPM—other people's money," Rupert explained.

It was surprising they bonded so quickly given their stark differences. Rupert operated with catlike cunning and could be painfully shy in social situations; Felker was a world-class kibitzer with a booming voice. Rupert hailed taxis and wore knockoff suits imported from Hong Kong; Felker traveled by limo and dressed in bespoke shirts from Turnbull & Asser of Jermyn Street. But beneath these surface contrasts lay a deeper kinship: both men were fascinated by power and saw their friendship as a means to acquire more of it.

TO WIELD REAL POWER in America—the market-moving and election-swaying kind—you needed to own a Manhattan newspaper or television network. In the early 1970s, New York's media establishment viewed Rupert as a carpetbagging schlockmeister, if they paid attention to him at all. His chances of buying a prestige media asset were virtually zero. But Felker's connections changed everything.

In the summer of 1974, Felker connected Rupert with the *New York Post*'s platinum-haired owner, Dorothy Schiff, known by everyone as Dolly. The seventy-one-year-old banking heiress turned crusading liberal was an eccentric character straight out of Tom Wolfe's seminal *New York* feature "Radical Chic." Schiff chain-smoked Kools from a white cigarette holder, married and divorced four times, and carried on a well-publicized affair with Franklin Roosevelt. "Everything about his body—except his legs—was so strong," she wrote in her memoir.

Schiff's operatic personal life didn't interfere with her steel-spined commitment to hard-hitting journalism. In the 1950s, the *Post* published a seventeen-part exposé on Senator Joe McCarthy at the zenith of the Red Scare. With Schiff's financial support, the *Post* was the only afternoon daily to survive New York's crippling newspaper strike of 1962–63. By the mid-1970s, however, her tolerance for sustaining endless losses had waned. Felker advised Rupert that Schiff would soon be ready to sell.

Felker greased the deal by hosting lunches for Rupert and Schiff at his East Hampton beach house that summer. Though almost incapable of small talk, Rupert could be deadly charming when pursuing a deal. He flattered Schiff by echoing her sentiment that *The New York Times* was arrogant and overrated. He claimed to share her progressive politics. He even noted they had the same birthday—March 11.

Schiff rejected Rupert's first offer. Felker advised patience. A few months later, Schiff's lawyers warned she faced a crushing tax bill if she passed the paper to her children. In September 1976, Schiff invited Rupert to lunch at her office in the *Post*'s Lower Manhattan headquarters. "I sensed she was very tired," Rupert later recalled. As they finished roast beef sandwiches, Rupert reminded her that he still wanted the *Post*. This time, Schiff said she would consider it.

But weeks passed without an answer. Growing annoyed, Rupert pounced on another opportunity—if only to pressure Schiff into deciding. In October 1976, he made an offer for one of the trophies of British journalism: *The Observer*. When Schiff heard, she panicked and called Rupert asking him to make an offer for the *Post*. On November 20, 1976, they settled on $31 million. "I may have paid too much for it, but it was the chance of my lifetime," Rupert later told Felker.

On the night the deal closed, Rupert celebrated with Felker at Elaine's, the Upper East Side haunt of the city's media and political elite. "You did it! You fucking did it!" Elaine Kaufman, the restaurant's brassy owner, cheered from behind the bar when Rupert walked in. Rupert took a seat at Felker's table with Felker's girlfriend, journalist Gail Sheehy; columnist Pete Hamill; Hamill's girlfriend, actress Shirley MacLaine; and Lazard banker Felix Rohatyn. There was much to look forward to. Later that winter, Rupert and Anna planned to go skiing in Switzerland with Felker and Sheehy. The trip never happened. Within weeks, their friendship imploded.

THE FUSE WAS LIT the night the *Post* deal closed. On the cab ride home from their triumphal dinner, Rupert vented to Felker that British journalists were protesting his bid for *The Observer*. The paper's Australian television critic, Clive James, was quoted in *The Sunday Times* saying: "Rupert Murdoch was one of the main reasons that people like me have come 12,000 miles to work in Britain." Feeling abused again by the London establishment, Rupert told Felker he was withdrawing his bid for *The Observer*.

Felker confided that he, too, was feeling disrespected. At a board meeting that summer, he had broken down when *New York*'s directors wouldn't give him a raise. "You've all got houses in East Hampton! You don't know what it's like to come up from the bottom!" he had shouted through tears. "You don't know what it's like to come from Webster Groves, Missouri, and make it in New York!" As the cab neared Rupert's apartment, Felker asked if Rupert could help him with his board troubles. "You've had a lot of experience with these things. Maybe you can give me some advice," Felker said.

The two met for lunch a week later in *New York*'s private dining room. What happened next would be fiercely disputed for years. Depending on whose version you believed, the unfolding melodrama was either a story of Rupert's ruthless treachery or Felker's tragic naivete about how dealmaking actually worked. According to Rupert, Felker asked him to buy out his antagonists on the board. "Clay let on that he might be looking for a buyer," Rupert later recalled. Felker vehemently disputed this. "I was asking personal advice on how to get out from under these guys," he said. Whatever the case, Rupert left lunch with his next takeover target.

Without telling Felker, Rupert instructed his investment banker, Stanley Shuman of Allen & Company, to explore a deal. Shuman called *New York*'s chairman, financier Alan Patricof, and asked if the board members would be open to selling to Rupert. The key, Patricof explained, would be winning over Carter Burden, a mercurial city council member and Vanderbilt heir who owned 24 percent of the stock. While Shuman courted Burden, Rupert wrestled with what to do about Felker. He was grateful for Felker's help engineering the *Post* deal, but he also thought Felker was reckless with money and couldn't be trusted to run *New York* if the takeover succeeded.

A week later, Rupert called Felker in California and said he had a proposal. Felker flew back immediately, anticipating Rupert would help him buy *New York*. Instead, at a meeting in Rupert's Third Avenue office, Rupert revealed he was buying the company himself. As a concession, he offered to sell *New West* to Felker for $3 million. Felker was enraged. He didn't have that kind of capital, and Rupert knew it. Rupert said Felker should have saved his money instead of spending it on limos and a personal chef. "It's a lifelong habit with you," Rupert lectured.

Felker's anger hardened into defiance. He believed his contract gave him the right of first refusal to buy out Burden—a poison pill that could block the deal. "It's you who are the forgetful one," Rupert countered. Felker's contract required Burden to offer his shares to Felker only if *New York* was profitable. But the company had lost money, which meant Burden didn't need Felker's permission to sell. Felker, spiraling, claimed the loss was booked only for tax purposes.

"Sorry," Rupert said. "The figures are down in black and white. You can't change the figures."

Felker, on the verge of tears, vowed to fight Rupert "tooth and nail."

"Teeth and nails are fine," Rupert deadpanned, "but it's money that wins this kind of scrap."

True to his word, Felker enlisted friends Rohatyn and Graham to make a rival offer for Burden's shares. When that failed, he filed a restraining order in federal court, but that, too, was unsuccessful. Felker played one last card, telling Rupert the magazine's entire staff would quit if he took over. "We won't work for you. Please go away," Felker pleaded. Rupert replied: "I can't back down. After losing the *Observer*, I'd be a journalistic untouchable around the world. I can't lose."

On January 7, 1977, Felker folded. He walked away with $1.2 million. Forty of his writers and editors resigned with him, but Rupert rebuilt the staff with his own people. Felker would go on to run several publications, but he never re-created the success of *New York*.

THE CONTENTIOUS *NEW YORK* takeover launched Rupert into the American consciousness. During a single week in January 1977, he appeared on the covers of both newsweeklies (*Time* depicted him as King Kong bestriding the Manhattan skyline). In July, *Rolling Stone* published a seventeen-thousand-word autopsy of the takeover by Sheehy, Felker's girlfriend. The scathing article portrayed Rupert as an amoral predator who had faked friendship with Felker to steal *New York*. The American media establishment turned bitterly against him, just as London society had done.

Ironically, the *New York* battle attracted so much coverage because Rupert paid little attention to the magazine once he owned it. The *Post* was his singular obsession. He had promised incremental change at first, but like many Murdoch assurances, the vow was soon disregarded. Rupert appointed himself editor in chief and replaced editors with Australian and British loyalists. Articles got shorter, headlines louder, editorials more conservative. He set a goal of surpassing the rival *Daily News* in circulation—an ambitious, some might say absurd, target. The *News* sold two million papers daily, more than four times the *Post*'s circulation.

Fortunately for Rupert, the long, hot summer of 1977 produced three infamous tabloid stories that the *Post* seized on to juice readership. First, the region's power utility failed on July 13, plunging New York into darkness. The *Post*'s front page blared "24 HOURS OF TERROR" and "A CITY RAVAGED." Circulation jumped by seventy-five thousand. Next, a murderer who called himself "Son of Sam" terrorized the city with a .44-caliber pistol, eventually killing six and wounding seven women. Rupert personally edited the *Post*'s hysterical coverage, smashing through barriers of ethics and taste. "There's only one game in town and that's Son of Sam," he told his staff. One story claimed mafia bosses had put out a hit on the killer (Rupert later admitted the article was fabricated). At one point, *Post* reporter Steve Dunleavy scored an interview with a victim's family by disguising himself as a grief counselor. On

August 10, the front page cheered "CAUGHT!" after police arrested twenty-four-year-old postal worker David Berkowitz—never mind that Berkowitz hadn't been convicted of any crime. A few days later, the *Post* ran a jailhouse photograph of Berkowitz that a freelance photographer had illegally obtained by bribing a corrections officer. Circulation doubled to one million copies.

The establishment struck back with fury. New York mayor Abe Beame labeled Rupert an "Australian carpetbagger" who "came here to line his pockets by peddling fiction in the guise of news." *New York Times* executive editor A. M. Rosenthal called him "a bad element, practicing mean, ugly, violent journalism." In the *Daily News*, Pete Hamill wrote: "Something vaguely sickening is happening to that newspaper and it is spreading through the city's psychic life like a stain."

Rupert punched back at his detractors. "I don't give a damn what the media critics say," Murdoch told an interviewer. He had a point. The *Post*'s sensational coverage reflected the visceral reality of readers living in a city whose social, financial, and political foundations were crumbling before their eyes. With the city's elite turned against him, Rupert set out to elect a mayor who would be in his corner.

New York was a one-party town, meaning the mayoral race would be decided in the Democratic primary. In August 1977, Rupert stunned observers by endorsing Ed Koch, a moderate congressman from Greenwich Village. Koch was hardly the obvious choice among the six candidates. He was Jewish, whiny, and rumored to be gay at a time when homophobia was rampant. Placards supporting his rival, Mario Cuomo, declared: "Vote for Cuomo, not the homo."

But Rupert liked Koch's plans to curb spending and rein in unions. In the final weeks of the race, he turned the *Post* into a virtual arm of the Koch campaign. His pro-Koch bias was so blatant that eighty *Post* reporters signed a petition protesting his interference. "We are dismayed at the kind of puff journalism that followed your endorsements," their statement read. Rupert crushed the mutiny. "It's my newspaper. You just work here and don't you forget it," he said.

Koch credited Rupert for his victory. "[Rupert] made the difference between winning and losing, and I am very grateful," he told a reporter. A year later, at Rupert's request, Koch lifted a ban on the *Post*'s delivery trucks using city highways. It was further evidence that Rupert used his newspapers to elect politicians who would increase his profits and power.

CHAPTER FOUR

BROKEN PROMISES

RUPERT COMPLETED HIS IDEOLOGICAL conversion by the end of the 1970s. Watergate had a particularly radicalizing effect on his worldview. While most journalists celebrated bringing down a corrupt president, Rupert saw something more sinister: the press had grown drunk on its own power. He watched Bob Woodward and Carl Bernstein become celebrities, and concluded that the "new cult of adversarial journalism" had turned what should have been a routine Washington scandal into a constitutional crisis that nearly paralyzed the government.

The lesson Rupert drew was characteristically contrarian. If liberal journalists thought they could destroy conservative politicians with investigations, then conservative media needed to be a bulwark protecting democracy. The real dangers, Rupert warned anyone who would listen, were the Democrats and labor unions who wanted to use the press to advance their leftist agenda. "The American press might get their pleasure in successfully crucifying Nixon," he told a friend, "but the last laugh could be had on them. See how they like it when Commies take over the West."

By the late 1970s, Rupert was ready to put these beliefs into practice. In the spring of 1979, he rocked Britain when *The Sun*—a working-class tribune—backed Margaret Thatcher for prime minister: "VOTE TORY THIS TIME.

IT'S THE ONLY WAY TO STOP THE ROT," the front page blared. Rupert's endorsement ushered in a historic political realignment not just in Britain but across the Western world. *The Sun* converted blue-collar readers into foot soldiers for Thatcher's right-wing revolution. It was a portent of the conservative populism Rupert would tap into to start Fox News in the 1990s.

Rupert's and Thatcher's fortunes rose in tandem over the decade as their alliance enhanced each other's power. Less than two years after Thatcher's election, she backed Rupert's long-shot bid for the crown jewels of British journalism: *The Times* of London and *The Sunday Times*. The papers' owner, Canadian industrialist Ken Thomson, declared in October 1980 that he would liquidate the money-losing papers if a deal couldn't be reached by March. Shortly before Christmas, Thomson and Rupert settled on a price of £12 million. Even the left-wing print unions supported Rupert's bid, seeing how he had added jobs at *News of the World* and *The Sun*.

To close the deal, Rupert told Parliament he would appoint an outside board that would protect the independence of Britain's "paper of record." "This new undertaking I regard as the most exciting challenge of my life," he told reporters gathered outside London's Portman Hotel. In private, though, Rupert admitted he had no intention of honoring the assurance. "You tell these bloody politicians whatever they want to hear, and once the deal is done, you don't worry about it," he told a friend. The government approved Rupert's takeover of the *Times* and *Sunday Times* in February 1981.

A month later, Rupert celebrated his fiftieth birthday in Australia. Anna planned the party at their sheep farm in Cavan. There was country music, fireworks, and a cake decorated in the shape of *The Times*. A plane circled overhead towing a banner that read: "Happy Birthday Rupie." Anna told people she hoped Rupert would finally slow down now that he'd achieved so much. To her dismay, his ambitions would only accelerate.

EVEN BEFORE THE *TIMES* deal closed, Rupert began wooing Harold Evans, then fifty-two and one of the most respected journalists in postwar Britain, to be his editor. Evans had made his reputation editing *The Sun-*

day Times for fourteen years, publishing exposés about government abuses and corporate malfeasance while fiercely defending editorial independence. Needless to say, Evans was wary of working for Rupert, especially after Clay Felker warned him about Rupert's duplicity.

Rupert deployed his raffish charm to lure Evans. On January 17, 1981, he hosted Evans and his then-fiancée, *Tatler* editor Tina Brown, for dinner at his London flat. Brown's diary entry brought the scene to life: "I had to admit I liked [Rupert] hugely. He was in an American country gentleman's three-piece suit and heavy shoes, and was by turns urbane and shady . . . But when he was standing by the fire with one foot on the fender laughing uproariously he seemed robust and refreshing. There's no doubt he lives newspapers." For Evans, the son of a Welsh railroad engineer, Rupert's pull was too strong. "Nobody could resist it," he later wrote.

Evans ultimately accepted Rupert's offer because he believed editorial protections built into the deal would restrain him. Rupert couldn't fire Evans without the approval of *The Times'* independent board. "No editor or journalist could ask for wider guarantees of editorial independence," Evans said.

But Evans's faith in those protections was misplaced. Even as Evans was negotiating his editorial protections, Rupert was secretly working to circumvent the government's regulatory oversight entirely. On Sunday, January 4, 1981, Rupert and Thatcher met for a secret lunch at Chequers, the prime minister's official country residence, according to a contemporaneous memo written by Thatcher's then–press secretary, Bernard Ingham. Thatcher instructed Ingham to mark his notes "In Confidence" and not to share them outside of 10 Downing Street. For the next forty years, Thatcher and Rupert would deny any meeting took place.

After the meeting, Thatcher shuffled her cabinet in ways that ensured Rupert would close the deal. That evening, she replaced her tough trade secretary with a more pliable official named John Biffen, who one colleague said "had no separate political existence." Rupert spun Biffen, telling him that the *Times* and *Sunday Times* were losing money, and he would shut them down if Biffen referred his bid to the Monopolies Commission. Rupert's threat took advantage of a loophole: companies at risk of going bankrupt were exempt from antitrust review. Rupert's friend Woodrow Wyatt knew of Rupert's lie and referred to it in his diary: "The Sunday Times was not really losing money and the pair together were not," he wrote.

The bid never came before the Monopolies Commission, and Biffen approved the takeover in February 1981. Not long after Evans started the job, Rupert ambled into the newsroom, picked up a page proof, and corrected a typo. Evans sent off a terse memo to Rupert instructing him never to touch copy. Rupert apologized, but his behavior got worse. Over lunch, Rupert told Evans there are "two kinds of politician in Africa, both chimps, only one has charisma." Evans remembered another instance when Rupert criticized a reporter's article about civil rights. "Why do you use these commies?" Rupert scoffed.

In Evans's view, these skirmishes were part of a wider war over the paper's political coverage. Evans told people Rupert pressured him to support Thatcher when her popularity plunged in the summer of 1981. Thatcher's policy of fighting inflation with high interest rates had deepened unemployment. According to Evans, Rupert jabbed his finger at headlines he thought were anti-Thatcher. "You're always getting at her," he complained. Evans received right-wing articles from Rupert that praised Thatcher's economic plans, marked "worth reading!"

Tensions reached a boiling point that October, only eight months into Evans's tenure. On their way to dinner at Evans's home, Rupert complained about an op-ed Evans had published by a liberal Nobel Prize–winning economist. "Intellectual bullshit!" Rupert fumed. Evans finally snapped. "What do you know? You said inflation would be down in single figures by now and it isn't." Evans recalled they nearly came to blows.

Ideology certainly fueled Rupert's animus. But his ire was also a result of financial stress. Accountants projected the *Times* and *Sunday Times* would lose $30 million in 1981. The *Post* was also burning cash in New York, despite circulation gains. The losses were potentially catastrophic because Rupert financed deals with debt. He could have raised money by issuing new shares to the public, but that would dilute his 46 percent ownership stake and weaken his control. Rupert instead slashed costs. On the morning of February 8, 1982, he sent a letter to *Times* staff announcing he would liquidate the newspaper in ten days if unions didn't agree to six hundred layoffs. "We are quite literally bleeding to death," Rupert wrote.

The ticking clock accelerated Evans's showdown with his boss. On the same day Rupert threatened to close *The Times*, Evans discovered Rupert had secretly transferred the paper's trademark from Times Newspapers to News International, which published *The Sun* and *News of the World*. This would allow Rupert to close *The Times* and *Sunday Times* and restart them with a skeletal staff. Evans assigned a reporter to expose Rupert's scheme in a front-page article. The story ignited public furor. Parliament members called for Rupert to be fined or jailed for breaching the agreement to protect *The Times*' independence. The threats were enough that Rupert returned the trademarks. But for Evans, it would be a Pyrrhic victory.

A few weeks later, Evans's father died. Evans was devastated—the Welsh railroad engineer had been his hero and inspiration for entering journalism. Rupert seemed to understand. He sent Evans a handwritten note of condolence that appeared genuinely heartfelt: "It was thirty years since my own father died and I remember it as yesterday. A good father and son relationship is one of the best experiences in life. You must take any time you need to attend to the necessary family arrangements."

Evans was touched by what seemed like rare empathy from his boss. The note suggested Rupert understood the profound loss Evans was experiencing, perhaps even creating a bond between two men who had both lost beloved fathers. The illusion shattered twenty-four hours after Evans returned from the funeral. Rupert summoned him to his office with no preamble, no acknowledgment of Evans's grief. "I want your resignation today," he said coldly. Evans was stunned not just by the dismissal but by its calculated timing. Rupert had used the grief they shared to manipulate Evans, offering false sympathy only to make the betrayal more painful.

But there was ultimately little Evans could do. On the night of March

15—the Ides of March—he resigned. He went home and cursed Rupert with friends at an impromptu party Brown threw for him. The following year, Evans published a scathing memoir, *Good Times, Bad Times*, about the tumultuous thirteen months he worked for Rupert. The bestseller further cemented Rupert's reputation for ruthlessness and deceit.

THE CONSEQUENCES OF EVANS'S ouster were immediate and devastating for *The Times*. In the eyes of critics, Rupert turned the sober paper into a pro-Thatcher propaganda sheet. *The Times* championed her quixotic war with Argentina over the Falkland Islands. "We're All Falklanders Now," *The Times* declared. The full extent of Rupert's editorial malpractice became evident a year later when he drove *The Times* into the worst journalistic scandal in its history: the Hitler Diaries hoax.

It started when Rupert learned in March 1983 that the German newsweekly *Stern* would be selling English-language rights to a trove of newly discovered Hitler diaries. The diaries' sketchy provenance should have immediately made Rupert cautious. A *Stern* reporter claimed he obtained the volumes from a secret East German source that he refused to identify. The source, in turn, said he got the diaries from peasants, who supposedly recovered them in the wreckage of a cargo plane that crashed with Hitler's personal effects on board at the war's end. Rupert flew to Zurich to inspect the volumes in a bank vault. *New York* magazine editor Ed Kosner remembered Rupert's giddy reaction. "I'm calling from Switzerland," Rupert whispered over the phone, "and do you know what's in the next room? Hitler's diaries . . . How big a story do you think this is?"

By asking how big the story would be, Rupert was really asking: How much money can I make? Enough that nothing would stop him from publishing the sensational news. For cost-cutting reasons, Rupert didn't allow *Times* journalists to investigate the diaries' authenticity independently. Instead, he dispatched a *Times* board member, the Cambridge historian Hugh Trevor-Roper—known as Lord Dacre—to inspect the fifty-eight bound volumes. Dacre didn't speak German, nor was he a handwriting expert. But his endorsement was good enough. In mid-April 1983, Rupert paid *Stern* $400,000 for the rights to publish the first installment in *The Sunday Times*.

As publication neared, even the authenticator began having doubts. But when editors called for permission to stop the presses, Rupert's response was swift: "Fuck Dacre. Publish!"

Within days, the story blew up in Rupert's face. The *Stern* reporter turned out to be a Nazi enthusiast who was dating Hermann Göring's daughter. His secret East German source was a petty thief and forger, who admitted to fabricating the diaries with stained school notebooks soaked in tea. Angry *Times* journalists confronted Rupert about the debacle. "I don't know why you're all so worked up. We put on 60,000 in circulation last week, and there's every evidence we're hanging on to it," Rupert told them. He had no patience for high-minded talk about journalistic ethics. "We are in the entertainment business," he said.

RUPERT'S CAPACITY FOR BREAKING promises wasn't limited to his professional relationships. Even as he was destroying Evans's career, he was making commitments to Anna that he had no intention of keeping. While Rupert was busy in London, Anna was isolated in New York with three young children and their live-in bodyguard, a former London police sergeant. Rupert's falling-out with Felker had left Anna with few friends in Manhattan. She told Rupert that she wanted to move back to Australia, and he agreed. They planned to live at the sheep farm and send Elisabeth, Lachlan, and James to Melbourne boarding schools. "They will grow up with better values in Australia than anywhere else," Rupert told a journalist.

Rupert blithely shredded his promise to relocate. His rationale was that Australia was too remote to oversee his British and American companies. His feint at a compromise was that Anna could choose to live anywhere in the Northern Hemisphere. Anna despised England even more than New York, so she decided to make the best of it in America. In the spring of 1981, Anna made a renewed effort to build a social circle in Manhattan. She called socialite Patricia Rose Gray and asked to be a bridesmaid at her wedding to media billionaire John Kluge at St. Patrick's Cathedral. "The guest list was going to be stellar. It was Anna's way of letting people know she was staying in New York," a friend said.

Rupert and Anna fought a lot during this period. "He is . . . very impatient and in some ways cold and remote," she told Wyatt, according to his diary. Anna also regretted having abandoned her journalism career to raise a family. "Have I given up my best work for them? Is that all there is?" she wrote in an essay. The tension between her and Rupert was palpable. "Oh Rupert, don't be daft," a friend recalled Anna saying dismissively in public.

After fifteen years of marriage, they had come to realize they were fundamentally different people. Anna valued culture and travel. Rupert cared about business and politics. "Art, music, hobbies, poetry, theater, fiction . . . have no interest for him," wrote former *Sunday Times* editor Andrew Neil. Anna was a socially conservative Catholic and despised lurid tabloids. "How can I teach the boys respect for women if every time they pass a newsstand they see some naked girl sprawled in their father's paper?" she told a friend. Rupert conceded by keeping nudity out of the *Post*. They also fought about Rupert's thriftiness. "His Scottish Presbyterian background makes him reserved about spending too much on the baubles of billionaires," Neil observed. (It was a trait he inherited from his mother, who clipped labels out of her designer dresses. "I like people to think I buy my clothes at Marks & Spencer," she once said.) Anna complained that Rupert refused to buy her a Rolls-Royce to replace their tired Jaguar and bristled that Rupert wore knockoff shirts from Hong Kong and underwear from Marks & Spencer.

Anna dealt with the cooling of her marriage by rekindling her dream to become a novelist. On a ski trip to Sun Valley, Idaho, around this time, she told Rupert she wanted to study creative writing. Rupert didn't take it well. "What about the household?" Anna recalled Rupert asking. Anna wasn't deterred. She enrolled in literature courses at Fordham and New

York University and was determined to be a published author by her fortieth birthday. By the early 1980s, she and Rupert were living functionally parallel lives. She told a journalist she knew Rupert wouldn't change: "I wish he would stop. I wish it would all slow down. But I don't think that's going to happen."

CHAPTER FIVE

CITIZEN RUPERT

BY THE MID-1980S, RUPERT HAD achieved what few immigrant entrepreneurs could imagine: he owned influential newspapers on three continents and was building a television empire in America. His success was now measurable in hard numbers. In October 1985, Rupert appeared for the first time on the *Forbes* list of the world's richest people. His matriculation into this gilded club marked an epochal shift in the global economy: the production and distribution of news and entertainment were now as valuable as extracting natural resources from the earth. His success only fed his appetite for more. But money was never Rupert's lodestar. He was motivated by deals—the bigger, the better. The question was no longer whether he could survive in America but whether America's media establishment could survive him.

In the heavily regulated media industry, dealmaking required political influence. After a decade in the United States, Rupert was frustrated that he played virtually no role in the national conversation despite having an ideological ally in the White House. To open doors in Washington, Rupert hired the notorious fixer Roy Cohn, who arranged a meeting with Reagan in the Oval Office. But Rupert's status in Washington barely changed after that White House visit. When Reagan visited New York and praised the rival

Daily News instead of the *Post*, Rupert was furious. The snub crystallized his frustration: he was still an outsider despite owning major newspapers.

Rupert lacked juice in Washington because of a fundamental difference between domestic and overseas media markets. In Britain and Australia, newspapers drove the news cycle, and Rupert owned more of them than anyone. But television shaped America's national conversation, and Rupert was shut out of this market. The obstacle was regulation: Section 310 of the Communications Act of 1934 made it illegal for noncitizens to own more than 20 percent of a domestic television station. Rupert was open to seeking American citizenship, but Anna rejected the idea. So Rupert looked for a loophole.

The nascent satellite TV industry had no rules against foreign ownership. In May 1983, Rupert invested $75 million in a start-up called Skyband. He saw the new technology's potential to smash the ideological monopoly of the Big Three broadcast networks. "There are really no limitations on what one can broadcast over this kind of TV," he told a friend. But Skyband's challenges exceeded Rupert's initial projections. Receiver dishes were too clunky and expensive for consumers to purchase at scale. Worse, Rupert couldn't secure programming because Hollywood studios refused to sell him shows and movies. The studios believed, correctly, that pay television would undermine the profitability of free broadcast networks. Rupert folded Skyband after less than a year and booked a $20 million loss.

Nonetheless, Skyband's failure taught Rupert a crucial insight that would fuel News Corp's next decade of growth: he had to control the content and distribution. If a satellite television service needed shows and films to build an audience, then Rupert would buy a studio to supply them. It was yet another example of how Rupert built his empire without a grand design. He simply relied on instinct, lessons learned, and a gambler's appetite for risk to put those lessons into practice.

IN THE SUMMER OF 1983, Rupert went after Warner Bros. The storied film studio's library included classics such as *Casablanca*, *Ben-Hur*, and

The Wizard of Oz. That August, Rupert flew by helicopter to East Hampton to meet Warner Communications chairman Steve Ross at Ross's beach house. The Brooklyn-born, silver-haired Ross was the era's dominant media mogul. He turned a small chain of funeral parlors into a global entertainment conglomerate worth $7 billion. At the time of Rupert's visit, however, Ross's empire was in crisis. Warner Communications reported a $302 million loss caused by the implosion of its Atari video game division. Warner stock plunged 70 percent, making the company a vulnerable takeover target. Despite this weakness, Ross told Rupert that his movie studio wasn't for sale. Rupert replied he wanted to buy some Warner stock, hinting he could pursue a hostile takeover if Ross didn't submit. "Be my guest," Ross replied.

Rupert marveled at Ross's arrogance given Warner's disarray. "This guy is living like Midas out on the Island, while his company is falling apart," he told a friend. Rupert returned to New York determined to pry the studio from Ross's grip. By early December, Rupert spent $78 million to buy 6.7 percent of Warner stock, making him the company's largest shareholder. But before Rupert could acquire more, Ross blocked the takeover by merging Warner with Chris-Craft Industries, which owned TV stations. Since foreign nationals couldn't own broadcast properties, this effectively shut Rupert out.

Rupert got the news while vacationing with Anna and the kids in Cavan over Christmas. "If they think they can beat me by exploiting the fact I'm not a citizen, I'll become a fucking citizen and shove the deal straight up their noses," he told a friend. Before he flew to New York, Rupert ordered his lawyers to launch a legal and PR war. News Corp sued Warner in federal court and filed complaints with the FCC. The company accused Ross and Warner executives of fraud and racketeering for enriching themselves as Warner stock cratered. As for the PR war, Rupert had no ethical qualms about enlisting his journalists as soldiers in a business brawl. He assigned the *Post*'s star reporter Steve Dunleavy to investigate Ross and brief Rupert's lawyers. The *Post* also began publishing nasty articles about Ross.

Warner, meanwhile, filed a countersuit in federal court that spotlighted

Rupert's underhand tactics. One filing quoted former *Times* of London editor Evans: "Rupert issued promises as prudently as the Weimar Republic issued marks." The judge described the dispute as a "corporate form of feudal warfare."

Ross had the legal advantage, but fearing a prolonged conflict, he folded. In March 1984, Warner bought back Rupert's stake at a premium. Rupert didn't get the film studio, but he walked away with a $40 million profit, plus $8 million in reimbursed legal fees.

LESS THAN A YEAR LATER, Rupert made a run at 20th Century Fox. The studio was then owned by wildcatter Marvin Davis, a six-foot-four, three-hundred-pound man of Falstaffian appetites. At one board meeting, Davis catered a nine-course lunch and had his secretary place Pepto-Bismol bottles at each seat. Davis and his wife lived in a forty-five-thousand-square-foot Beverly Hills mansion named the Knoll, where they threw Christmas parties featuring the Radio City Rockettes and violinists from the Los Angeles Philharmonic. But running a successful studio proved to be more than Davis could stomach. In 1984, Fox lost $36 million and was teetering on bankruptcy. Making matters worse, Davis was locked in a power struggle with his forty-three-year-old studio chief, Barry Diller, whom Davis recruited from Paramount only months earlier. Davis wanted out of Hollywood. He had followed Rupert's pursuit of Warner in the press, so he called Rupert and proposed he invest in Fox.

The two outlined the contours of a deal over lunch at the 21 Club in Manhattan. Davis told Rupert he would only sell a 50 percent stake in Fox. Rupert normally demanded full control of his assets, but he made an exception to get a toehold in Hollywood. On March 21, 1985, Rupert and Davis announced Rupert would buy half of Fox for $250 million. Only in hindsight would the deal's significance become clear: it was the moment Rupert transformed News Corp from a newspaper publisher into a fully integrated global media company.

Rupert had scant experience in the movie business. His biggest foray to date was financing the 1981 Peter Weir war film, *Gallipoli*, in part to honor his father's legacy. Rupert needed a Hollywood rabbi, someone who could teach him the baroque ways in which the town operated. Diller could fill this role. He was a show business wunderkind, having taken over Paramount at thirty-two and presided over such hits as *Raiders of the Lost Ark*, *Flashdance*, and *Terms of Endearment*. Broad shouldered and balding with a perpetual tan, booming voice, and boundless energy, Diller was a creative impresario and a boardroom killer, a rare combination that made him a once-in-a-generation executive. Over lunch at the Hillcrest Country Club across the street from the Fox lot, Rupert convinced Diller to work for him. "The hot bath of Rupert Murdoch's enthusiasm is something quite extraordinary," Diller recalled.

Diller became Rupert's Hollywood whisperer. Rupert complained of inefficiency, but Diller explained that creative output took time to nurture. Diller hosted lunches to introduce Murdoch to the top producers in town like Stephen Cannell, whose hits *21 Jump Street* and *The A-Team* dominated the ratings. Murdoch deferred to Diller, mostly, but at times his patience wore thin. "You're costing me a fortune!" he said. "Then go out and buy your own fucking movies!" Diller brayed. Because Murdoch lacked a show-business background, he allowed Diller far more autonomy than his editors—for the time being.

A month after the Fox deal closed, Diller invited Davis and Rupert to a cocktail party for media billionaire John Kluge in Diller's office on the Fox lot. The German-born Kluge stood just over five feet. His rotund frame and bald head gave him the appearance of a human bowling ball. Despite his diminutive size, Kluge was a giant in the broadcasting industry. Kluge had become an American citizen and built his company, Metromedia, into the country's largest operator of independent television stations. Diller had heard Kluge, now in semiretirement, might be ready to cash out. Then seventy, Kluge and his third wife, Patricia, had moved to a forty-five-room Georgian estate Kluge built for her in rural Virginia.

As Diller hoped, Kluge admitted he was thinking of selling some stations. Rupert immediately recognized the potential. Metromedia owned stations in major markets, including Los Angeles, Dallas, and New York. With one investment, Rupert could establish a fourth national broadcast network and smash the liberal monopoly of ABC, CBS, and NBC, the gatekeepers that dictated what Americans watched. "There is no dog with hearing as sharp as Rupert Murdoch's when opportunity calls. It took him less than a second to say, 'Ha! Let's go after this!'" Diller recalled.

Buying Metromedia, however, required Rupert to gamble more than he ever had. Kluge wanted $2 billion for his seven stations—50 percent more than what analysts projected they were worth. "I just thought it was crazy," Diller recalled. Rupert admitted the price was high, but it was worth the risk. "You're paying a premium for [the stations] all coming together. It's the one time in life when wholesale is more expensive than retail," Rupert said.

Rupert stayed in Los Angeles that week to lock down the Kluge deal. While attending financier Michael Milken's investment conference—also known as the "Predator's Ball"—Rupert asked Milken to fund the Metromedia purchase with $1.15 billion in junk bonds. Negotiations continued the following week in New York. "What a great adventure! We're betting the company!" Rupert told Diller in a cab on the way to Kluge's apartment. "He's never happier than when there are huge obstacles to overcome in pulling off something wildly ambitious," Diller recalled. "He's a warrior when fighting to establish something in enemy territory—usually against the Establishment."

On May 6, 1985, Rupert and Davis announced Fox would buy Metromedia's stations. But Davis pulled out of the deal a month later because he'd soured on media investing, leaving Rupert with a $775 million hole to fill. "You can't rely on anything he says," a furious Rupert later complained. Rupert didn't know where he would get the money, but one thing was clear: the Rupert-Davis partnership in Fox was over. According to Rupert, he challenged Davis to a coin flip to determine which of them would buy the other out of the studio. Davis agreed, then waffled. Rupert bought Davis's 50 percent of Fox for $325 million and proceeded with the Metromedia purchase alone.

News Corp's Bronx-born chief financial officer Richard Sarazen scribbled projections on a yellow legal pad that indicated Rupert could handle the debt. Over the years, Sarazen developed complex strategies to legally exploit differences in accounting and tax laws among the countries News Corp did business in. This increased News Corp's borrowing capacity. "[Rupert's] father, a famous newspaper editor in Australia, was a manager who made a fortune for others. Rupert decided he'd never do it that way," Sarazen said.

Even if Rupert could raise the money for Metromedia—a big if—he faced a gauntlet of regulations. Federal law prevented one company from owning a TV station and newspaper in the same city. Rupert applied for an FCC "cross ownership" waiver, hoping he could hold on to the *Chicago Sun-Times* and his beloved *New York Post*. Reagan's FCC granted Rupert a two-year reprieve and signaled it would extend it further. The citizenship requirement was one regulation Rupert couldn't change. "It's not a problem, I can take care of it," Rupert told Diller.

Just a few years earlier, Rupert had sold himself as Australian to the core when he bought Melbourne's Channel Ten. "I love Australia. I carry an Australian passport, my children are Australian. I have a home in Australia. I hope to send my children through Australian universities." Now he was breaking the news to Anna that he would become an American to buy more TV stations. "I was shocked. I never thought he'd do it," she later said. "I realized then how strong his ambitious drive was." His mother was disapproving as well. "It was quite a bit to swallow," Dame Elisabeth told a Sydney newspaper.

On the Wednesday after Labor Day 1985, a pair of limousines spirited the Murdoch family into a parking garage beneath the federal court in Lower Manhattan. Anna and the kids—Elisabeth, seventeen; Lachlan, thirteen; and James, twelve—watched Rupert stand with a group of 185 immigrants from forty-four countries. District Judge Shirley Wohl Kram delivered an emotional introduction about the meaning of citizenship and then asked the aspiring Americans to place their right hands on their hearts and recite the Oath of Allegiance. Murdoch swore to "renounce and abjure all allegiance and fidelity to any foreign prince, potentate, state or sovereignty, to whom or which I have heretofore been a subject or citizen."

That Christmas, the Murdoch family spent the holiday at their Aspen ski house, with its wooden beams and swimming pool built incongruously in the living room. For Anna, it was a moment to celebrate. William Morrow recently published her debut novel, *In Her Own Image*, about a mother and two estranged sisters set in rural Australia. The book received positive reviews, a salve to her ego that was bruised by Rupert's criticism of her early writing. Anna would later tell a friend that writing gave her independence, and showed Rupert she wasn't dependent on him.

For Rupert, the Aspen trip was a chance to recharge after the grueling Fox-Metromedia deal. He had achieved his mission to become a force in American television. But he didn't have time to slow down. If he failed to repay Milken's junk bonds within three years, the debt would convert to equity. Rupert's ownership of News Corp would be diluted, and he would lose control of the company. Put simply, Rupert wagered his empire on the Metromedia deal working out.

CHAPTER SIX

RAMBO

TO SAY RUPERT HAD NO passions beyond business and politics wasn't entirely accurate. In his twenties, he had become an avid yachtsman. He sailed his fifty-four-foot ketch *Ilina* to second place in the 1964 Sydney–Hobart race, a harrowing seven-hundred-mile open-water voyage down Australia's east coast to Tasmania. Years later, Rupert commissioned renowned Italian shipbuilder Perini Navi to build him a 158-foot yacht named *Morning Glory*. "Why should I wait till I'm too old to enjoy it?" he asked a friend. So surely a man of the sea like Rupert recognized that the debt he incurred to buy Metromedia's TV stations bore down on News Corp like a menacing storm. In business terms, this meant Rupert needed to tack from being a buyer of companies to a seller. He was in a race to raise cash.

One weekend in February 1985, Rupert summoned his top London executives to his Upper East Side duplex. Rupert had recently sold off the *Village Voice* and would soon jettison the *Chicago Sun-Times*. Even with the divestitures, News Corp's balance sheet remained dangerously off keel. Rupert assembled his executives to discuss his secret plan to slash costs by destroying the British printers' union. Their contract mandated each press be staffed with eighteen men when only five were required. The union repeatedly thwarted Rupert's efforts to modernize his hot-metal presses with computerized equipment, by then standard in the industry. Rupert complained the union's intransigence forced him to print papers "in conditions that combined a protection racket with a lunatic asylum."

Bruce Matthews, a genial Australian who ran Rupert's print operations in London, explained that the unions could be pressured into cost cuts. But Rupert was in no mood to negotiate. He wanted to smash the union with one blitzkrieg assault. The key to the attack would be the vast new printing plant Rupert built in Wapping, an industrial district in East London. Even Rupert would admit Wapping looked as attractive as a high-security prison: it was a drab, gray monolith surrounded by a twelve-foot-high iron fence topped with coiled razor wire. Giant floodlights illuminated the fifteen-acre complex at night. Rupert publicly maintained Wapping would produce only a new evening paper—the *London Post*—but this was "just a ploy," he later told Woodrow Wyatt. Rupert stealthily outfitted Wapping's automated machines with enough capacity to print all four of his London papers with 90 percent fewer workers. Rupert expected the printers would strike rather than accept layoffs to move production to Wapping. When they did, he would fire them en masse and staff the facility with workers from the rogue electricians' union. Rupert's accountants projected the job cuts would increase the value of his London newspapers from $300 million to $1 billion.

After the meeting, Rupert sent his executives to execute the plan with military precision. By January 1986, Wapping was operational, just as contract negotiations with the printers' union broke down. The printers had no hint what Rupert had in store for them. They believed Rupert would countenance their demands because News Corp had taken on so much debt, and Rupert couldn't afford a work stoppage. It was a grave miscalculation. Shortly after 7:00 p.m. on Friday, January 25, 1986, Rupert was on the Wapping floor when he got word that 6,500 printers had gone on strike. "That's just what I wanted," he said.

Rupert hustled around in a cardigan, faded trousers, and sneakers, barking orders at the skeleton crew. As deadlines slipped, Rupert's temper flared. "You fuckwit! You bastard! Get this fucking newspaper out!" he screamed at a managing editor, jabbing his finger into the poor guy's chest to drive home the point. That weekend, Wapping published four million newspapers with just six hundred workers. Rupert used a fleet of private trucks to make deliveries, thereby circumventing the unionized railways that would have shut down in solidarity with the printers. *The Sun*'s Monday front page celebrated: "We Beat Strike Thugs." "I feel like a man who has been on a life sentence and has just been freed," Murdoch said.

Soon, hundreds of unemployed printers marched on Wapping. "Scab! Scab! Scab!" picketers screamed at employees crossing the lines. Workers set fires and overturned a truck. "I hate you!" they yelled, when Rupert's limo drove by. A group called Women Against Murdoch chanted, "Burn, burn, burn the bastard!" In the midst of it all, News Corp chairman Richard Searby hosted Rupert's fifty-fifth birthday dinner in London. Wyatt noted in his diary that Rupert looked "tired and thin. The strain of all the Wapping move has obviously told on him."

As the strike dragged on, the crowd swelled to ten thousand protesters. But Murdoch had briefed Thatcher, and she promised heavy security. Riot police clashed with picketers outside the gates. The bloody strike lasted 375 days, leaving a trail of broken lives. "There were suicides, marriage break ups; people lost their homes," recalled former union official Barry Fitzpatrick. When it was over on February 5, 1987, Murdoch had dealt a decisive blow to the British labor movement, from which it would never recover. Murdoch steered his company into calmer waters for the time being. But the journey to safe harbor came at a personal cost that extended beyond the balance sheet.

RUPERT'S NONSTOP TRAVEL MADE him a fleeting presence at home. "He was like a visiting comet, and the mysterious astronomy of Rupert made it impossible to know when he would appear and how long he would stay," longtime News Corp executive Les Hinton recalled. During the times when Rupert flew through the family's Manhattan apartment, Anna woke the children at dawn for breakfast with their peripatetic father. "Pop had precious little time to spend with us, so the breakfasts were crucial," James recalled. The household staff arrayed the morning's newspapers on the table, and Rupert critiqued them to teach the children. "My dad would be handing out the stories and saying, 'Read that,' or he'd say, 'Look at the headline, that's a shocking headline,'" Lachlan said.

At times, the kids felt ignored. "Is Daddy going deaf?" James asked Anna. "No, he's just not listening," she replied. Rupert avoided deep conversations about the facts of life. In a diary entry, Woodrow Wyatt recounted Anna describing her awkward attempt to get Rupert to talk about the birds and the bees. "Anna said she had said to him the other day he must tell the boys about sex. He said, 'Why?' 'Well they've got to know about it. They're in their puberty.' Anna said to him later on that day, 'Did you tell them about sex?' He said, 'Yes. I told them in the lift going down.'" Anna concluded he did not tell them anything.

Adolescence can be a painful journey of self-discovery. This was especially true for the Murdoch kids. Elisabeth spent ninth grade in Australia at Geelong Grammar, Rupert's alma mater. But the following year, she enrolled at Ethel Walker, an all-girls boarding school in Connecticut. "I had only lasted about six months. I got suspended. I bought a bottle of rum, and everyone was smashed," she recalled. Elisabeth finished high school at Brearley in Manhattan. Lachlan also struggled. In the fall of 1987, he enrolled for his freshman year at Phillips Andover Academy, the elite Massachusetts boarding school that counts six U.S. presidents among its alumni, but left after one year. Anna moved Lachlan to Aspen, and he finished high school at the Aspen Country Day School. When James was about sixteen, his parents began spending most of their time in Los Angeles while Rupert focused on the Fox studio. James recalled he was looked after by a butler named George while he finished high school at Horace Mann.

The kids learned from an early age that shoptalk was the surest path to their father's heart. "We don't talk about our personal affairs. But we can talk about business forever," Lachlan said. "We were brought up with the company as an ever present force in our lives," added Elisabeth. Family gatherings could be as pressurized as a board meeting. "Rupert's presence brought tautness to the atmosphere; he was always the patriarch, and his children were anxious to impress," Hinton observed. Rupert drafted the kids into the business during school vacations. Lachlan did a stint at *The Times* and *The Sun*; Elisabeth at the *New York Post*; and James at *The Australian* in Sydney. James learned the hard way that the media obsessively chronicled the Murdoch children as if they were royals: James fell asleep while covering a press conference in Sydney. A photographer snapped a picture of him napping on a sofa, and *The Sydney Morning Herald* printed it the next day. "Everybody knew who I was. I wouldn't do it again," he recalled.

Succession was decades away, but the contours of the competition were already coming into view. Lachlan seemed closest to Rupert. They shared an atavistic love of conservative politics, newspapers, and Australia. James, meanwhile, struggled to relate to his father, perhaps because he was acerbic and literary like his mother. James studied Roman history and read novels like Rushdie's *Shame* and *The Moor's Last Sigh*. Elisabeth seemed to be a combination of Rupert and Anna. She was whip-smart but also something of a larrikin, which is how Rupert described himself in his rebellious youth.

The kids were notoriously competitive, but in distinctly different ways. Lachlan, the golden child, competed for his father's approval through displays of physical prowess. James, more intellectual and rebellious, seemed to compete by bucking authority. Elisabeth, sharp-tongued and fearless, refused to be overlooked simply because she was female. At the Aspen ski chalet, these dynamics played out in everything from chin-up contests that left Lachlan's and James's palms bleeding to game nights that devolved into shouting matches. Ski outings turned into downhill races.

Watching these spectacles of ambition, Anna worried that the kids would destroy their relationships competing to inherit their father's throne. Perhaps as a way to process these feelings, Anna published a novel in 1987 titled *Family Business*, about a fictional media dynasty that implodes when the patriarch dies, and his widow watches her three children battle for control of the empire. "I thought you would come to trust and respect each other," the mother tells the children in one passage. "I thought that responsibility would teach each of you humility. I was wrong. It taught you greed and disloyalty and hatred."

But in the late 1980s, Rupert showed no sign of wanting to relinquish the throne.

AFTER PROFITS AT RUPERT'S London papers doubled in the second half of 1986, the threat of the Metromedia debt went into remission. Rupert responded to the clean bill of financial health by borrowing aggressively to finance ever-riskier deals. It was as if Rupert were a chain smoker who, after surviving lung cancer, decided to crank up his habit from two packs a day to three.

The deal frenzy started while Rupert and the family vacationed in Aspen in November 1986. He learned that his father's former employer—the Herald Times Group—was in play. Rupert had waited thirty-four years for this moment. He abandoned his family vacation, flew to Melbourne, and paid $1.5 billion for the newspaper chain that had humiliated his grieving mother in 1952, forcing her to sell Sir Keith's Adelaide newspaper after his sudden death. The purchase gave Rupert control over 75 percent of the Australian newspaper market—and something far more valuable: revenge. "It gives me a great thrill," Rupert said at the press conference announcing the Herald takeover, as Dame Elisabeth beamed at his side, finally watching her son settle the family's oldest score. "His father dying so young was a great challenge to Rupert. Subconsciously, he wanted to prove he was worth," Dame Elisabeth said at the time.

The deals came in a relentless cascade. Rupert snapped up Hong Kong's *South China Morning Post* for $105 million, then paid $300 million for storied publisher Harper & Row, merging it with his London house, Collins. He bought a $5.8 million Spanish colonial mansion in the Hollywood Hills, and a Gulfstream jet—after the humiliation of arriving in Aspen on a commercial flight while Barry Diller stepped off his own plane. Even the Black Monday market crash in October 1987 didn't slow the spree. Rupert called this period his "expansionary lunge."

The acquisitive burst was interrupted by a wrenching setback. In December 1987, at the height of the Reagan presidency, Massachusetts senator Ted Kennedy slipped language into a one-thousand-page congressional spending bill that would force Rupert to sell his cherished *New York Post*, which one journalist noted "would be like Dracula selling his coffin." On February 8, 1988, Rupert sold the *Post* to New York real estate developer Peter Kalikow for $37 million. News Corp executives privately rejoiced that Rupert was getting rid of a tabloid that burned $20 million a year. But the sale stung Rupert deeply. "It was a nightmare," he later said. Without the *Post*, Rupert appeared lost and depressed. "We had never before lived in a town where we did not have a paper," Anna said.

Some people try therapy after suffering a terrible loss. Rupert found relief in doing deals. Months after selling the *Post*, he paid a record $3 billion for Triangle Publishing, the parent company of *TV Guide* and *Seventeen*. The price appalled News Corp executives—Rupert struck the deal without consulting lawyers or bankers. "I don't know where the money is coming from," he admitted. At the closing meeting, longtime News Corp executive Les Hinton sensed Rupert knew the deal could be his Waterloo. "I saw a red smear on his fingers, staining the white handkerchief he had taken from the breast pocket of his jacket. He had picked at the cuticles of his fingers until they were bleeding," Hinton later remembered.

In just three years, Rupert had grown News Corp's assets by 600 percent, entirely on borrowed money. He now controlled 150 newspapers and magazines, a satellite channel, book publishers, Ansett Airlines, television stations, and the newly launched Sky television service. But he was also $5.5 billion in debt. A board of a normal public company would rein in a reckless CEO. But News Corp in the late 1980s was not a normal company. It was the singular expression of one man's limitless ambition. "You can't build a strong corporation with a lot of committees and a board that has to be consulted at every turn," Rupert told a journalist around this time. "You have to be able to make decisions on your own."

By the end of the 1980s, Rupert acted like a man who believed the laws that governed mortals—how much sleep one needed, how much debt a company could handle—did not apply to him. His deals got bigger, his politics more right-wing, his views more socially conservative. In the 1988 Republican primary, he supported televangelist Pat Robertson. "Our master is becoming uncontrollable," Bruce Matthews told *Sunday Times* editor Andrew Neil. The executives privately began referring to Rupert as "Rambo," the Hollywood archetype of 1980s go-it-alone masculinity. After a decade of conquest, Rupert was about to discover the price of hubris.

PART TWO

DOMINANCE

CHAPTER SEVEN

"I HAVE TO THINK OF MY CHILDREN"

ANDREW NEIL, WHO SPENT ELEVEN years editing Rupert's *Sunday Times*, compared the senior ranks of News Corp in the late 1980s to the court of France's Louis XIV—the Sun King. "All authority comes from him. He is the only one to whom allegiance must be owed, and he expects his remit to run everywhere, his word to be final," Neil said. A courtier understands that his livelihood depends on the monarch's benevolence. This was also true inside News Corp.

Executives constantly worried they might fall out of favor with The Boss. They watched how, months after Bruce Matthews orchestrated the successful move to Wapping, Rupert dumped him. "He turns on lovers and chops them off," Matthews said.

The effect was that executives never knew where they stood. Rupert could seem like a best friend one moment only to turn scarily distant the next. "I became good at providing therapy to executives and editors who suddenly felt out in the cold," longtime News Corp executive Les Hinton recalled.

In the summer of 1988, Rupert flew senior executives from Los Angeles to Aspen aboard a fleet of Learjets for News Corp's first corporate conference. The event was designed to bring order to the motley collection of companies Rupert acquired. What people remembered most, however, was that career-ending consequences awaited executives who dared question the Rupert way.

During a presentation by *Sun* news editor Tom Petrie, a recently hired *Melbourne Herald* editor named Bruce Guthrie raised his hand. "Tom, do you have any ethical framework at all at the London *Sun*?" It was a fair question. *The Sun* was then being sued by Elton John for libel after the tabloid falsely printed the pop singer hired male prostitutes ("ELTON IN VICE BOYS SCANDAL," the headline screamed).

Guthrie later recalled his colleagues' reaction: "The place simply erupted. 'Ethics? At *The Sun*? You've got to be joking,' shouted one of the execs . . . All around were shouts of derision, raucous laughter and general hysteria." Finally, when the jeers subsided, Petrie said, "To tell you the truth, we don't really have any kind of ethical framework at all." Word later got around that Rupert called Guthrie a "wanker" for asking the question. "I now was the social equivalent of a leper. No one came near me," Guthrie said. He resigned a little over a year later.

Executives felt Rupert's presence even when The Boss was thousands of miles away. "The mythology of Murdoch perpetuated the idea he was all-seeing and everywhere," Les Hinton said. No matter what time zone Rupert was in, he called executives with the avidity of a hungry reporter chasing a hot story. "Murdoch, here," he would say in an unmistakable Australian warble, before probing the executive for information about the business. During these fact-finding calls, Rupert toggled between aggression and steely silence. But not getting called at all was equally unnerving. An executive then wondered if he had lost the king's favor.

The element of surprise kept everyone on edge and gave Rupert an aura of omnipotence. "Telephone terrorism [was] his weapon of choice to make sure his word extends through his worldwide empire," Neil recalled. Rupert's phone habit bordered on a compulsion. "Murdoch without a telephone was like an alcoholic without a drink. He would grow agitated, fidgety, desperately looking for a fix," recalled former executive Bruce Dover. Rupert's London butler, Philip Townsend, recalled that Rupert once cut short a vacation with Anna to the English countryside because the inn's bedroom lacked a phone. "I had to stand in the hall and make my calls," Rupert complained upon returning to his St. James flat.

Executives tried to preempt Rupert's ire by anticipating his demands. "The most highly regarded people at News are little more than Rupert robots, programmed to consider him first and the issue second," Guthrie recalled. Rupert rarely dictated what editors should print in their papers. "Instead, by way of discussion he would make known his personal viewpoint," Dover recalled. "What was expected in return, at least from those seeking tenure of any length in the Rupert Empire, was a sort of 'anticipatory compliance.'" Piers Morgan, whom Rupert tapped at twenty-eight to run *News of the World*, deduced early into his editorship that Rupert's offhand political comments were, in fact, veiled marching orders. "I'm beginning to understand more about the true scope of Murdoch's influence, and the way he does business. And it's quite scary," he noted in his diary.

Rupert prized loyalty above all. He elevated executives who would never attain similar positions of power at another media company. "[Rupert] cares little about university degrees, excuses workplace indiscretions and will even forgive egregious journalistic errors," Guthrie said. "Deep down he knows that the culprits will be even more indebted to him: they are his forever." Executives went to nearly spiritual lengths to display their loyalty. "I'd do anything for him," said Sky CEO Sam Chisholm. "This job isn't just a matter of life and death to me. It's far more important than that."

But this hiring strategy carried risks. Rupert's employees sometimes went too far or broke laws because they thought it would impress The Boss. This would be the case years later when Rupert's London tabloids allowed a culture of illegal phone hacking to run unchecked until the scandal nearly destroyed the company.

Spreading gossip was another strategy executives tried to impress Rupert. The Boss loved a juicy anecdote about a business rival or political enemy. "Give him some good inside information and he will go away happy," Neil remembered. But oftentimes Rupert couldn't be placated. *The Sun's* pugnacious editor Kelvin McKenzie was a frequent target of Rupert's telephone rages. "You're losing your touch, Kelvin. Your paper is pathetic," Rupert would snarl at McKenzie. *Sun* colleagues noted how Rupert's calls seemed to dictate McKenzie's emotional state. "Kelvin used to go into great depressions after Rupert's onslaughts," remembered managing director John Dux. McKenzie was a loutish bully himself, and he coped with Rupert's abuse by treating his staff as badly as Rupert treated him. "Don't speak. Take your bollocking. Then fuck off," McKenzie would scream at an unlucky *Sun* staffer, before launching into an expletive-laden tirade that could run to thirty minutes.

Some executives blamed Rupert's dark moods on his nonstop travel, which left him perpetually sleep-deprived and irritable. Many nights he slept as little as three hours. In the 1970s, Rupert began taking the sedative temazepam to combat jet lag, but the medication just made things worse. McKenzie called them "angry pills." Rupert's growing reliance alarmed his staff. "I had become increasingly worried about his dependence on sleeping tablets," his butler Townsend recalled. One time, Townsend panicked Rupert had overdosed and he would find him in a coma. Rupert's longtime secretary, Dot Wyndoe, grew so concerned she began intercepting his pill bottles. "I'll take those," she would say when new deliveries arrived.

This culture of fearful compliance would prove nearly catastrophic when Rupert's empire faced its greatest existential threat. By the summer of 1990, none of his courtiers dared tell him that his debt-fueled expansion had left News Corp dangerously exposed.

THE FINANCIAL EARTHQUAKE THAT nearly toppled his empire began when banks raced to tighten lending standards as the world economy slid into recession. But Rupert's courtiers had trained themselves never to deliver bad news. The same executives who anticipated his every whim about editorial content had learned to stay silent about the company's precarious finances. When the crisis struck, Rupert discovered he had built a court of flatterers rather than counselors—and none of them could save him from himself.

News Corp's spiral toward insolvency accelerated. On September 1, Rupert tried to reassure investors by appointing a new chief financial officer, David DeVoe. The financial situation was worse than DeVoe anticipated. The company needed a $600 million credit line to keep operating until the end of the year. Its debt was spread amongst 146 banks around the world in ten different currencies. Untangling the Gordian knot of loans would be like trying to repair a Rube Goldberg machine in the dark. On October 4, DeVoe called an emergency meeting in London with News Corp's seven biggest lenders to secure a lifeline. One banker described Rupert's financial condition as "somewhat terminal."

For a man accustomed to absolute control, Rupert found himself dependent on people who owed him nothing. Rupert's bankers agreed to fund a bailout under the code name Project Dolphin. The rescue would be organized by News Corp's biggest lender, Citibank. The bank assigned a thirty-four-year-old vice president named Ann Lane to lead the mission. Rupert had retrograde ideas about women in business—none sat on News Corp's board because Rupert said women "talked too much"—but Lane wasn't part of his court system, meaning she couldn't be fired for delivering bad news. For the first time in decades, Rupert faced an adviser who would tell him hard truths rather than what he wanted to hear.

The clock was ticking. Lane stalked around her office in an Armani suit and sneakers, quickly drafting two rules that would govern the bailout. First: "We are where we are," she told bankers. They simply didn't have time to waste criticizing Rupert's heedless borrowing that brought them to this precipice. Second: "No one gets out." If even one lender got repaid before another, every bank would demand their money and start a run on News Corp that would tip the company into bankruptcy. The banks grudgingly agreed to Lane's terms because they had no choice. News Corp's liabilities were the size of Ecuador's sovereign debt. Liquidating the company risked the possibility of triggering a global financial meltdown. "We were dealing with a really fragile banking system," Rupert said, proving the timeless observation: "If you owe the bank $100, that's your problem. If you owe the bank $100 million, that's the bank's problem." Lane convinced the bankers to roll over loans, which bought Rupert time.

The bankers, however, demanded a painful concession: Rupert needed to merge his cash-burning Sky TV service with rival British Satellite Broadcasting (BSB). The two were locked in a grinding war of attrition to sign subscribers. Rupert hated the merger idea. Rupert saw BSB as a bloated and elitist company that lavished executives with high salaries and perks like leased BMWs. Rupert believed that BSB—then losing $10 million a week—would go bust, leaving Sky with a monopoly. But bankers were calling the shots. On November 2, Rupert agreed to merge Sky with BSB.

The deal required the British government's approval because Rupert didn't have a license to operate a satellite TV service in the United Kingdom. He had ingeniously infiltrated the market in 1989 through a loophole: Sky used the Luxembourg-based Astra satellite to beam programming into the UK. Rupert feared his enemies in the Labour Party would block the merger on the grounds that he didn't have a license. "They hate the idea of a competitive society, and it's only companies like ours that have the guts and strength to risk everything," Rupert fumed. Rupert needed Thatcher's protection more than ever. "He doesn't want [the deal] suddenly to be taken up by some Department of Trade Minister," Rupert's longtime friend Wyatt noted in his diary after speaking with Rupert.

Alarmingly, it was unclear if Thatcher could help. In the fall of 1990, her political capital was as depleted as Rupert's bank accounts. On October 29, Rupert visited Thatcher at 10 Downing Street to brief her on the deal, later telling Wyatt "he had a good meeting . . . and talked about the BSB business." Thatcher ultimately was able to bless the corporate marriage. Shortly after 3:00 a.m. on November 3, Sky and BSB inked the merger, forming a new company called BSkyB. It would be Thatcher's parting gift to Rupert.

A little over a week later, Michael Heseltine, a fifty-seven-year-old Tory MP with big hair and even bigger ambition, challenged Thatcher's leadership. Rupert unleashed his newspapers to crush the mutiny. *The Sun* labeled Heseltine's allies "spineless saps, tinpot Judases, and two bob traitors."

But Rupert's anti-Heseltine campaign wasn't enough to save Thatcher. On November 22, she resigned after eleven years in power. With Rupert's debt crisis still raging, he seemed poised to suffer a similar fall from grace.

ON THE MORNING OF DECEMBER 6, 1990, Rupert and DeVoe were in Zurich meeting bankers when they received news that was akin to a corporate death sentence: News Corp would not be allowed to extend a billion-dollar Australian loan that was due in twenty-four hours. After some digging, Rupert uncovered the problem: the Australian bank that had originated the loan sold a $10 million tranche of the debt to the Pittsburgh National Bank. This regional Pennsylvania bank was now demanding repayment with no exceptions. News Corp was hours away from default.

Rupert and DeVoe flew to London to handle the crisis. Rupert strode into his flat and was shocked to find contractors working on an extensive renovation. "Good God, Philip. What's this mess?" Rupert asked his butler. Townsend reminded Rupert he had approved Anna's remodeling plan. "Oh yes, I'd forgotten," Rupert said. He turned to DeVoe and grumbled: "At a time like this, Anna has to spend money on decorating." Rupert ordered that the project be immediately scaled back.

In Rupert's study, DeVoe called the chief loan officer at Pittsburgh National. Rupert later recounted the harrowing exchange:

"Give us the money," the loan officer demanded.

"We can't," DeVoe said. "We'd go out of business."

"That's right," the banker said.

DeVoe was incredulous. "You're telling us to liquidate our company?"

"Yes," the officer said.

Rupert saw the walls closing in. "It was horrific!" he later recalled. "The chief loan officer said, 'Liquidate your company.' All for ten million dollars!"

DeVoe made one final plea, but the loan officer wouldn't budge. "We don't think you have the ability to repay us. Let's put it into receivership," he said.

Rupert raced over to the law firm representing Citibank. When Rupert arrived, Lane ushered him into a conference room and explained she had already asked Citibank chairman John Reed to call Pittsburgh National's chairman. Now it was Rupert's turn to call the Pittsburgh bank and beg. In London, it was approaching midnight and near the end of the business day on the East Coast of the United States. Rupert dialed the number, but the chairman wouldn't take the call. Rupert said it was all over. Lane tried to project confidence. "Nothing is over till it's over," she replied. She later recalled she saw Rupert visibly trembling.

AND THEN: SALVATION: within minutes of Murdoch's failed attempt to reach the Pittsburgh chairman, he was patched through to a loan officer from the bank. He told Rupert the bank would extend the due date. "We don't want to be that difficult," Rupert recalled the officer saying. But why did the bank relent? Rupert's account of those agonizing hours elided this pivotal beat. Was it pressure from Citibank? Or simply luck? Rupert never said.

His butler had a plausible explanation. Townsend wrote in his memoirs that, before Rupert left to meet Lane, he saw Rupert in his apartment study call the White House and ask President George H. W. Bush to intervene. "I've called the president of the bank a half dozen times," Rupert told Bush, according to Townsend, "but he won't take my calls. Without them, the whole pack of cards will come tumbling down. Can you help?" Townsend said the Pittsburgh bank extended Rupert's loan shortly after Rupert and Bush allegedly spoke. "Phew, that was a close one. I may be broke, but I'm still here," Rupert told Townsend, wiping his hand across his brow. For the second time in a matter of weeks, it appeared that Rupert's conservative political allies leveraged their government positions to protect him from financial ruin.

Nonetheless, News Corp had more than $2 billion in loans due at the end of January, and the existential threat of bankruptcy remained. Lane told Rupert to spend Christmas in Aspen with the family to rest. The dark mood was brightened by the success of the Fox broadcast network, which was already profitable with hits like *Married . . . with Children* and *The Simpsons*. But on January 16, 1991, the world economy took another hit when American warplanes bombed Baghdad, starting the First Gulf War.

News Corp stock crashed to three dollars a share, an 80 percent decline from August.

For the first time since leaving Oxford, external forces dictated Rupert's fate. People noticed how Rupert retreated inward, like a patient confronting an inoperable diagnosis. "It's not a pretty sight to see a great man like that," Lane said. Townsend said Rupert stopped using his Grecian 2000 hair formula, which caused his chestnut hair to turn ash white. "I have to say he aged visibly in the weeks that brought the crisis to a head," Townsend recalled. "As things got worse, he sat in his study for hours on end, sometimes on the telephone, sometimes in silence." Lachlan recalled taking a walk with his father through London late one night and learning how dire the outlook actually was. "I wanted to put my arms around him and hold him up," Lachlan remembered.

And then, in the predawn hours of February 1, 1991, it was over: Lane cajoled all 146 banks to sign the bailout agreement, which extended News Corp's $8.2 billion debt for three years. The rescue bought Rupert time to sell assets and stabilize his balance sheet. Looking back on the 116-day credit crisis, Rupert expressed a desire to repair Wall Street's broken trust. He said he would travel less and delegate more. He appointed a Swiss executive named Gus Fischer to be News Corp's first chief operating officer. "This has been a chastening experience," Rupert told *Variety* editor Peter Bart during an interview in his office on the Fox lot.

On March 11, Rupert turned sixty. Anna had organized a family cruise down the Nile, but the Gulf War forced her to cancel the trip. She and Rupert instead checked into the Canyon Ranch Spa in Tucson, Arizona. He had become highly health conscious as he got older to avoid the fatal heart attack that killed his father. "Rupert, who, like many tycoons, is something of a hypochondriac," former *Sun* editor Larry Lamb said. "He stopped smoking long ago, now drinks only wine, and that in moderation, and exercises regularly." He even dabbled in New Age fads, ordering herbal supplements and muesli cereal. "I'm into yin and yang and all that shit," he told Townsend after visiting a renowned Swedish biopath. Rupert's budding sense of mortality motivated him to secure his children's patrimony.

———

EVEN AS RUPERT TREMBLED in conference rooms and aged visibly under the strain, his predatory instincts never switched off. At the nadir of his debt crisis, he spotted an opportunity that would transform his greatest vulnerability into his most brilliant victory: he could use his sisters' terror about the company's survival to buy their shares in the family trust at a steep discount. Rupert believed his children should inherit the company upon his death. It was only fair since Rupert single-handedly built the empire, while his sisters Helen, Janet, and Anne benefited passively. His mother, Dame Elisabeth, however, didn't see it this way. "I can't go on making money for all of you forever. I have to think of my children," Rupert told her during a tense phone call.

In January 1991, Rupert took advantage of the stock's historically depressed price to buy his sisters' shares for a song. He offered them $650 million—roughly half of what their stake was worth a year earlier. Some family members protested. Dame Elisabeth didn't know how to handle the conflict, expressing a mother's hope that everyone could just get along. "I cannot imagine that one branch of the family would ever be competing against another," she told a reporter. During a family meeting, she buried her head on the boardroom table and said, "This is all a bit uncomfortable."

In the summer of 1992, Rupert and his sisters struck a deal during an Alaskan cruise. His sisters thought they were cutting their losses on a dying company. Rupert knew better. He had turned the worst crisis of his career into the deal that would give him absolute control of his empire. It was vintage Rupert: even when cornered, he found a way to win. It came at the price of damaged relationships. "Rupert didn't like it one bit that any member of the family would be anything but grateful and say anything but 'Whatever you say, Rupert,'" said Matt Handbury, his sister Helen's son. "As an illustration of Rupert's sense of entitlement and the family being behind him, when he bought everyone out, he basically offered a future payment at a current price."

Now he was ready to welcome Lachlan, James, and Elisabeth into the company to commence the competition to see which of them would one day inherit his throne.

CHAPTER EIGHT

FIRST AMONG EQUALS

RUPERT'S POLITICS SHIFTED LEFT TO RIGHT over the years, but one position remained fixed: he detested the British class system. Growing up in Australia with Scottish heritage, Rupert loathed the idea that he was a subject of a distant and unelected power. "The Queen? Nice little woman. Nothing special," he said after meeting Elizabeth II in June 1990. Rupert was suspicious of anyone with aristocratic aspirations, so much so that he fired *Sun* editor Larry Lamb in 1981 after Lamb accepted a knighthood and insisted people address him as "Sir Larry."

Of course, Rupert's antipathy to hereditary monarchs was deeply ironic because he ruled News Corp like one. "I'm a great believer in nepotism," he told a board member in the late 1980s. Although Rupert had no intention of vacating his throne for decades—he once declared "my retirement plan is to be carried out of here"—he nevertheless planned for the inevitable. In 1990, he appointed Anna to News Corp's board to ensure that power would remain in the family if he died prematurely. "She's there because I just want the assurance, should anything happen to me, that there'll be someone keeping the door open for the children to come along," Rupert told a journalist.

Primogeniture determined hierarchy in the British aristocracy. The same was true in the Rupert family. "Lachlan was the golden child," a person close to the family said. Rupert's favoritism toward Lachlan seeded resentments with siblings Prue, Liz, and James that would grow to disastrous proportions in later years. But in the early 1990s, Lachlan's primacy seemed natural, in part because he shared his dad's right-wing worldview. In 1987, Lachlan cofounded the Trinity School's Conservative Society to redress the "imbalance of political ideology in the school community." Lachlan expressed his dad's hostility to "elites." "What the criticism in Britain is about is an upper-class elite being scared of the masses," Lachlan would later tell a *New York Times* journalist in 1998. "In our papers they see a reflection of society that's not Oxford or Cambridge and they don't like it. There's a fear of democracy. My dad's Australian and that's where they sent everyone they didn't want."

Crucially, Lachlan imbibed his father's love of newspapers. "He was the one who was always most interested," Rupert told friends. "When he was a 13-year-old kid, he worked as an apprentice with the printers in the pressroom, cleaning all the oil and the grease off the press." During other school vacations, Lachlan trained as a reporter at the *San Antonio Express-News* and London *Times*. Rupert also made sure Lachlan learned the art of dealmaking. In October 1990, Rupert invited Lachlan to sit in on meetings during Sky's merger with BSB.

Lachlan was then a month into his freshman year at Princeton. The Ivy League university attracts the world's wealthiest progeny. Lachlan, however, seemed determined to remain anonymous. "There was a small minority who knew who he was, but the reality was, most people didn't," said former Princeton student Glenn Polin. The school's social scene centered around eating clubs, but Lachlan didn't join one and instead lived in a small apartment off campus. "He was not a super social guy. He spent his weekends going to New York City," said George Richards, who took a junior-year course with Lachlan called the Truth Paradox. Polin said Lachlan rarely talked about his powerful father, although there were signs he came from serious money. "When Lachlan went shopping for music, he would come home with forty or fifty CDs," Polin recalled.

Lachlan majored in philosophy with a concentration on German idealists Kant and Hegel. He titled his senior thesis "A Study of Freedom and Morality in Kant's Practical Philosophy." Lachlan began the paper with an epigraph from the Romantic poet Lord Byron: "Between two worlds life hovers like a star, / 'Twixt night and morn, upon the horizon's verge. / How little do we know that which we are! / How less what we may be!" Read a certain way, the quote reflected a young man struggling to balance his father's dynastic ambitions with his own desire for independence.

By Lachlan's own admission, he felt most himself at Princeton's indoor rock-climbing gym, where he befriended Peter Hunt, a flaxen-haired grad student ten years his senior. The pair motivated each other through punishing training sessions that included scaling the wall weighted down by twenty-pound vests. "He pushed very hard," Hunt recalled. Lachlan dedicated his thesis to Hunt, writing that climbing together was "the two most happy and fulfilled years of my adult life."

A few months before Lachlan graduated, Rupert summoned him to Aspen to discuss his future. "How would you like to go work in Australia for a while?" Rupert asked. Lachlan suppressed whatever ambivalence he harbored and set out on the career path his father had mapped for him.

IN AUGUST 1994, Rupert sent Lachlan to Australia to be groomed by Ken Cowley, News Corp's longtime Australian CEO. Cowley installed Lachlan as the general manager of the Brisbane *Courier-Mail*. The newspaper was freighted with historical significance for the Murdoch family: Sir Keith bought the broadsheet in 1933 and intended for Rupert to inherit it after he completed his studies at Oxford. But when Sir Keith died in 1952, Dame Elisabeth was forced to sell the paper to cover his debts. Twenty-five years later, Rupert bought back *The Courier-Mail*, thus fulfilling his father's dream to pass it to an heir.

Lachlan's debut started inauspiciously. On his first day, his boss thought he was a copy boy and ignored him. But pretty soon, Lachlan became an object of almost Christlike fascination among the staff. At *The Courier-Mail*, reporters called Rupert "God." They began referring to Lachlan as "Son of

God." Lachlan reacted smartly. He humanized himself by cultivating the paper's rank and file. He played in touch football games and invited junior staffers to dinner at his house to brainstorm how the paper could attract younger readers. "That really sort of established him in our eyes, because he was very, very normal. It was amazing how natural and down-to-earth he was," reporter Christine Jackman later told a journalist.

After ten months in Brisbane, Rupert moved Lachlan to Sydney to be publisher of *The Australian*, the company's flagship national daily. The promotion, however, didn't automatically grant Lachlan new powers. Rupert kept job descriptions purposely vague because he wanted employees to fight for turf and responsibility. This required Lachlan to stand up to men more than twice his age. And he did. Lachlan forced out *The Australian*'s esteemed editor in chief, Paul Kelly, after Kelly resisted Lachlan's cost-cutting edicts and calls to make the coverage more populist. "Paul Kelly did a fantastic job of making it the paper of record," Lachlan later said. "However, nobody wanted to read it."

Even as he flexed his corporate muscles, Lachlan didn't seem entirely comfortable in his role as mogul-in-training. He was quiet and surprisingly earnest in an industry where ruthlessness prevails. "I love you, Dad," Lachlan would say at the end of every business phone call, even if others were in the room. Also, being a nepo hire at a proudly anti-elitist company led to awkward moments. During a staff meeting, one young reporter asked Lachlan if he thought Australia should hold a referendum to abandon the British monarchy. Lachlan replied he didn't like monarchies because they were made up of people who inherit money and power from their parents. The reporter deadpanned: "Isn't that what you've done?"

Meanwhile, Lachlan chafed at executives who pressured him to conform to protocols about how a successor should act. Cowley sent Lachlan home after Lachlan came into work with a mohawk, and told Lachlan to return with an appropriate haircut. At a black-tie corporate gathering in Sydney, attendees did double takes when Lachlan rolled up his sleeves to reveal a blue and black tattoo circling his left forearm. "I thought it was quite odd—a young thing to do, as if he was with a bunch of twenty-year-old blokes at the pub," a partygoer later told a reporter.

Despite his power and wealth, Lachlan was a twentysomething trying to find his way after college with the challenge of a gold-plated pedigree. "I'm not a movie star or a celebrity, and I feel uncomfortable tooting my own horn," he told a journalist. Lachlan avoided interviews and declined to participate in a *Vanity Fair* article about Rupert's heirs. The press nonetheless burnished Lachlan's image as a playboy. Sydney papers reported he purchased a $6 million harbor-front home, raced around the city on a lime-green Kawasaki motorcycle, and competed in offshore yacht races. Society reporters breathlessly noted when "Lachie" showed up at a movie premiere or charity event with a different beautiful woman. "It's not a natural position to be in, nor is it a position I want to be in, in terms of that much publicity," Lachlan told a journalist in 1996.

At the same time, Lachlan's friendship with Australia's only openly gay rugby star, Ian Roberts, fueled rumors that Lachlan was in the closet. The gossip grew so loud that the Murdoch family asked a business journalist if there was any truth to the chatter. She said there wasn't. Speculation about Lachlan's sexual orientation must have been especially painful given Rupert still called gay people "poofters" and his tabloids were ruthlessly cruel toward the gay community—*The Sun* once published an article that quoted an anonymous "psychologist" who called for genocide against gay men to stop the AIDS epidemic.

Lachlan displayed admirable maturity during this time. He kept his head down and earned his father's trust to handle bigger tasks. In April 1995, Lachlan spearheaded a secret plan to launch a new professional rugby league that News Corp would broadcast on its Australian cable television service Foxtel. The $500 million project ignited a war with the rival Packer family. After a year of bruising legal and PR battles, Lachlan brokered a truce with James Packer during a trip to Fiji aboard Packer's yacht.

In December 1995, Rupert promoted twenty-four-year-old Lachlan to be deputy CEO of News Corp's Australian division. For the first time, Lachlan publicly declared his ambition to be his father's successor. "If you don't think you can conquer the world when you are 24, you are never going to be able to do it," he told the Melbourne *Age*. "I'm ambitious enough on a personal level to say, yes, I want to run this company, and I can do a good job at it." Lachlan's growing confidence and public declarations of ambition didn't go unnoticed by his siblings, who were fighting their own battles for recognition.

As Lachlan accrued more power, he began cutting Cowley out of conversations with his father. In April 1997, Cowley tired of being undermined by Lachlan and resigned. "Ken wasn't prepared to wear it anymore," one source said at the time. "He has great loyalty to Rupert and to Lachlan but it wasn't working."

Years later, Cowley revealed how he felt stung being sidelined by Lachlan after decades of service. "I like Lachlan. He's a nice man, but he's not a great businessman," he said. Back in New York and London, Lachlan's siblings were watching his Australian triumph with growing alarm. Each newspaper story about the "golden child's" latest promotion felt like another door slamming shut on their own ambitions. If Lachlan was already running newspapers and brokering deals at twenty-five, what hope did they have of proving themselves worthy heirs? The pressure to distinguish themselves—and fast—was becoming unbearable. The battle lines were drawn: Lachlan was destined to hold the crown, but his siblings would spend the next two decades fighting to take it from him.

WHILE LACHLAN ASCENDED THE corporate ladder in Australia, Prudence, Elisabeth, and James fought to earn their father's approval on their own terms. As a teenager, James's politics veered left—just as Rupert's had at Oxford—and he cultivated an intellectual persona at the Horace Mann School, an academic hothouse filled with children of New York's elite. James was into music; wore long, black wool trench coats and Chuck Taylors; and bleached his hair blond. "He was that type in the John Hughes movie that was the really cool, aloof guy," a schoolmate recalled. During several summers, he volunteered at an archeological dig in San Vincenzo al Volturno,

Italy, under Richard Hodges, then director of the British School in Rome. When people tried to engage in political debate, James would say, "I'm not my father."

James enrolled at Harvard in 1991 and further honed his counterculture identity. He studied history and film, drew comics for the satirical *Lampoon*, and cultivated an aesthetic that seemed designed to horrify his conservative father—piercing his eyebrow and growing a scraggly beard. Shortly before graduating, James shocked his family by dropping out entirely and spending several months following the Grateful Dead on tour. It was the ultimate act of rebellion for the son of a media mogul: disappearing into anonymity among the tie-dyed masses.

He then launched a music label called Rawkus Records that put out groundbreaking acts like Mos Def and Talib Kweli. *News of the World* editor Piers Morgan recalled James once boasting he packed heat at work. "I keep a gun under my desk because some of these rap guys come in to negotiate their contracts with Uzi machine guns stuffed into their jackets," James said, adding, "Don't tell dad—he'd go mad!"

For a moment, it looked like James would pursue a career outside the family empire. But Rupert lured him back in 1996. First he agreed to buy Rawkus. Then he named James chairman of News Corp's Australian music label Festival Records. Soon, James's interest shifted from music to technology. Liz, meanwhile, had to fight twice as hard for her father's attention, never easy in a family focused on the sons. "Liz [was] the most overtly ambitious of the three kids," a former News Corp executive said. "She was driven to prove to her dad that she could more than hold her own with the boys." Liz attended high school at Brearley and went to Vassar in 1986. While she was college friends with fashion designer Carolina Herrera, the actress Catherine Kellner, and filmmaker Noah Baumbach, she also waited tables at the Dutch Cabin, a scruffy bar and restaurant in Poughkeepsie, New York, where Vassar is located. "She ran in the cool crowd, but she wasn't inaccessible," a friend said.

Growing up, Liz had lost herself in television during her father's many absences, soaking up reruns of *I Love Lucy*, *The Brady Bunch*, and *The Partridge Family*. At Vassar, Liz worked for the campus television station to gain experience for a career in entertainment. When she graduated, her father helped her get a job in Sydney working for Channel Nine, Australia's biggest network, which was owned by the rival Packer family. "Australian television was a bit like the world of *Mad Men*," Liz said years later. "There was a bar in the boardroom, salesmen drank Martinis at lunch, and there was not a single woman in senior management." After a year down under, Liz moved back to America and did stints at Fox stations in Los Angeles and Salt Lake City.

Liz was at the time engaged to a Vassar graduate named Elkin Pianim. They had met while Liz did interviews for a show she created on Vassar's student TV channel. Pianim was the son of a prominent Ghanaian dissident economist and a Dutch mother, was popular on campus, and known for his rakish wit and charm. For Liz, dating a black man was an act of defiance in a family whose social world was entirely white. When Liz planned to visit London, Anna called her butler to warn him. "She will be bringing her boyfriend with her, and by the way, he's black," Anna said.

Liz and Pianim married in August 1993 in a lavish Beverly Hills ceremony that combined Christian and African traditions. The Murdochs barred the media from covering the event. Longtime Murdoch confidant Woodrow Wyatt recalled receiving a nasty phone call from Anna when the Murdochs learned that Wyatt's journalist daughter, Petronella, who was friends with Liz, planned to attend. "If Petronella comes to Los Angeles and goes to the wedding and one word appears in any of the newspapers, the *Sunday Telegraph* or anywhere else, it's the end of our friendship," Anna said icily. "I am much tougher than Rupert and I'm telling you that now." Wyatt later marveled at Rupert's hypocrisy "considering the intrusions into privacy which all his newspapers have gloried in for years."

After the wedding, Liz and Pianim moved to Carmel, California, and paid $35 million to acquire a pair of local NBC affiliates with a loan guaranteed by Rupert. When a reporter brought up her father's name several times during an interview, Liz snapped, "Is this an interview about us or about my father?" Her early management decisions infuriated the staff at the stations. To cut costs, she required staffers to dial an access code before making long-distance calls. Within months, several staffers quit.

Despite the turmoil, Liz made a fortune on the deal. A little more than a year after buying the stations, she sold them for a $12 million profit. "I felt I had to prove something to myself by being on the outside," she later said. Around this time, Elisabeth gave birth to her first child and planned to attend business school at Stanford. "You don't need a fucking MBA!" Rupert told her. "I'll give you an MBA. What you need to do is to go to London and work for BSkyB and see the amazing things they're doing to introduce digital television." Buoyed that her father finally recognized her business prowess, Liz agreed to come into the fold. But going to work for Rupert presented its own risks.

In 1996, Liz joined BSkyB as head of broadcasting and programming during a time of rapid expansion. She pushed CEO Sam Chisholm to develop original programming beyond acquiring shows like *Friends* and *ER*, but Chisholm resisted and openly mocked her as a "management trainee." When Chisholm resigned in June 1997, Liz expected a promotion. Instead, Rupert passed her over. "He never told her the job was open," an executive recalled. The timing was especially painful: she told *The Wall Street Journal* the previous year that she accelerated her plan to have a second child because "once in News Corp, I can't extricate myself." For Elisabeth, who had battled twice as hard for recognition in a family obsessed with sons, being passed over wasn't just professional disappointment—it was confirmation that no amount of talent or ambition could overcome the accident of her gender. The rejection stung even more when she learned through the press that same month that Rupert had declared Lachlan his official successor.

Anna's fears about sibling rivalry were prescient. Growing up, the children's relationship to their father was expressed through the business, making them equate paternal love with corporate advancement. So when Rupert told *The Guardian* that Lachlan would inherit the empire, it felt like a public ranking of his children's worth—and their siblings' devastating rejection. James read the article in disbelief, then crushed the paper into a ball and stomped on it. "It's not fucking true," he said—though what hurt most wasn't the accuracy of the reporting but the brutal reality of his father's favoritism laid bare for the world to see. Elisabeth demanded Rupert retract the statement publicly, but he refused.

Prue made it clear from childhood that she had no interest in competing for the crown. But bowing out of the succession race left her adrift. She bounced between various private schools and failed to attend college. Rupert repeatedly tried to bring her into the fold. "Dad was like, 'Why don't you come and work for me?' and I was saying, 'No, I don't want to work for you,'" Prue later recalled. Prue's early romantic life was equally turbulent: her first marriage to financier Crispin Odey in 1986 lasted about a year. The contrast with her half-siblings was stark. Rupert's butler recalled delivering clothes to Prue's house in south London and finding "overflowing ashtrays, unwashed wine glasses and half empty bottles—a far cry from the pristine order of St. James Place."

Perhaps most devastating was Prue's complete erasure from Rupert's public life. After a lifetime of watching her father build an empire, she wasn't even worth mentioning. "I rang up, I screamed at him, I hung up," she recalled. "He then sent the biggest bunch of flowers—it was bigger than that sofa—and two clementine trees. The flowers kept coming, and he felt awful . . . It caused a huge amount of hurt."

Yet in some ways, Prudence's exclusion from the business freed her to be the one thing her siblings couldn't: honest with their father. Known as the truth teller, Prudence was unafraid to challenge Rupert precisely because she didn't want to be in the business. But if Prudence felt liberated from business competition, she couldn't escape other forms of sibling rivalry. She was acutely self-conscious about how glamorous and attractive her half-siblings were. "They are all taller than me," she told a journalist years later. "That's the worst thing, so they all look chicer wherever they are, but especially on a boat, where everyone is in shorts or a swimsuit and I'm the short, fat one."

Rupert knew Prue's independence would make her both invaluable and dangerous in the years ahead—the one person in his inner circle who couldn't be bought, threatened, or manipulated. So he sought leverage over her indirectly: he hired her husband, Scottish financier Alasdair MacLeod, against her wishes.

Liz's yearning for Rupert's approval trapped her in a toxic cycle of rejection that Prue was spared. Her professional frustrations were also taking a toll on her marriage. Around the time she was thinking of leaving BSkyB, Liz started working with Matthew Freud, the raffish London PR executive whose famous bloodline—great-grandson of Sigmund, nephew of artist Lucien—came with its own psychological baggage. "I loved his mind. I loved his intensity. I found him incredibly attractive," Liz later said. Freud also uniquely understood Liz's daddy issues. Freud's own father, Sir Clement, was celebrated in public—he was a member of Parliament, writer, and TV personality—but a gruff bully at home. "He was incredibly narcissistic," Freud told a journalist. Both Liz and Freud had spent their lives trying to win approval from brilliant, ruthless fathers who withheld love. The recognition was instant.

But their courtship was messy. Rupert fumed when Freud and Liz's affair appeared in the London tabloids. Freud's wife was pregnant at the time, and Liz was not yet divorced. Rupert felt Liz was spurning his family values. Liz saw it as another of his hypocrisies, especially when Rupert soon decided to blow up his thirty-year marriage to Anna. The man who demanded absolute control over his empire couldn't tolerate the one person who tried to control him.

CHAPTER NINE

A NEW FRONTIER

IN THE SUMMER OF 1993, the Murdochs spent a month sailing the Mediterranean aboard their new 158-foot yacht, *Morning Glory*. Rupert had struggled to justify the extravagance of the Italian-built boat. "Maybe I should wait before buying," he told Andrew Neil. Anna convinced her husband to get over it. To her surprise, Rupert embraced the languid days at sea. He even allowed her to disconnect the boat's fax machine for a while. One night, they anchored off the Tuscan coast and hosted a dinner for twelve. "There were vast quantities of caviar and champagne," recalled Rupert friend and *News of the World* columnist Woodrow Wyatt, who was among the guests. Wyatt later said he hadn't seen Rupert and Anna "so happy together for a very long time."

Off the boat, however, Rupert wasn't happy. After the debt crisis, he was ready to launch new conquests, but everyone was trying to hold him back. Banks wouldn't lend like they used to; doctors told him to take at least thirteen weeks of vacation a year; and Anna nagged him to work less. For a man whose identity was conquest itself, talk of retirement felt like a death sentence. Rupert decided he might find the answer to his malaise in the city of reinvention: Los Angeles.

In 1991, Rupert and Anna moved full-time into their Spanish-style mansion on six acres in Beverly Hills, which was once owned by MCA founder Jules Stein. Most mornings, Rupert rose before sunrise to exercise for forty minutes and then drove his BMW to his office on the Fox lot, which he decorated with cream-colored furniture, and abstract landscapes of the Australian countryside.

Hollywood briefly reinvigorated Rupert. Fox's 1990 comedy *Home Alone* earned $476 million worldwide on a budget of just $18 million. But the excitement faded. Rupert disdained Hollywood's excesses, and called the executives "Hollywood ignoramuses."

Rupert's attempt to impose his will on the studio brought him into conflict with Barry Diller, Fox's charismatic and fearsome CEO. It was disorienting for Rupert to work alongside a veteran executive like Diller who was unafraid to challenge him. "He's as smart as a barrel of monkeys and as tricky," Rupert told a colleague. Les Hinton recalled attending a meeting during which Diller exploded because Rupert referred to Fox executives as "you Hollywood people."

"This is our town and these are good hard-working people!" Diller snapped.

According to Hinton, "Rupert didn't say a word. He just threw down his pen and sent it bouncing down the long table. The meeting soon ended."

The relationship ruptured when Rupert heard Diller had complained to Anna that he was "just a hired hand." Diller wanted Rupert to make him a full partner. At News Corp there was, and only ever would be, one owner. In February 1992, Diller quit.

For Rupert, the worst part of living in Los Angeles was being cut off from his newspapers. "The movie business," he complained to a journalist, "can't compare with owning and running a newspaper." In March 1993, Rupert repurchased his beloved *New York Post*, but only found time to visit the tabloid once or twice a month. He was also dispirited by the political scene. In the 1992 American election, Rupert voted for independent Ross Perot. In Britain, Rupert loathed Thatcher's successor, John Major, to such a degree that *The Sun* supported Labour for the first time since the 1970s. "He's a dead duck. The Tories are hopeless," Rupert complained to *News of the World* editor Piers Morgan. A *Vanity Fair* writer who visited Rupert around this time noted he "was gray and drawn, and he seemed somewhat depressed."

It was in this restless, dispirited state that Rupert flew to Beijing in April 1993 to pitch Fox shows to state broadcaster China Central Television. The talks went nowhere because the regime banned Western programming, which it labeled "spiritual pollution." Nevertheless, Rupert returned to Los Angeles flush with excitement. Here was the answer to Anna's retirement demands: the world's final media frontier—an untapped market of 1.2 billion consumers. While his wife wanted him to slow down, Rupert had found the ultimate reason to speed up.

ON HIS 1993 MEDITERRANEAN SAILING TRIP, Rupert got word that Pearson plc, owner of the *Financial Times*, was negotiating to buy Hong Kong–based Star TV. The satellite service was the brainchild of Richard Li, the twenty-three-year-old, American-educated son of Hong Kong billionaire Li Ka-shing. Because Star was based outside of mainland China, the government couldn't censor the BBC, MTV, and other Western channels it carried. By the summer of 1993, Star claimed to have forty-five million viewers in eleven million homes.

Rupert was determined to snatch the deal from Pearson. He invited Li aboard *Morning Glory*. Anchored off Sardinia, the two reached a deal for Rupert to buy a majority stake in Star for $525 million. "Murdoch didn't bother to inform his own board until later," recalled Bruce Dover, an Australian who ran Rupert's China strategy in the 1990s.

Two months later, Rupert invited several hundred media executives to a party at London's Banqueting House. Done in a Palladian style with a ceiling painted by Rubens, the building is the last surviving structure of the original Whitehall Palace, where British monarchs resided from 1530 until fire destroyed it in 1698. Against this imperial backdrop, Rupert intended to extol the liberating power of satellite television to spread free-market capitalism. Instead, he instigated the worst political setback of his career.

Addressing the grandees from the podium, Rupert argued that George Orwell had been wrong. The dystopia in *1984* didn't come to pass because "advances in the technology of telecommunications have proved an unambiguous threat to totalitarian regimes everywhere." He went on: "Fax machines enable dissidents to bypass state-controlled print media; direct-dial telephone makes it difficult for a state to control interpersonal voice communication; and satellite broadcasting makes it possible for information-hungry residents of many closed societies to bypass state-controlled television channels."

In Beijing, officials reacted to Rupert's speech like it was an attempted coup d'état. According to Dover, China's premier Li Peng "was incandescent with rage" when he heard Rupert assert technology would topple dictatorships. A hard-liner's hard-liner, Premier Li was known as the "Butcher of Beijing" for authorizing the 1989 Tiananmen Square massacre. Rupert had never faced an adversary like him. Within a month of Rupert's speech, Li issued a decree banning satellite dishes throughout China. Dover later told a colleague that Rupert's remarks "were probably the costliest ever uttered by an individual." Each setback only deepened Rupert's obsession. The more impossible China became, the more it justified his refusal to retire. How could he slow down when the biggest prize remained just out of reach?

RUPERT REFUSED TO ALLOW a few sound bites to scupper his China dream. He immediately sent word to Beijing that his London speech had referred to the former Soviet Union, not China. The Chinese were unmoved. Doing business in China requires one to have *guanxi*—powerful connections—of which Rupert had none. So he took the extraordinary step of dictating editorial decisions to placate the regime.

What was remarkable was the dexterity with which Rupert shed his Cold War militancy. Neil recalled Rupert wanted Thatcher to risk World War Three rather than surrender Hong Kong to China: "She should hold out, make no concessions, and tell the Chinese that there's a Trident submarine off their coast," Rupert said. "If the Red Army moves into Hong Kong, they should be left in no doubt that we'll nuke Beijing."

In the winter of 1994, Rupert told HarperCollins to publish a hagiography of Deng Xiaoping by the former leader's youngest daughter, Deng Maomao. Despite terrible reviews—*The New Yorker* called her book a "turgid, barely literate propaganda piece"—Rupert promoted it like a bestseller. HarperCollins threw Maomao a New York book party on the top floor of the Waldorf Astoria hotel while Rupert personally fêted her with a dinner at Le Cirque attended by the Chinese ambassadors to Washington and the United Nations.

Six months later, Rupert went further: he dropped the BBC from Star and replaced it with a Mandarin channel. Rupert censored the BBC after learning the Chinese were outraged by a recent BBC documentary that reported on Mao Zedong's penchant for sex with "hundreds" of young women. The press excoriated Rupert, accusing him of suppressing news to appease a brutal regime. Rupert brushed off the opprobrium. "The BBC was driving them nuts, it's not worth it," Rupert later said. He was hopeful Beijing would reward his favors by allowing Star to broadcast in China.

In July 1995, Rupert doubled down and purchased the remaining stake in Star for $300 million. But Li Peng wouldn't lift the dish ban. Rupert grew impatient as he watched his rivals like Time Warner CEO Jerry Levin and Viacom chairman Sumner Redstone get meetings with Chinese president Jiang Zemin. Rupert's grievances spilled out when he met mid-level officials in Beijing. "Look," Rupert snapped, "I don't know why you don't just stop all this nonsense and just lift the ban on satellite dishes and allow us to broadcast in here. We're not going to broadcast news or information that is going to upset anyone." The interpreters across the table stared back in shock. The meeting soon ended.

Rupert's persistence generated a small victory. In 1996, the Chinese let Rupert invest in Phoenix TV, a Communist Party–approved satellite channel that broadcast on the mainland. But even the minor success left Rupert wanting. He abhorred joint ventures and wanted full control, something the government would never allow.

In late 1997, Rupert's desperation to win friends in Beijing created one of the worst public relations scandals in News Corp history. Rupert ordered HarperCollins to cancel a contract to publish Christopher Patten's memoir about serving as Britain's final governor in Hong Kong. Patten was an outspoken China critic, and Rupert was certain his book would antagonize Beijing. The Chinese press had called Patten "a criminal of a thousand antiquities," "a serpent," and "a whore."

Obviously, HarperCollins couldn't reveal the real reason it killed Patten's book—Rupert wanted a favor from Beijing—instead the publisher claimed it spiked Patten's book because it was "boring." This smear was quickly exposed when newspapers reported that Patten's editor had written a memo that described the manuscript as "the most lucid, best written and compelling book I have read by any politician of any persuasion." Patten sued HarperCollins and received a settlement and a public apology.

Even the Chinese were shocked at the sacrifices Rupert made to win their approval. According to Dover, officials were "astounded by the level of criticism Rupert had endured in China's interest." In December 1998, Rupert achieved his long-standing goal of meeting President Jiang Zemin in person in Beijing. Nonetheless, the satellite ban remained in force. Rupert's China project was turning into a financial and reputational disaster.

As Rupert's China dream crumbled, so did his marriage. Anna watched her husband sacrifice principles for a fantasy while rejecting the life they'd built together. Every humiliation in Beijing drove him further from home.

Of course, no one at News Corp would be so bold as to tell Rupert he was failing. Except for one person. In the summer of 1997, Rupert addressed Star employees at the inauguration of the company's new headquarters. After his remarks, a tall, stylishly dressed young Chinese woman with pixie hair raised her hand. "Why is your business strategy in China so bad?" she said in accented English.

Her insubordination sucked the air out of the room. Was she trying to get fired on the spot? Rupert defended his track record.

"That's not a good explanation," she shot back.

Rupert answered again, showing his irritation. "Does that satisfy you?" "No," she said.

Afterward, the woman approached Rupert. She introduced herself as Wendi Deng, a Yale MBA student whose own journey to that Hong Kong boardroom had been as ruthless as any corporate takeover. She represented everything Anna was asking him to abandon: ambition, risk, the pursuit of the impossible. Rupert turned to a colleague: "We need more people like that in the office," he said.

Two years later, she would be Wendi Deng Murdoch.

THAT GALE-FORCE PERSONALITY HAD been forged by necessity. Wendi arrived at Star in spring 1996 for an internship while studying for her MBA at Yale. "Her arrival was a revelation," Dover recalled.

For starters, Wendi was a twenty-eight-year-old native Chinese woman working at a company staffed by older Australian men. "Usually the women pushed the tea trolley," Wendi later said. Her unchecked ambition could have alienated colleagues—as if she were the Chinese Tracy Flick—but instead she endeared herself with guileless confidence. "Hello, I'm Wendi, I'm the intern . . . um, who are you?" she would say to people she met. She also had a provocatively flirtatious sense of humor that made men in the office enamored of her. One colleague remembered the time Wendi snuck up behind a senior executive and tugged his ponytail. "He turns around with this I-can't-believe-someone-did-that-to-me look and sees Wendi standing there, grinning and saying, 'Hi-ii, it's Wendi, I'm the intern,'" the executive recalled. Colleagues found her impishness refreshing. "She was self-confident, optimistic, brave," Star's CEO Gary Davey said.

Wendi was the talk of the office, although people knew little about her. When asked about her past, Wendi spoke opaquely, which added to her mystique. "All we knew is that she was at Yale for her M.B.A. and had spent time in California," Dover said. A few years later, a front-page article in *The Wall Street Journal* filled in the details of her remarkable—and scandalous—journey.

Wendi was born Deng Wen Ge on December 8, 1968, in Xuzhou, an industrial city about four hundred miles south of Beijing, where her father managed a factory. Her name means "Cultural Revolution," which families of the era gave children to prove allegiance to the Communist Party. "We didn't have hot water. We were four children: three girls and a boy," Wendi later told a journalist. She grew tall—nearly six feet—and starred on the local volleyball team. After a while, the family moved to more prosperous Guangzhou and enrolled Wendi in medical school. "It was not my choice. It was 1985, and I did what I was told," she said. Wendi excelled academically but her superpower was seizing opportunities.

In 1987, Wendi began taking English lessons from an American expat in Guangzhou named Joyce Cherry. Joyce's husband, Jake, then fifty, advised local factory owners. In the fall, Joyce, then forty-two, moved back to California to enroll their two children in school while Jake stayed in China to complete his work. Soon, Jake was asking Joyce to sponsor Wendi's student visa so she could study economics at California State University Northridge, a commuter college in the San Fernando Valley. In February 1988, Wendi, then nineteen, moved into the Cherrys' suburban Los Angeles home. She shared a bunk bed with their five-year-old daughter.

The arrangement combusted when Joyce found "coquettish" photos Jake had taken of Wendi in his hotel room. Jake admitted to having an affair, and Joyce kicked Wendi out. Jake soon followed.

Wendi and Jake married in February 1990, but the union was brief. By this point, Wendi was dating a wealthier man in his twenties named David Wolf, who ran an import-export business and spoke some Chinese. Wendi and Jake divorced after two years and seven months—enough time for her to earn a green card. "She told me I was a father concept to her, and it would never be anything else," Jake later told the *Journal*, adding, "I loved that girl." When asked in 2011 by *British Vogue* if the details of her time living with the Cherrys were true, Wendi simply replied "yep."

After graduating from Yale, Wendi returned to Star full-time, working in business development. It was only a matter of time before she'd cross paths with the boss again. One day in the winter of 1998, Star's CEO assigned her to be Rupert's interpreter on a business trip to Shanghai. When they landed, Wendi gave Rupert a personal tour of the city, and Rupert got a haircut for less than a dollar. Dover accompanied them on the trip and sensed the chemistry. "He was radiating pleasure and excitement," Dover recalled. At 6:00 the next morning, Dover arrived at the hotel's gym to find Rupert and Wendi sweating away on exercise bikes, giggling like teenagers.

Star employees began speculating about Rupert and Wendi's relationship. Not long after the Shanghai trip, Rupert's longtime assistant Dot Wyndoe told executives that Rupert would be unreachable for four to five days because he was taking "a walking tour of Wales." At the same time Rupert was supposedly walking in Wales, Wendi was out of the office. She told colleagues she needed to make a last-minute trip to New York. Rupert soon confirmed their suspicions.

"Look, you may have noticed Wendi isn't back from vacation," Rupert told Gary Davey. "She is currently with me, and she won't be coming back to Star TV."

EVERY MARRIAGE IS A BLACK BOX. But by the late 1990s, people around Rupert could sense he and Anna were in a bad place. The ostensible conflict was a negotiation about where they would live. In late 1993, Rupert convinced Anna to relocate to Hong Kong while he focused on China. They moved during winter when the city was blanketed in fog. Anna hated the gloom and returned to LA after six weeks. Rupert then complained he missed New York and wanted to move back east. "You're a perpetual motion machine," Anna snapped. "I've had enough of keeping pace with you. I'm staying in LA."

The dispute over geography was a proxy battle in a much bigger fight: Anna wanted Rupert to retire, or at least slow down. She had traipsed around the globe as he built the empire, endured his absences and emotional unavailability, all while raising three children and a stepdaughter. Anna now wanted Rupert to make her the priority.

Perhaps what Rupert needed, Anna reasoned, was a visual reminder that he had achieved more than anyone thought possible, certainly more than his father ever did. In January 1998, Anna unveiled a thirty-six-foot-high mural of Rupert's right index fingerprint she commissioned for the lobby of the Fox building in LA. The piece's not-so-subtle theme: Rupert put his stamp on the world. It was okay to stop, even if he had yet to conquer China.

Retirement talk depressed Rupert. "Makes me feel like I'm getting to be an old man or something," he groused to a colleague. He told another person he feared what retirement might bring. "I'd probably die," he said. So instead, Rupert made Anna a counterproposal: "Let's divorce," he said.

Anna was blindsided. She flew to London to stay with Liz, who was also going through a separation from her husband, Elkin. "I wanted to save my marriage at all costs," Anna said. Rupert showed no desire to reconcile. "You've got to get on with life," he would say. It was the Rupert method: when he ended relationships, he never looked back. "Even the wife was expendable," Andrew Neil observed.

On April 21, 1998, Rupert announced—in the pages of the *New York Post*, no less—that he and Anna were splitting after thirty-one years of marriage. The novelist in Anna couldn't have missed the timing's significance: it came only a few weeks after Rupert turned sixty-seven—the age his father was when he died of a heart attack. Rupert denied there was another woman, but Anna was sure Rupert was having an affair. "It's not an original plot," she later said. Anna spoke from experience—she had begun an office romance with Rupert while he was married to Patricia. Rupert soon confirmed Anna's writerly hunch: there was another woman. "I've met a nice Chinese lady," Rupert told the children. Prue later recalled her first thought was, *"You dirty old man!"*

Next to stories about sex, schadenfreude sells newspapers. Rupert's messy divorce was the perfect tabloid scandal that combined both. The London press especially relished the dark irony that Rupert—whose tabloids ruthlessly invaded private lives for profit—was seeing his own infidelity splashed on the front pages. At the same time, some of the coverage carried a racist undercurrent that cast Wendi in the role of a predatory Asian gold digger.

An exposé in the British magazine *Punch* described Wendi as "Rupert's Dragon Lady."

The *Post* announcement described the split as "amicable." It was anything but. "This is war, make no mistake about it," one News Corp executive said. In June 1998, Anna filed for divorce in California, a state with communal property laws that entitled her to half of Rupert's $8 billion fortune. Rupert went on the offensive. He was, in Anna's later telling, "extremely hard, ruthless, and determined."

In September, Rupert announced he would sell the Beverly Hills home that Anna loved. The next month, he booted Anna off News Corp's board, telling her she was "an embarrassment." Anna insisted on formally resigning in person. "You don't hurt people for your own happiness," she told board members. Lachlan escorted her out of the meeting in tears.

The divorce unfolded as Rupert said a final goodbye to his first wife. That December, Patricia died at the age of seventy after a long struggle with mental illness. Rupert and Prue flew to Adelaide for the funeral. In March 1999, the Murdochs were back in Australia to attend Lachlan's wedding to Wonderbra model Sarah O'Hare in Cavan, the family's sheep farm outside Canberra. The pouring rain reflected the sodden mood. Dame Elisabeth was furious about the divorce. "I was very fond of Anna and very upset when they split," she later recalled. Rupert was angry at Prue for giving a front-page interview to *The Sydney Morning Herald*, which the paper published that morning. Anna used her toast as an opportunity to twist the knife. "Now I have the microphone, and one man in the room must be rather nervous," she said.

Unexpectedly, James broke the stalemate. In June, Rupert and Anna reached a deal that required Anna to sacrifice money to secure the children's future. Rupert would pay her $100 million instead of the $2 billion she originally sought. In exchange, Rupert amended the family trust so that the empire would be divided equally between Prue, Liz, Lachlan, and James. Each child received one vote. After Rupert died, control would fall to the children. Crucially, any subsequent children Rupert had would get no votes. "We have something set that cannot be touched," Anna later told a journalist.

As Rupert reached an accord with Anna, he was dragged into another negotiation, this time with Wendi. "He wanted to be with me, and I said no," Wendi later told a Chinese TV interviewer. She told Rupert she didn't want to leave her job at Star in order to date him. "If the relationship fails, then I lose everything." That's when Rupert proposed. "He said, 'Don't worry. I will marry you.'"

Late on the afternoon of June 25, 1999—seventeen days after finalizing the divorce with Anna—Rupert married Wendi on the deck of *Morning Glory* in front of eighty guests as the yacht circled Manhattan. A string ensemble played Mozart. The ceremony was timed so that the couple exchanged vows as they sailed by the Statue of Liberty. "Rupert gave a long speech—that he loved her and would take care of her, forever and ever," remembered one of the guests. Wendi was barefoot. "You will not be hearing from me for a month," Rupert told Les Hinton as he and Wendi departed for a honeymoon to Tuscany. Within a few days, however, Rupert summoned executives to his Italian villa to plot new deals.

A few months later, Anna married a retired financier named William Mann in a small ceremony at St. Patrick's Cathedral in Manhattan. "He's a kind, gentle, very spiritual man," Anna said. She especially looked forward to sailing aboard *Morning Glory* with him. Murdoch had promised her use of the boat. But in March 2000, Rupert sold it to Silvio Berlusconi, the Italian media mogul and future prime minister. Like everything else in their marriage, it was just another promise that didn't survive his next conquest.

CHAPTER TEN

"IT'S EASIER TO BE A MURDOCH OUTSIDE OF NEWS CORP THAN INSIDE"

O**N A MARCH MORNING IN** 2000, Rupert sat in his doctor's office absorbing the words that would shatter his illusion of invincibility: prostate cancer. The diagnosis hit like a hostile takeover. Rupert's father had suffered multiple bouts of prostate cancer—the last occurring four months before his death. For a man who proclaimed "my retirement plan is to be carried out of here," this was the one adversary he couldn't intimidate, acquire, or outlast.

Getting married for the third time was supposed to inaugurate Rupert's second youth. At seventy, he was determined to prove that age was just a number. Under Wendi's influence, he moved from the Upper East Side to Soho, traded his rumpled suits for black turtlenecks, and bulked up with a personal trainer. News Corp executives gossiped about the Boss's protein shake diet, his suddenly orange hair, and the feng shui adviser who left lucky objects around the office. It was awkward to witness, but also . . . sort of sweet. Here was Rupert—exponent of ruthless capitalism—clearly besotted with his new wife. "He was definitely in love," recalled former News Corp executive Scarlett Li.

As Murdoch reinvented himself, he was also trying to transform his business. He was yearning for a new corporate conquest. He was certain that his empire had room to grow. So when China rebuffed him, he spent billions on sports rights and teams he never watched—seeing them purely through a monopolist's lens. Then he chased the next big thing: the Internet. When AOL and Time Warner announced their $350 billion merger in January 2000, Rupert suffered serious FOMO and scrambled to play catchup. But on March 10—the eve of his sixty-ninth birthday—the Nasdaq crashed, killing those dreams just as his cancer diagnosis arrived. It was a double blow to his sense of invincibility.

The carnage on Wall Street turned out to be the least of Rupert's problems. After meeting with the doctor, Rupert called Wendi. "I didn't know what is prostate cancer. It was a really scary experience," Wendi later told a journalist. The health crisis was a corporate emergency. Like Steve Jobs and Apple, Rupert and News Corp were impossible to separate. He *was* the company, and any hint of mortality would send the stock crashing. Rupert ordered Wendi not to tell anyone he was sick—including his adult children.

The secret held for all of a few weeks. On April 16, 2000, the news leaked after Rupert was spotted at Memorial Sloan Kettering. Rupert's PR team raced to control the narrative by announcing he had "low grade" cancer and a "very good" prognosis. A company spokesperson declared, "He has no intention of changing his work schedule." Investors still freaked out. News Corp's market cap plunged by $10.9 billion on the Australian stock exchange where it was traded—the biggest single-day decline in the country's history.

As Rupert managed the financial fallout, he fielded panicked calls from his children. They loved their father and desperately wanted to know he would be okay. At the same time, they were confused and angry that he made them learn he was sick via a press release. *Did he consider them senior executives or his kids?* It was a mindfuck. "He's impossible to figure," Liz later said.

Rupert's cancer hit at a particularly turbulent moment in Liz's life. Her marriage was collapsing. She was miserable working for BSkyB's chauvinistic CEO Sam Chisholm. And she resented her dad for having never taken her seriously in the succession competition. In Liz's battles to assert herself, she had a powerful ally, one who was in many ways as mercurial, combative, and gossip-loving as her father: her boyfriend and future husband, Matthew Freud. Not long after Liz and Freud began dating in 1998, Freud encouraged her to go her own way. Seeing her dad get cancer was, for Liz, a stark reminder that life can be cut short. In May 2000, she followed Freud's advice and quit BSkyB to launch Shine, a television production company.

Tearing a page from Rupert's playbook, Liz faxed a press release to his office announcing her resignation. Rupert called her immediately, and things got heated. "I was not thrilled," Rupert later recalled. During the conversation, Liz broke more news: "Dad, you are so pissed at me now you might as well know I'm pregnant with Matthew's child." Rupert viscerally disliked Freud, whom Rupert regarded as an untrustworthy interloper. Executives referred to him as "Matthew Fraud." Rupert later told a colleague Liz was a "very silly girl" for heeding Freud's advice.

In May 2000, Rupert began two months of radiation treatment. He fought the disease like it was a corporate rival he wanted to vanquish. Optics were paramount: the world needed to know nothing changed. That spring, James announced he was going to marry Kathryn Hufschmid, a PR executive and former model. Rupert went to Las Vegas for the bachelor party, spending the weekend with James's friends gambling and shooting machine guns at a desert firing range. He kept dealmaking, too. In August, News Corp bought ten television stations from Chris-Craft Industries for $3.5 billion. The deal was sweet revenge: Chris-Craft had thwarted Rupert's takeover of Time Warner decades earlier. By October, doctors pronounced Rupert in remission. "I'm now convinced of my own immortality," he declared at News Corp's annual meeting. Yet even as Rupert declared his intention to live forever, the succession battle was about to claim its first casualty.

It was the paradox at the core of Rupert's dynastic project: he proclaimed he wanted Lachlan to succeed him, but he also didn't want to let go. The closer his firstborn got to the throne, the more Rupert fought to keep it.

Eventually, this toxic dynamic would force a choice. Who did Rupert love more: The business or his son?

IN OCTOBER 2000, Rupert promoted Lachlan, then twenty-nine, to be News Corp's deputy chief operating officer. The lofty title came with an expansive brief: Lachlan would continue to oversee News Corp's Australian operations while taking charge of the *New York Post*, HarperCollins, the Fox broadcast stations, and the newspaper coupon business—a portfolio that accounted for 20 percent of News Corp's revenues. As if to punctuate Lachlan's primacy, Rupert exiled James to Hong Kong to be CEO of failing Star TV.

Lachlan's promotion required him to relocate to New York. He struggled with the idea. In Australia, Lachlan and his wife, Sarah, were treated as quasi-royals. Lachlan loved Sydney's laid-back culture. He could race his yacht *Karakorum* or go rock climbing in the outback. At the time Rupert summoned him to America, Lachlan was looking forward to taking delivery of an even bigger $7 million yacht. "I'm most myself when I'm in Australia," Lachlan confided to a friend. At a goodbye party with employees, Lachlan broke into tears.

In New York, Lachlan and Sarah settled into a 3,200-square-foot Soho loft, where their neighbors included music legend David Bowie and hotelier Ian Schrager. But Lachlan's troubles began even before they moved in. News Corp's stock dropped 5 percent on the day Rupert announced his promotion—a sign Wall Street had doubts about Rupert's succession plan. Part of Lachlan's challenge was bad timing: the bursting of the dot-com bubble was ravaging New York's economy. One couldn't help but think Lachlan got to the party just when it was over.

Economic devastation was followed by literal destruction when Islamic terrorists flew jets into the World Trade Center three days after Lachlan's thirtieth birthday. Lower Manhattan, where Lachlan lived, became an ash-strewn war zone. For weeks, the smell of smoke and death hung in the air around his Soho loft. It was a brutal introduction to America's challenging 2000s—arriving just as the economy collapsed and the country came under attack. If this was his inheritance, Lachlan couldn't help but wonder what kind of empire he was supposed to inherit.

Lachlan's biggest challenge, though, was navigating News Corp's vicious office politics. Rupert's court—officially known as the Office of the Chairman—was populated by cutthroat rivals who saw the prince as a pretender. At board meetings, James and Lachlan sniped at each other over business decisions. Lachlan had needed speech therapy as a child and struggled to debate his hyper-articulate younger brother. "There was always banter going on," a former senior News Corp executive recalled. Executives grew uncomfortable, but Rupert never intervened. He wanted to see which brother would emerge on top.

Another antagonist was Peter Chernin. Rupert hoped Lachlan would be mentored by the polished fifty-year-old chief operating officer. Lachlan even bought a house in Los Angeles in anticipation of working alongside Chernin, but the relationship didn't gel. Of anyone at News Corp, Chernin had the strongest claim on being Rupert's rightful successor. He had no interest in being a regent. Lachlan and Chernin clashed over business strategy. "Lachlan thought because he was the son he could outwit Chernin," a former executive recalled. But Rupert backed Chernin.

Iced out by Chernin in Hollywood, Lachlan put his stamp on the *New York Post*, the money-losing business no one except Rupert paid much attention to. But this eventually brought Lachlan into conflict with Fox News chief Roger Ailes. In 1995, Rupert recruited Ailes—the pugilistic Republican political operative turned cable television executive—to launch a right-wing news network to challenge CNN. Ailes, then fifty, had an ego as massive as his Falstaffian girth and an explosive temper. He was like a human grenade with the pin pulled. Ailes was also pathologically paranoid: he carried a concealed handgun and outfitted Fox News's offices with bulletproof glass and surveillance cameras. Rupert tolerated Ailes's belligerence because Ailes gave Rupert the megaphone to influence American politics he'd coveted. By 2001, Fox was about to overtake CNN as the most-watched cable news network.

The schism between Lachlan and Ailes ripped wide open on October 18, 2001, when a *New York Post* staffer showed symptoms of anthrax poisoning. The FBI ordered Lachlan to keep the potential exposure strictly confidential until test results came back. Around midnight, Lachlan learned that Ailes had barged into Fox News shouting, "We're under attack! We're under attack!"

Lachlan raced down the elevator to find Ailes—still in his white-tie tuxedo from the Al Smith dinner—barking orders at terrified staffers.

"Roger, you need to let the FBI handle this," Lachlan said, his voice steady despite his fury.

Ailes wheeled around, his face flushed. "Fox News is my turf and I'll manage my people as I see fit."

The confrontation lasted only minutes, but staffers knew they were watching something seismic. Nobody talked to a member of the family like that. The next morning, executives predicted Ailes would be fired.

But Ailes had survived by going on offense. He raced to Rupert's office and threatened to resign, claiming Lachlan "hated" him. Rupert, who couldn't afford to lose his programming Svengali, offered Ailes a new three-year contract. For Lachlan, it was another devastating betrayal. First Chernin. Now Ailes. His father's pattern was becoming clear.

As Lachlan nursed his wounds, he confronted a formidable new adversary: his thirty-three-year-old stepmother.

WHEN RUPERT AND WENDI WED, she was living a fairy tale few Chinese women had known. She used to wash her clothes with the same soap she used for her face, but now there she was posing for Annie Leibovitz in *Vanity Fair*, meeting world leaders at Davos, renovating their collection of homes from London to Beijing to Soho.

Still, signs of Wendi's restless ambition were bubbling. "I'm not going to be a stay-at-home society wife," she told a colleague shortly after the wedding. She was bold, provocative, and unafraid to be the alpha in the marriage. "Are you going deaf, old man?" a colleague overheard her once teasing

Rupert. With her Yale MBA, Wendi had always seen herself as more than an ornament. "She's a bit frustrated by it—she'd love to work," Rupert acknowledged in an October 1999 interview. "She could get a job anywhere, but the fact is she cannot do that and travel with me. So we'll just have to resolve that somehow."

Wendi resolved the issue by forging an alliance with James. The two began traveling to China to invest in digital start-ups. Though she had no official title and drew no salary, she took meetings and handed out News Corp business cards inscribed with her name. This unusual arrangement— the CEO's young wife conducting company business with the CEO's son— got the attention of reporters at *The Wall Street Journal*. On October 31, 2000, the paper published a vicious 3,500-word profile of Wendi that chronicled her tempestuous journey out of China, including her affair with Jake Cherry, the American father who sponsored her student visa. The article enraged Rupert. Before publication, Murdoch's PR chief unsuccessfully tried to kill the story by lobbying the paper's editor and threatening to cut off the reporter's access.

The article humiliated Wendi. After its publication, she retreated to focus on her role as a new mother. In 2001, she gave birth to daughter Grace, followed by Chloe in 2003. She also embarked on a multiyear renovation of a trophy apartment. With Wendi's encouragement, Rupert bought Laurence Rockefeller's Fifth Avenue triplex for $44 million—then the most expensive purchase in New York history. The twenty-room apartment overlooked Central Park from the same building where Anna had raised the children. The symbolism was unmistakable: Rupert had traded up, literally.

Managing the house became part of Wendi's job. According to a former nanny, the Murdochs employed a pair of secretaries, a chef, two housekeepers, a tutor, and a part-time laundry person. Though Wendi insisted she did much of the work herself. "I quit work to work at home. To care for Rupert, slaving, don't get paid. Construction, chef, and cooking and house cleaning!" she told a journalist. Having paused her media career, she poured her ambitions into her children's future and securing their place in the Rupert dynasty.

In the fall of 2004, Rupert approached his adult children with an indelicate request: he wanted to include Chloe and Grace in the trust. It was more than just estate planning—it was Wendi's attempt to rewrite Anna's legacy. The divorce settlement that had secured the older children's inheritance was now under assault by the new wife and her daughters. Elisabeth, Lachlan, James, and Prue rejected the offer. As Lachlan saw it, Anna sacrificed half of what Rupert owed her—*billions*—to ensure that Lachlan and his siblings would control the company after Rupert died. Wendi refused to relent. According to the former nanny, Wendi and Rupert had a screaming match on Christmas that year over the trust structure. "They were fighting all night over the estate for the kids," the nanny recalled.

It was under this escalating pressure that Lachlan's relationship with his dad fractured. In the summer of 2004, Lachlan and Rupert fought bitterly over Rupert's plan to relocate News Corp's stock listing from Australia to New York. Doing so, Lachlan argued, would diminish the company's Australianness that sustained its buccaneering culture. Lachlan lost the debate, an outcome that stung all the more because his pro-Australia position would have spared the company grief. During the brief window when News Corp's shares moved from Australia to New York, cable mogul John Malone—the only media executive Rupert feared—doubled his stake in News Corp from 9 to 18 percent. It was a huge position from which Malone could threaten Rupert's control of the company. Lachlan wanted to be respected for his foresight. Instead, he felt increasingly marginalized.

In the summer of 2004, Disney courted Chernin to succeed Disney's longtime CEO Michael Eisner. Rupert, fearing Chernin might decamp to work for a rival, signed him to a massive new contract that ensured Chernin, not Lachlan, would be CEO if Rupert died suddenly. Chernin flexed these expanded powers to essentially bully Lachlan out of the company. Meanwhile, Ailes continued to make Lachlan's life miserable. According to a former Fox executive, Ailes fanned rumors around the company that Lachlan was gay. In the summer of 2005, Ailes pressured Lachlan to broadcast a reality show called *Crime Line* on Fox TV stations. Lachlan resisted, so Ailes went around him and lobbied Rupert directly. In early July, Lachlan stopped over in Los Angeles en route from Sydney when he heard his dad had told Ailes, "Do the show, don't listen to Lachlan." Lachlan called Joe Cross, a longtime friend in Sydney, and unloaded. "Fuck it. I'm out. If they're going to go around my back and whatever, then fuck them," Cross remembered Lachlan saying.

The programming dispute was trivial. But the emotional valence of his dad's betrayal triggered in Lachlan something like an existential crisis. Old resentments exploded into the open. For the past eleven years, Lachlan had climbed the ranks and proved himself—his prescient investment in the Australian real estate website REA Group would become one of News Corp's most successful deals ever—and yet Rupert allowed Ailes and Chernin to treat him like a callow interloper. Meanwhile, Rupert was plotting his takeover of *The Wall Street Journal* with forty-four-year-old *Times* of London editor Robert Thomson. The two had become close. Thomson was married to a Chinese woman and vacationed with Rupert and Wendi. It was painful watching his dad treat an employee like a surrogate son.

It was Rupert's dream that Lachlan would succeed him, but was it Lachlan's? Lachlan was the outgoing son, more like his mother, Anna. He enjoyed socializing, and was the outdoorsy type. He once told a News Corp associate that in another life, he might have been a forest guide. Lachlan was also confronting these questions as a new dad to a ten-month-old son named Kalan. "Are you your own man?" he imagined his son wondering. As Lachlan wrestled with his identity, he called Liz. She told him she was a lot happier since she quit the family business years ago. "It's easier to be a Murdoch outside of News Corp than inside," she said. Years later, she would recall the hurt Rupert caused by not protecting Lachlan from Ailes and Chernin's vicious campaign. "It wasn't the most emotionally intelligent way for Dad to handle it," she said. "He doesn't really have the tools to express that he's sorry."

On July 25, Lachlan called his dad and asked him to lunch the next day. They met at one of their usual spots, but this wasn't business as usual.

"I'm resigning," Lachlan said, lowering the boom. "I'm moving back to Sydney."

Rupert's face went through a series of emotions—shock, anger, desperation. He tried to negotiate, offering the same deals that had worked with countless executives over the decades. More money. More responsibility. Different reporting structures. But this wasn't a corporate defection. Rupert saw the company as an extension of himself, so Lachlan's decision was a personal rejection of everything he represented. The conversation grew emotional as the devastating irony became clear: Rupert's succession planning had driven away the very person he wanted to succeed him.

With his voice heavy but full of resolve, Lachlan told Rupert that if he didn't leave now, their relationship might not survive. "I have to be my own man," he said. Then the prince walked away from the throne, leaving his father to contemplate the wreckage of his dynastic dreams.

CHAPTER ELEVEN

"I'M DOING IT MY WAY"

AFTER LACHLAN'S ABDICATION, Rupert confronted an uncomfortable reality: the son he'd never fully trusted was now his only viable heir. This turn of events surprised News Corp executives because Rupert sometimes openly mocked James. When James illustrated a comic strip for the satirical *Harvard Lampoon,* Rupert told people the prestigious college paper was more about "drinking than journalism." Rupert's obvious preference for Lachlan was such that a 1999 profile in *The Sydney Morning Herald* dubbed James the "forgotten Murdoch."

Another mark against James: unlike affable Lachlan, he was combative and hotheaded. "Lachlan is very solid, and James is more volatile," their grandmother Dame Elisabeth once said. Les Hinton recalled a dinner hosted by Prime Minister Tony Blair at 10 Downing Street during which James spewed expletives at his dad as they debated Middle East politics. "After [James] had used the words 'fuck' and 'fucking' a dozen or so times, I became uneasy," Hinton remembered. "I know the feeling of being attacked by adult children who think they know everything, but we weren't at home sitting around with a few beers."

James was also willing to criticize Rupert in larger settings. At a News Corp retreat in the late 1990s, James lambasted his dad's lack of an Internet strategy. "We are woefully unprepared for this digital tidal wave that is now only minutes from shore. And there is no one to blame but ourselves," James told hundreds of executives. Before the speech, Rupert's longtime adviser Irwin Stelzer lobbied James to tone it down, to no avail. "I told James that it might not bode well for his future to insult people with whom he would have to work," Stelzer recalled.

Worse, James displayed no affinity for tabloid journalism, Rupert's abiding love. In 1997, James rejected his dad's offer to become deputy publisher of the *New York Post* and instead asked to spearhead News Corp's digital investments. James adopted the persona of a media futurist: he wore tailored black suits, thick-framed glasses, and peppered conversations with Internet speak. "We're basically agnostic about information platforms," he said in one interview. James may have looked the part, but he actually had little responsibility. "You've given me no money and no staff, and this is a bullshit job," he vented to his dad, according to a former colleague.

James's persistence convinced Rupert to open the purse strings, leading to a disastrous $400 million bid for Internet company PointCast just before it collapsed. After that debacle, Rupert gutted James's division and sent the furniture to HarperCollins. "The feeling was James was the mistake maker," a former executive said.

FOR THREE YEARS, James languished in corporate purgatory. Then in early 2000, while James was licking his wounds, Rupert called with a seemingly innocuous question: "Do you like Chinese food?"

James knew his dad was congenitally averse to small talk, and suspected the question masked an agenda. James was right: Rupert wanted James to move to Hong Kong to become CEO of Star TV. On paper, it looked like Rupert was banishing his twenty-seven-year-old son. China was where careers at News Corp went to die. Rupert had recently ousted Star TV's CEO, a Chinese-American MBA named Gareth Change, after just eighteen months in the job.

But James, smartly, recognized the opportunity. By running Star TV from Asia, he would be far removed from the viperous politics of Rupert's court. In May 2000, James and his new wife, Kathryn, headed to Hong Kong. They met in the winter of 1997 in Australia, where Kathryn was modeling. On a charter flight, James struck up a conversation with a beautiful blonde reading one of his favorite novels, *Midnight's Children* by Salman Rushdie. Two years later, they married in a small ceremony on the banks of the Connecticut River. James read poetry by Pablo Neruda. She read James Joyce.

The perception of James among Star TV executives was that he needed to be rehabilitated after his failed Internet investments. "This is going to be a nightmare," one former executive remembered thinking. But James quickly proved doubters wrong. The irony of James being considered the black sheep was that he was the most Rupert-like of the children. "He's ruthless like Rupert," a former colleague said. James gave speeches attacking the BBC and cravenly courted the Chinese government. Human rights advocates denounced James's pro-Beijing propaganda, but the strategy paid off: in December 2001, the Chinese government finally granted Star a license to broadcast in the mainland. By April 2002, the network turned its first profit. James juiced Star's revenues by expanding into India. At one point, Star broadcast fifty of the top Hindi-language shows.

In the fall of 2003, Rupert rewarded James's success by naming him CEO of BSkyB in London. The decision was controversial. James was just thirty, and BSkyB was a publicly traded company. The financial community complained that Rupert was promoting his son to advance his nepotistic succession plan. BSkyB's stock plunged nearly 20 percent during the ninety minutes that James gave his first investor presentation. The stakes couldn't have been higher. In April 2003, News Corp bought a majority stake in DirecTV for $6.6 billion. Rupert wanted to make the American satellite service the centerpiece of a global broadband network, of which BSkyB was a major node. Rupert's entire strategy would be imperiled if James failed in London.

James again converted skeptics into believers. He brazenly predicted Sky would hit ten million subscribers by the end of the decade, and hit the number ahead of schedule. James benefited from good timing: streaming services were still years away from eroding traditional television, giving satellite providers a brief window of dominance that James exploited. He also made gut decisions that struck fear into the heart of opponents. In 2006, James swooped in and bought a big stake in ITV while Richard Branson's Virgin Group was angling to buy it. "By the time we did ITV, [James] was confident and ready to play the pantomime villain," a colleague said. Rivals began referring to Sky as the "Death Star." James embraced the image and installed a life-size Darth Vader statue outside his office.

But James also aspired to be respected by the establishment. He threw around MBA buzzwords and cared deeply about how News Corp was perceived—it bothered him that, because of Rupert's right-wing tabloids and Fox News, the company was seen as downscale and predatory. "When I'd say things like 'compliance,' they'd be like, 'Oh my God, he uses business-school speak!'" James later recalled. "And it's like, 'No, it's the English language, and it's kind of an important idea.'" Early on, James drafted a set of corporate values for Sky and organized a retreat at a Cotswold spa where his executives sat on a circle of stones and discussed Sky's future. "All these grumpy, old English guys were looking around like, 'What the fuck is this guy talking about?'" James later said.

Whereas Lachlan and Sarah became celebrities in Sydney, James and Kathryn kept decidedly low profiles in London. The couple rarely attended red-carpet premieres, preferring to stay home with their two young children. In this way, James was more like his private half-sister Prue. "James was a decent guy who was home to bathe his kids. He tried to learn from his dad's actions and he didn't want to be absent like him," a former executive said.

James's smartest maneuverings were directed at his own rise within News Corp. Rupert jettisoned flashy executives like Barry Diller when their profiles threatened to eclipse his own. James shrewdly stayed out of the press and told his PR adviser that he would be successful when people began referring to him as the "reclusive James Murdoch." Watching Lachlan's battles with Chernin and Ailes, James avoided their fiefdoms. "James played it so right. He left the country and established himself," a former senior News Corp executive said. James's career strategy could be summed up by a Chinese proverb he would quote often: "The mountains are high and the emperor is far away."

It also helped James that the emperor was distracted by new conquests—conquests that, ironically, vindicated James's earlier warnings about the digital revolution.

A LITTLE OVER A year after James arrived at Sky, Rupert bought MySpace for $580 million. Rupert boasted the social network would change the world but paid it almost no attention. In the summer of 2005, he was plotting another takeover that had much deeper emotional resonance: he wanted to buy *The Wall Street Journal*.

Since arriving in New York in the early seventies, Rupert longed to own one of the crown jewels of American journalism. Irwin Stelzer recalled Rupert once musing he would sell News Corp to own *The New York Times*. In financial terms, it was an absurd hypothetical: News Corp generated roughly $23 billion in revenues in 2005, the *Times* just $3.4 billion. The only possible explanation was that the *Times* had greater psychogenic value for Rupert—as if owning the paper would finally win the approval of his dead father. In any event, Stelzer never took the idea seriously because America's media dynasties—the Sulzbergers of the *Times*, Grahams of *The Washington Post*, and Bancrofts of *The Wall Street Journal*—would never sell their papers, especially to a pirate like Rupert.

That all changed in late spring 2005. Rupert got a tip from a money manager named Andy Steginsky that several Bancroft heirs were growing restless as the *Journal*'s financial performance deteriorated. The clan had controlled Dow Jones since 1902. Subsequent generations lived off generous dividends while the last Bancroft to run the company committed suicide in 1933. Rupert saw them as entitled elites sucking the newspaper dry to fund hobbies like show-horse breeding and opera singing. Steginsky told Rupert that he was friendly with a dissident Bancroft cousin named Billy

Cox III who lived in Rome (of course). Rupert dispatched him to meet Cox and explore a deal.

But first, Rupert needed to tamp down two rebellions that weakened his control of News Corp. The first was instigated by his family. Wendi continued to demand that their daughters, Grace, four, and Chloe, three, be treated as full heirs with equal voting rights in the trust, which his four adult children opposed. After months of acrimony, Rupert broke the stalemate with money: he gave each of his children $150 million cash. Then on July 20, 2006, he appeared on *Charlie Rose* and declared that Chloe and Grace would be financial equals but would get no voting rights—essentially defining the kids as second-class citizens of Rupertland.

Rupert next had to deal with John Malone. The Colorado-based media mogul had been circling Rupert since Malone's company, Liberty Media, bought nearly 20 percent of News Corp stock during the chaos of the domicile change. That gave Malone serious leverage, and he extracted painful concessions. Three days before Christmas 2006, News Corp announced it would swap its $6 billion stake in DirecTV for Malone's News Corp stock. The deal killed Rupert's dream to build a global satellite broadband network. Rupert viewed it as a necessary sacrifice. By getting back Malone's shares, Rupert boosted his ownership of News Corp from 31 percent to an unshakable 38 percent, and cleared the path for the Dow Jones takeover.

On April 9, 2007, Rupert offered the Bancrofts $5 billion for Dow Jones—a 67 percent premium over the company's share price. The bid juiced the value of the Bancroft trust by $500 million. It was classic Murdoch: strike with such overwhelming financial firepower to force the other side to capitulate. The Bancroft family soon tore itself apart as various factions debated whether to resist Rupert or sell to him.

Rupert deployed a canny strategy to flip the holdouts: he summoned James from London to meet the Bancrofts on a rain-slicked afternoon in June. "I brought in James so they could see that we're a family company," Rupert later explained. James flew by private jet across the Atlantic, arriving two hours late from a charity speech in London.

James strode into the conference room and made a showy display of hugging his dad in front of the skeptical Bancrofts. What the Bancrofts saw as cynicism, Rupert and James experienced as love language: corporate machinations were how the family communicated. Rupert was using James as a prop, but James was also playing his dad: he knew his father would be focused on transforming the *Journal* after acquiring it, and that distraction would let James build a rival power base in London. When the Bancrofts questioned Rupert's editorial independence, James jumped to his father's defense. These dilettantes had run their company into the ground; who were they to challenge his father's business ethics?

In December 2007, Rupert got his prize. But victory came with an unexpected emotional cost. Steginsky later recalled Rupert was anguished that his takeover shattered the Bancrofts. "How could you feel good about it? It wasn't the route he hoped the family would take," Steginsky said. It was a cruel paradox: Rupert, who prized family loyalty above all else, had torn apart another dynasty to expand his own. Perhaps Rupert glimpsed his own family's potential future in the wreckage he'd created.

A WEEK BEFORE THE *JOURNAL* DEAL CLOSED, Rupert promoted James to run all of News Corp's businesses in Europe and Asia. James remained chairman of Sky. It was more power than Lachlan had ever attained. In London, James and Kathryn socialized with Liz and her husband, Matthew Freud, at their white stucco house in Notting Hill and their country estate. James and Liz shared the same ideas about where the culture was going and what News Corp should become. They admired their dad but loathed his tabloid ventures, especially Fox News (even if James respected Fox's nearly $1 billion profit). They wanted News Corp to be as respected as its rivals Comcast, Disney, and Time Warner. "Liz and James talked all the time. They complained about Rupert together," a London-based media executive said.

Surprisingly, Rupert seemed open to their liberal influence. After marrying Wendi, Rupert's friend group expanded to include the "Google guys," Larry Page and Sergey Brin; Queen Raina of Jordan; Arianna Huffington;

David Geffen; Nicole Kidman; and Hugh Jackman, among others. News Corp's senior ranks liberalized, too: along with Chernin, there was General Counsel Lon Jacobs and Communications Chief Gary Ginsberg, a former lawyer in the Bill Clinton administration and college friend of John F. Kennedy Jr.

Rupert was adopting progressive positions on climate change and immigration reform. In July 2006, Rupert invited Al Gore to speak at News Corp's retreat in Monterey, California. Kathryn was so inspired by his presentation—a version of the slide show that was the basis of his Oscar-winning documentary, *An Inconvenient Truth*—that she became an environmental activist. "I decided to switch everything I was doing," she later said. "I wanted to be able to look my children in the eye and say 'I did everything I could.'" At her urging, she and James convinced Rupert to pledge to make News Corp "carbon neutral" within three years. In 2007, Rupert hosted a fundraiser for Hillary Clinton and even flirted with endorsing Barack Obama for president.

James's liberal allies encouraged Rupert to cooperate with *Vanity Fair* columnist Michael Wolff for his book on the Dow Jones deal, hoping to ease Rupert toward retirement. When the book was published in December 2008, the plan backfired spectacularly. Ailes threatened to resign after reading Wolff's claim that Rupert was ashamed of Fox News. "The embarrassment can't be missed—[Rupert] mumbles even more than usual when called on to justify it; he barely pretends to hide the way he feels about Bill O'Reilly," Wolff wrote. "And while it is not possible that he would give Fox up—because the money is the money; success trumps all—in the larger sense of who he is, he seems to want to hedge his bets."

"Is this true?" Ailes demanded in a September 2008 meeting.

To prove his loyalty, Rupert signed Ailes to a new five-year contract that also enshrined Fox News's editorial independence. Ailes soon put conspiracy theorist Glenn Beck on the air. "That was the beginning of when the network went crazy," a Murdoch adviser said.

James was angry with Wolff, too. Despite the access, Wolff portrayed News Corp as a carnival of clashing egos. James blamed Ginsberg for authorizing the project. But the crisis also presented an opportunity for James to reshape News Corp's power structure. In February 2009, Chernin announced he was leaving, creating a leadership vacuum. James moved quickly to fill it. He told his dad he wanted Ginsberg, a Chernin loyalist, to leave. "What James figured out is, whoever controls the press and investor relations controls James's image," a person close to Ginsberg said. Ginsberg soon resigned.

The pattern was unmistakable to News Corp veterans: James had already gotten his human resources director moved to New York in 2007, and now he wanted his PR chief, Matthew Anderson, stationed there as well. News Corp executives began referring to James's management team as the "Shadow Government"—a parallel power structure that could operate independently of Rupert's New York headquarters. This was a step too far for Rupert, who had spent decades ensuring no executive accumulated enough influence to challenge him. He rejected James's request to promote Anderson.

It was a momentary setback. In the summer of 2009, James advocated for Rupert to let him bid for the 61 percent of Sky that News Corp didn't own. If successful, the $11.5 billion deal would make James's London operation as powerful as his dad's in New York. James also cultivated News Corp's biggest outside shareholder, Saudi prince Alwaleed bin Talal. During an interview with Charlie Rose, the prince advocated for James to be Rupert's successor.

But the pathway to a deal was fraught with risk. James's aggressive leadership of Sky had drawn the ire of Britain's media regulator, Ofcom. Rivals charged that the Murdochs already controlled too much of the country's media. They were certain to mount a furious campaign to prevent James from increasing News Corp's reach. Rupert was also chafing at James's power grab, seeing Prince Alwaleed's interview as James's backhanded way to pressure him into retirement.

When James most needed allies, his personality became a liability. James had Rupert's killer instinct but none of his innate charm. Worse, James began breaking his own rule to fly below the radar. After the *Independent* newspaper ran an advertisement criticizing News Corp, James barged into the editor's office and snapped, "What the fuck are you playing at?" "Prue feared that the Real James was being lost in the Corporate James," a former colleague said. "It's what happens when you get too close to Rupert." The cautionary tale was clear: James was sacrificing his identity to win his father's favor.

James's unchecked ambition was on full display in August 2009 when James delivered the MacTaggart Lecture at the Edinburgh International Television Festival, where twenty years earlier, James's dad had attacked the BBC as "innately unsympathetic to markets and competition." In the weeks before James's speech, he drafted a similarly Ayn Randian polemic that sanctified the free market while casting the BBC as an Orwellian instrument of government thought control. James's speech inspired panic amongst News Corp executives, the last line especially: "The only reliable, durable, and perpetual guarantor of independence is profit." Rupert and Liz also lobbied James to tone down the language. "Someone had sent the thing to Rupert. Rupert saw it and said 'Fuck, you can't say that, it's too extreme,'" a former executive recalled. Sky's communications chief drafted a new ending that made the point in a less incendiary way.

That night, Sky and News Corp executives gathered for dinner at Martin Wishart, a Michelin-starred restaurant in Edinburgh. James strode in and said he'd made up his mind. "I know you don't like what I've done and you've even tried to get my dad involved, thank you very much," he said, according to an attendee. "You've given me this alternative ending and I've considered it very carefully and you know what? Fuck the lot of you and fuck my dad, I'm doing it my way." As Rupert and others predicted, James's speech inspired fierce and immediate backlash from the British media establishment.

James, however, remained defiant. A couple of weeks later, James put the second phase of his Sky takeover strategy in motion: he would topple Prime Minister Gordon Brown. On the night of September 10, 2009, James met Brown's opponent, David Cameron, the forty-two-year-old Tory leader, at a Mayfair members club. Cameron, a former television company PR executive, planned to run in the general election the following year on a free-market platform that would be friendlier to News Corp's Sky acquisition. Over drinks, James told Cameron that *The Sun* would be flipping its endorsement to the Tories after backing the Labour Party for the last dozen years.

The decision was another measure of James's willingness to usurp his dad's authority. In 2006, Rupert gave an interview calling Cameron "totally inexperienced." Cameron aggressively courted Rupert, flying to meet aboard his yacht *Rosehearty* off the coast of Santorini, but a relationship didn't blossom. In the 2010 election, Rupert supported Brown, whose father had been a Scottish Presbyterian minister, just like Rupert's paternal grandfather. "Gordon has a Calvinistic approach to life, and there is a lot to be said for it," Rupert told a journalist.

James and *The Sun*'s flame-haired editor, Rebekah Brooks, planned the Cameron endorsement to maximize the damage to Brown. *The Sun* released its front-page headline—"Labour's Lost It"—on September 29, 2009, the same day Brown addressed Labour's nominating convention in Brighton. The timing ensured that Brown's impassioned speech was drowned in the torrent of articles about *The Sun*'s historic political switch.

A few days later, *The Sun* struck again. A front-page article alleged Brown misspelled the name of a soldier killed in Afghanistan in a condolence letter he'd sent to the soldier's grieving mother. Even Rupert loyalists thought it was a deeply unfair attack. Brown's poor eyesight was well documented, and journalists knew he routinely misspelled words. "It was a low blow and Brown [was] said to have snapped over the story," Hinton remembered. Rupert later testified that Brown called him and seethed, "Your company has declared war on my government, and we have no choice but to declare war on your company."

Brown denied he made the threat, but no one doubted that he wanted retribution. The phone hacking scandal would soon give him the opportunity—and James would become its primary casualty. In his ruthless campaign to prove himself worthy of his father's empire, James had made himself the perfect target for its destruction.

PART THREE

COLLAPSE

CHAPTER TWELVE

THE FOURTH OF JULY

DAVID CAMERON'S ELECTION VICTORY IN May 2010 was also James's triumph. With direct access to 10 Downing Street secured, James was ready to launch the biggest deal of his life: on June 15, 2010, he greenlighted Operation Rubicon, the internal code name for his $11.5 billion takeover of BSkyB. James viewed the acquisition as the final step to earning his father's approval—and his succession. The deal would effectively tie Rupert's hands, making James's London fiefdom bigger than Rupert's empire in New York. "James wanted BSkyB to use up all News Corp's debt headroom so Rupert couldn't buy anything else," said a person who spoke frequently to James during this time.

Other family members were also challenging Rupert's power. On the morning of January 9—five months before James made the BSkyB bid—Rupert was on his Boeing 737 returning to New York from Los Angeles when he got an email from Freud. "I've given a quote to the New York *Times*, and you're probably not going to like it," Rupert read in disbelief on his BlackBerry, which he'd only recently begun using. Freud's quote lived up to its advance billing—and quite a bit more: "I am by no means alone within the family or the company in being ashamed and sickened by Roger Ailes's horrendous and sustained disregard of the journalistic standards that News

Corporation, its founder and every other global media business aspires to." The quote revealed the deep ideological fault line running beneath the facade of family unity: Rupert knew that James, Liz, and Prue wanted to steer News Corp to the political middle, but now the rift was out in the open.

Rupert, pushing eighty, responded to this rebellion with a mounting alarm. "I'm just sick of being told I'm dying," he complained during a shareholder meeting. Perhaps sensing James's swelling confidence, Rupert moved to undermine him by trying to recruit Lachlan and Elisabeth back to News Corp. It was a calculated cruelty. When Lachlan quit in 2005, Rupert cut him off. "Don't let him into the fucking building—when you're out, you're out," Rupert growled to the CEO of News Corp Australia. Humiliated, Lachlan launched an investment firm called Illyria—the island of transformation in Shakespeare's *Twelfth Night*. But Illyria failed. For Lachlan, returning to News Corp would validate his dad's judgment that he couldn't be successful on his own.

In 2009, Liz had refused her dad's invitation to join the News Corp board. But now she was more receptive to Rupert's overtures. She had proved, more than any of her siblings, that she could thrive outside the family. Her company, Shine, produced global television hits like *MasterChef* and had acquired Reveille, the American production company behind *The Office* and *The Biggest Loser*, for $200 million. As James pushed the BSkyB deal forward, Rupert told Liz he wanted News Corp to buy Shine. James warned her it was a trap, but Elisabeth listened to his concerns skeptically. Wouldn't that precisely be the advice of a rival threatened by her success?

With his children still resisting his control, Rupert took an extraordinary step: he asked them to do family therapy. In the fall of 2010, a therapist met with Rupert and the kids—no spouses allowed—in Cavan, the family's Australian sheep farm. Ostensibly, the family wanted to use the exercise to help James and Rupert get along. But the sessions were doomed to fail. The Murdochs were emotionally stunted in different ways, and the family talked about business as a proxy for ever having a difficult conversation. According to a source familiar with the meeting, the therapist asked each family member to stand with their back to others and let them vent their grievances. "It was a car crash," James later said. "Everyone was more alienated from each other at the end." But Rupert had achieved his real goal: forcing his children to confront their powerlessness against him.

A couple of months after the therapy, around Christmas 2010, Rupert gave James an ultimatum: move to New York or be fired. Rupert presented it as a promotion. James would be elevated to News Corp's deputy chief operating officer, a title that suggested he had a lock on succession. But really it was Rupert's opportunity to dismantle James's London operation before James could finish the BSkyB takeover.

At the same time, Rupert positioned Liz as James's in-house rival: News Corp bought Shine for $670 million. Playing to her ambitions, Rupert promised Liz a seat on News Corp's board and told her that she—not James—was his preferred successor, according to a source who was briefed on the discussions at the time. The plan was for Liz to debut her new status by appearing alongside Rupert at the annual Consumer Electronics Show in Las Vegas in early January 2011. But once she signed the paperwork on the Shine deal, Rupert stopped talking to her. "He disinvited her from CES literally a week after he told her she was going to be his successor," a person close to Liz said. "She was heartbroken."

By spring 2011, Rupert had crushed his children's putsch and seemed to have restored order to his empire. But his victory was illusory. While he'd been focused on the enemy within, a far greater threat had been building outside the castle gates for years.

ON SATURDAY EVENING, JULY 2, 2011, Liz and Freud threw what would become the fin de siècle celebration of the Chipping Norton set, a clique of political, media, and business elites who owned sumptuous homes in the verdant Oxfordshire hills. At their twenty-two-bedroom Cotswold estate, the annual summer party was in full swing. A jazz band played on the landscaped gardens as guests, including Bono and Helena Bonham Carter, mingled between two opulent restaurant marquees—Pizza East and Cecconi's—created by Soho House founder Nick Jones. Freud, wearing leather trousers, greeted Cameron's education secretary, Michael Gove, and former Labour ministers Peter Mandelson and David Miliband—old enemies united by proximity to power. CNN's Piers Morgan surveyed the crowd and remarked to his wife, "I've never seen so many people who hate each other together in one room."

But at the center of the festivities, something was off. James huddled with News International CEO Rebekah Brooks discussing something urgent. The forty-three-year-old Brooks's carrot-colored curls, aquiline nose, and piercing blue eyes normally made her the magnetic center of any gathering. "Usually, Rebekah flits around having a word with everyone. But that night she spent nearly all her time with News International people," one guest remembered.

Twenty-four hours later, the source of Brooks's apparent agitation became clear: *The Guardian* reported that a private investigator working for Rupert's *News of the World* had hacked into the cell phone of Milly Dowler—the thirteen-year-old whose 2002 kidnapping and murder had gripped Britain. The newspaper had deleted Dowler's messages—thereby giving her parents false hope that she was alive. The revelation outraged the public and ignited a crisis that News Corp had been trying to contain for years.

The newspaper had been exposed once already for hacking. Years earlier, on January 26, 2007, a British judge sentenced a *News of the World* reporter to four months in prison for illegally accessing voice messages on Royal Family phones, describing his actions as "reprehensible in the extreme." The tabloid's editor Andy Coulson resigned, insisting he knew nothing about the hacking. Cameron hired Coulson months later as his communications director, binding the Conservative Party to the scandal. As the rival newspaper *The Guardian* continued to break story after story about more hacking transgressions, the victims sued News Corp. The company claimed the surveillance was the work of a single "rogue reporter." But a *New York Times* investigation in September 2010 reported Coulson had authorized widespread hacking, leading Cameron to finally dump him. When the Dowler revelation came to light, it set a new bar for exploitation: this time, a tabloid deepened the grief of a murdered child's family.

The hacking scandal was an existential business crisis and public relations disaster. But at its core it was a battleground for the Rupert family to wage emotional warfare against each other. James was furious he was becoming the face of the scandal. The hacking had occurred years before he assumed responsibility for the London tabloids. Nevertheless, James was linked to it because *The Guardian* revealed that, in 2008, he approved a £1 million settlement with hacking victims. James insisted he had just been following advice of the company's lawyers. The answer smelled like a cover-up.

James felt under siege. Paparazzi camped outside his London house. Kathryn begged James to defend himself in public. "You cannot just sit here and hide!" she said. "My father won't let me," James said. The cocky executive who'd defied Rupert when he ran Sky was now acting like the scared child.

Muzzled, James worked damage control behind the scenes. In the wake of the Dowler report, James told Rupert they needed to apologize and shut down *News of the World* to save the BSkyB takeover. News Corp's stock was plummeting. Rupert and Lachlan were attending the annual Allen & Company media retreat in Sun Valley, Idaho, and pushed back. The 168-year-old tabloid was the first British newspaper Rupert bought when he left Australia, and he did not want to let it go. Rupert wanted to counterattack. On July 8, when Coulson was arrested for his alleged role in hacking, Rupert agreed to shutter *News of the World.* But almost immediately Rupert began telling people it was a mistake and blamed James for caving to public pressure.

For Rupert, closing a newspaper was like cutting off a limb—and it seemed to age him overnight. Les Hinton was shocked at Rupert's diminished state when he walked into the living room of Rupert's London flat on July 12. "He was slumped forward in a chair. His elbows rested on his knees and the fingers of his old hands were locked together. His head was drooped and still," he recalled. James told people his dad's addled behavior was making things much worse. Rupert told reporters his top priority was saving Brooks, who had edited *News of the World* when the Dowler hacking occurred. He complained to a *Wall Street Journal* reporter that he was "getting annoyed" at the barrage of bad press. James was angry at his dad but also genuinely frightened. The media titan they would catch breakfast with at 5:00 a.m. with their blazers on now seemed fragile and confused. "Dude, our old man has gone crazy. This is terrible," James told Lachlan, his voice breaking slightly.

Liz also found the entire situation galling. In the space of a week, the narrative of the self-made daughter, the one who'd made good on her own before returning to the fold, had been forgotten. As Freud had warned, now she was just another Murdoch, entitled and corrupt. In the United States, shareholders had filed a lawsuit claiming Rupert overpaid for her company and treated News Corp like a "candy store." If News Corp hadn't bought Shine, Liz would have essentially been an observer. But now she had a stake and as much right to hold her brother and Brooks accountable as anyone. She blamed James for mismanaging the crisis. On a family conference call on Monday, July 11, Liz argued James and Brooks should resign. Rupert said no decisions regarding the resignations should be made until Lachlan flew in from Sydney in two days. "I'm not throwing innocent people under the bus," Rupert had said.

On July 13, Liz went to Wapping, News Corp's fortress-like London headquarters, to take control of the crisis. The tenth-floor executive offices were, at that point, more war zone than war room. "The place was going nuts," an executive who was present recalled. When Liz arrived, Rupert told her that he now agreed with her that James should resign. Rupert then made as cruel a request as a father could make: he told Liz to fire James. It was Anna's deepest fears realized: Rupert was pitting their kids against each other in a corporate *Hunger Games*.

Liz was desperate for her dad's approval—and to take out a sibling rival—so she went to James's office. As she walked down the hall, she replayed all the problems with the family business, trying to convince herself this was justified. She loved James as a brother, but she saw his favoritism as undeserved.

She was the talented one. This was only fair. She knocked on James's office door and poked her head in. "I was chatting with Dad, and we think the only way to stop the noise is for you to step down," she said. James was gutted, not only by his sister's betrayal but also by their father's cowardice. He told Liz that if Rupert wanted to fire him, he should say it to his face. The siblings wouldn't speak for years. "It's one of the greatest regrets of my life," she later said.

TWO DAYS LATER, Rupert met the Dowlers at a London hotel and was forced to confront the cruelty of his tabloids. Rupert told the anguished parents that it was "the worst day of my life." He said his father had been a crusading journalist who had exposed the Gallipoli military disaster and never would have condoned the *News of the World*'s invasive criminality. The Dowlers' lawyer Mark Lewis told Rupert that his mother, Dame Elisabeth, now 103, must be ashamed of him. Rupert buried his head in his hands. When Rupert left the hotel, a scrum of reporters pressed microphones in his agitated face as protesters shouted "shame on you!" "Rupert was shaken by the fact that so many press were out there. He was used to giving it and wasn't used to getting it," Lewis recalled.

But Rupert had little time for moral accounting—plus looking back was anathema to him. By mid-July 2011, the phone hacking crisis escalated from a media scandal into a national reckoning that exposed a corrupt relationship between tabloids and government. The BBC and others reported that News Corp had buried "smoking gun" emails that revealed Coulson authorized bribes to police for information. Politicians who had courted Rupert for decades and feared his tabloids now went on the attack. Gordon Brown, still bitter over his election loss, accused News Corp of "law-breaking on an industrial scale" and likened the Murdochs to a mafia. On July 13, Parliament issued a summons for Rupert and James to testify. News Corp abandoned its bid for BSkyB, destroying everything James had been working toward. As if to punctuate the point that James's star had burned out, Lachlan arrived from Sydney that day and became a constant presence at their dad's side.

The scandal went global. On July 14, the FBI launched an investigation into allegations that Murdoch tabloids hacked the phones of 9/11 victims. Rupert needed to give his critics scalps. To protect himself, he told James he should resign, but changed his mind after a sleepless night. Others would take the fall instead. On July 15, Brooks resigned along with her predecessor, Les Hinton. They were the closest thing to family: Rupert adored Brooks like a daughter, and Hinton had worked for Rupert for more than fifty years. On July 17, London police arrested Brooks on charges of phone hacking and bribery. James's wife, Kathryn, later said the sound of a police siren made her panic that James, too, would be arrested.

Rupert and James were scheduled to appear before Parliament on July 19. The Murdochs did their best to unify beforehand. Prudence arrived from Sydney. Even Anna flew in to support James. Though she despised talking to her ex-husband, she called Rupert and told him to publicly support their son. The media built anticipation for the televised session like it was a Watergate hearing. One notable absence was Liz. As James prepared to testify, Freud and Liz skipped town, spending two weeks on a yacht.

On the afternoon of July 19, James and Rupert sat for their Parliamentary interrogation. Rupert had been a shadowy force in British politics for decades, and now, finally, he was appearing in broad daylight, forced to answer questions under oath as his callow son looked on. What the world witnessed was the great revelation: behind the curtain was not a fearsome media wizard but a confused eighty-year-old man with shorn white hair whose empire was crumbling on live television. "This is the most humble day of my life," Rupert said, feebly. The image was complete when Wendi leapt to Rupert's defense and spiked a foam pie from the hands of a protester who was attempting to hurl it at Rupert's face.

The scandal's human cost was staggering. More than ninety Murdoch employees and associates were arrested for alleged roles in hacking. At least one, former *News of the World* reporter Sean Hoare, was found dead under suspicious circumstances. During the trials that followed, salacious details emerged—including that Brooks and Coulson had had an affair while running the tabloid—adding soap opera elements to the corporate tragedy.

The financial and reputational toll was equally devastating. News Corp paid out hundreds of millions in settlements and legal fees. Brooks was eventually acquitted, but Coulson was sentenced to eighteen months in jail. Most damaging of all was Parliament's verdict in May 2012: Rupert was "not fit and proper" to run a major international company. The ruling carried no legal weight but was devastating symbolically—the British establishment had formally declared him unworthy of the power he'd wielded for decades, validating their view, going back to 1968—when Rupert bought *News of the World*—that Rupert was a malevolent influence on the country.

AFTER GROUP THERAPY IN THE FALL OF 2010, Rupert's four adult children had signed a family constitution called "Murdoch Principles." The goal was to institute rules that might prevent succession from causing a sibling rupture. "We commit to undertake active dialog with each other at all times and to relentlessly communicate openly, with trust and humility," read one clause. Another promised: "We will be vigilant of and defend against divisiveness, either between us or that which could infiltrate from without." The document now reads like a prophecy of everything that was about to go wrong. The phone hacking exploded any hopes that the constitution would prevent the family unraveling that Anna most feared.

James suffered the worst. Unlike his dad, who appeared doddering before Parliament, James came across as both robotic and testy. The Watergate parallels were impossible to miss: What did James know and when did he know it? James asserted repeatedly that he signed hacking settlements with victims in 2008 because News International lawyers told him that hacking was isolated to one rogue reporter. This assertion was undermined by Tom Crone, a *News of the World* lawyer, and Colin Myler, the tabloid's former editor, who claimed under oath that they told James about pervasive hacking. If true, James was complicit in a cover-up. James's reputation—and career future—hinged on which version people believed.

Family relationships wouldn't survive the scandal. James and Kathryn blamed Liz and Freud for orchestrating a whisper campaign in the press to damage James and boost Liz's succession chances. For their part, Liz and Freud told people that James should have admitted he mismanaged the hacking crisis. In September 2011, the Murdochs gathered off the coast of Spain on Rupert's 184-foot new yacht *Rosehearty* for Lachlan's fortieth birthday, but Liz left before James and Kathryn arrived. The tensions between Freud and the Murdochs ultimately strained Liz's marriage and ended their reign as London's dominant power couple. Their previous summer's grand party would be seen as the Chipping Norton set's finale. "It was like *The Last Hurrah*, the moment when politicians, newspaper editors, financiers, and celebrities could be together," one guest said.

Anna watched from afar as her worst predictions came true. The children she'd tried to protect from their father's manipulations were now destroying each other exactly as she'd warned they would.

In February 2012, James left London in disgrace for exile in New York. He resigned from the chairmanship of BSkyB, the satellite broadcaster that, if it were not for hacking, would have been his stepping stone to the CEO suite. James's handling of the hacking scandal confirmed Rupert's suspicions that James didn't have the temperament to be his successor, and he redoubled his campaign to recruit Lachlan back to the company. James and Kathryn felt deeply betrayed. It was confirmation that the sibling competition was rigged from the start. Kathryn later realized that Rupert had used James's "promotions" as opportunities for James to fail so Lachlan could inherit the company. "He was pitting them against each other," she later said, "but there was always going to be one winner."

Liz spent the next year distancing herself from the family. She told Rupert she would not be joining News Corp's board following the Shine purchase. In August 2012, she decided to address the scandal publicly for the first time by delivering the MacTaggart Lecture at the Edinburgh International Television Festival. Liz spent weeks on her speech and wrote as many as a dozen drafts. Hitting the appropriate tone was like walking a tightrope with no net to catch her: she would be criticizing her family and Shine's parent company. Addressing the audience in a conservative black sleeveless dress, Liz pitched herself as the enlightened Rupert, praising the BBC and quoting Nelson Mandela. She aimed her harshest criticism at James, who on the stage three years prior had declared profit was the only guarantor of journalistic independence. "Profit without purpose is a recipe for disaster," she said. James felt betrayed. Rupert refused to read it and didn't speak to Liz for months. "I thought it was falling in line too much with the sort of BBC and establishment," Rupert later said. The media celebrated Liz. The Australian Broadcasting Corporation hailed it "as the best speech given by any of the Murdoch family."

It was fitting, perhaps, that the next time the Murdochs gathered was for Dame Elisabeth's funeral. The Murdoch matriarch died at 103 in December 2012. In his eulogy, Rupert told the one thousand mourners packed into Melbourne's St. Paul's Cathedral about Dame Elisabeth's moral influence on his life. She was the one person Rupert felt obliged to please. He had launched the upmarket *Australian* newspaper in 1964 to prove he could do more than tabloid journalism. "She just wanted to make sure we understood the gravity of our actions and the impact our choices had on others," he said. Now she was gone, and Rupert had no one to answer to but himself.

CHAPTER THIRTEEN

SPLIT

THE PHONE HACKING CRISIS WAS a cancer metastasizing inside Rupert's empire. In the summer of 2012, Rupert excised the malignancy: he announced that his toxic tabloids would be quarantined at News Corp while faster-growing assets like the film studio and Fox News would be owned by a new company called 21st Century Fox. Rupert had opposed the operation at first. "It was emotional," he later said. He relented because the corporate chemotherapy was necessary to save what mattered most.

While Rupert was cleaving his empire, his marriage was splitting as well—though publicly no one knew it. The previous summer, at Parliament, Wendi became world famous when she spiked the shaving cream pie before the protester threw it in Rupert's face. It was an indelible image: a fierce wife defending her husband's honor. "Nothing characterizes her more than that moment," fashion mogul Diane von Furstenberg told *The New York Times*. But by that point Rupert and Wendi were essentially living parallel lives. A former employee recalled they slept separately at their Fifth Avenue triplex.

The breakup traced back to a moment when Rupert blindsided Wendi on national television. In July 2006, Rupert unilaterally announced on *Charlie Rose* that Chloe and Grace wouldn't get voting rights in the trust. Rupert apparently hadn't given Wendi a heads-up, and she called his cell phone screaming about his announcement, according to a News Corp executive who overheard the conversation. The problems didn't end there. Charlie Rose was coincidentally scheduled to moderate a panel at a News Corp retreat in California a few days later, and Wendi demanded that Rupert disinvite him. In a detail that would become a company legend, Rupert told executives that when he arrived at their Carmel ranch, Wendi made him sleep in the garage.

The girls' inheritance might have been a resolvable issue; Rupert and Wendi's thirty-eight-year age gap wasn't—and it became evident when Wendi insisted on turbocharging her career. After giving birth to their second daughter, Chloe, in 2003, she led MySpace's failed expansion into China—that imperial dream never died—and then pivoted to Hollywood. In July 2011, she produced *Snow Flower and the Secret Fan*, a poorly reviewed drama about female friends in nineteenth-century China that grossed just $11 million.

The failures didn't daunt Wendi. In this way she was like her husband—always moving forward. By 2011, she infiltrated the fashion and art worlds. Wendi's stamina was legendary. She'd abandon Rupert to work the room and then party till dawn at venues like the Box, the downtown Manhattan club known for performances by nude women and a cross-dressing dwarf. "You could feel his loneliness," a friend said.

Publicly, Rupert and Wendi presented themselves as happily married. "Who wouldn't fall in love with such a beautiful woman like her?" Rupert told a Chinese TV program in June 2011. But the couple fought constantly. "It would start with how he was dressed. Or the schedule for the kids. Or something the nanny said. Just anything would set her off," said a friend. An executive recalled Wendi screaming at Rupert in his London office, "Fuck you, Rupert! You're stupid! What are you going to do when I'm gone!?" The verbal brawls allegedly even turned physical. According to what Rupert later told doctors, in early 2011, Wendi shoved Rupert into a piano at their Fifth Avenue triplex. Rupert broke vertebrae in the fall and required hospitalization.

The mask finally slipped in June 2012. A sixty-nine-year-old Mandarin tutor gave an interview to *Gawker* that described the Rupert household as a "war zone." She said Wendi abandoned a nanny on a roadside for some perceived slight. "Everyone who works for [Wendi] hates her and is scared of her," the tutor said. The cruelest detail involved Grace. The tutor alleged that Wendi berated her ten-year-old daughter about her weight, restricting her food so she stayed "skinny like Zhang Ziyi," the delicate star of *Memoirs of a Geisha*. (The Murdochs denied the claims from a "disgruntled employee.")

Meanwhile, Wendi was becoming a divisive figure inside News Corp. James heard from a foreign official that Wendi was a Chinese intelligence asset. Ailes told executives that Rupert ordered him to water down Fox's coverage of China because Wendi wanted it. *Gawker* reported that someone, most likely Ailes, hired private detective Bo Dietl to spread gossip about Wendi's alleged affairs. Dietl admitted that his firm anonymously emailed a dossier to *Gawker* that alleged Wendi's "path to [Rupert's] boardroom and bedroom [was] paved with betrayal, infidelity, adultery and continuous scandalous affairs."

For a man who built an information empire, Rupert was, ironically, one of the last to hear the rumors. "Everybody was talking about these things and never telling me anything," Rupert later said. In the winter of 2013, it fell to Lachlan to open his dad's eyes to the allegations. "Of course she's cheating, Dad. Everyone knows that but you," he claimed.

The conversation with Lachlan motivated Rupert to discreetly investigate. During the phone hacking investigation, News Corp lawyers had found emails from Wendi that suggested she slept with a tennis coach in Carmel, and with Google CEO Eric Schmidt and Tony Blair. "That really took him aback," a former News Corp executive said. The Blair allegation was particularly devastating. Rupert's newspapers helped elect Blair, and the two became close friends during Blair's ten years as prime minister. In 2010, Rupert made Blair the godfather of his daughter Grace.

From household staff, Rupert learned that Blair and Wendi met alone and acted like lovers. A ranch staffer told Rupert they were seen feeding each other at dinner. One alleged encounter particularly infuriated Rupert:

on October 7, 2012, while Rupert was in Australia visiting his 103-year-old mother, Dame Elisabeth, after she was hospitalized, Wendi invited Blair to the ranch.

But Wendi's own words suggested there was fire behind the smoke. Lachlan told his dad that the butler at Rupert's New York penthouse found a crumpled note from Wendi in the garbage. The letter, written like an angsty teenager speaking in broken English, began: *"Oh, shit, oh, shit . . . Whatever why I'm so so missing Tony. Because he is so so charming and his clothes are so good. He has such good body and he has really really good legs Butt . . . And he is slim tall and good skin. Pierce blue eyes which I love. Love his eyes. Also I love his power on the stage . . . and what else and what else and what else . . ."*

Rupert, feeling betrayed and humiliated, prepared a counterattack. In May 2013, he bought a place to move into: a $28.8 million Bel Air estate called Moraga, one of the only working vineyards in Los Angeles. A month later, Rupert filed for divorce in New York, blindsiding Wendi. Within a day, *The Hollywood Reporter* published the allegations about her Blair romance. Both Wendi and Blair denied the story and called Rupert repeatedly, but he refused to pick up. Rupert later told people to let Blair know he never wanted to speak to him again.

On the night Rupert filed the divorce papers, Lachlan and James stayed by his side in New York. The brothers competed feverishly for their father's love, but the outside threat united them all. The comity wouldn't last.

EVER SINCE LACHLAN QUIT IN 2005, Rupert lobbied his prodigal son to return. "He was always going to come back," Rupert assured a journalist. Wendi's presence had been an obstacle—of the children, Lachlan was most hurt by Rupert's betrayal of Anna. "I'm not thinking about returning," Lachlan told a friend during the phone hacking scandal. "I have my own business. Leaving News Corp is the best decision I've ever made apart from marrying my wife and having kids." But there was satisfaction in being courted by a lonely father who had once driven him away.

In August 2013, two months after divorcing Wendi, Rupert corralled his sons at Sun Valley's Allen & Company retreat—having first ensured Blair was disinvited from the conference. Rupert's pitch was direct: come back to News Corp, he told Lachlan. Both brothers resisted. Lachlan didn't want to leave Australia. He and Sarah were happily raising three children in Sydney and renovating a $21 million white stucco mansion that formerly housed the French consulate. Meanwhile, James clung to the fantasy that he was Rupert's successor despite the phone hacking scandal. Lachlan's return would undermine his status as heir apparent.

Then, a health crisis: six months after the Sun Valley meeting, Rupert suffered a scary fall in a San Francisco hotel room. He smacked his head and fractured his spine. A friend sent a neurosurgeon racing over to evaluate Rupert. Luckily, there was no concussion. Rupert spent the next three weeks at the ranch recovering. As his eighty-third birthday approached in March, the timing felt symbolic. The man who had built a global media empire was suddenly confronting his mortality—and his sons could see it, too.

On March 11, 2014, Lachlan and James flew to Los Angeles to be with Rupert on his birthday. Rupert was being inducted that night into the Television Academy Hall of Fame. Fox is a "family company," Rupert told attendees during his speech. After dinner, father and sons retired to Beverly Hills for a nightcap. Notably absent was their sister Elisabeth—she and Rupert were in a period of estrangement after the phone hacking crisis. Perhaps moved by Rupert's recent injury, Lachlan agreed to come back and take the title of non-executive chairman, though he insisted on being based in Australia. James would be promoted to co–chief operating officer and work "alongside" 21st Century Fox president Chase Carey. James hoped the new title signaled he was still in line to inherit the throne.

Two weeks later, Rupert convened his board for a secret conference call to make Lachlan's homecoming official. Rupert clearly savored luring Lachlan back like he had closed a major deal. "Rupert has a lot of emotional momentum right now," a confidant said at the time. "I haven't seen him this energized about the future."

With his warring sons back in his court, the aging king prepared for one final corporate battle. Tech giants like Netflix and Amazon were transforming entertainment with streaming. Rupert feared his empire was too small to compete, and he needed to scale up. On July 14, 2014, he made an $80 billion takeover offer for Time Warner. Buying the parent company of HBO, CNN, and Warner Bros. would be the biggest deal of his career—and also repay a grudge he'd nursed since the 1980s when Time Warner had thwarted his attempted takeover. But once again, the media giant rebuffed Rupert's offer. Investors, alarmed by how much debt Rupert would incur to do the deal, drove down 21st Century Fox's stock price. Less than three weeks later, Rupert withdrew his bid. It was a humbling defeat that signaled Rupert's empire-building days might be over.

AS RUPERT NURSED HIS corporate wounds, two family developments helped ease the sting of failure. Weeks after Rupert dropped his Time Warner bid, Liz divorced Freud, whom Rupert openly loathed. Their rift had put Liz in an impossible position—after Freud attacked Ailes in *The Times* in 2010, she sent Ailes an apology email. A final straw had occurred in November 2013 when Freud invited Blair—but not Rupert—to his Noah's Ark–themed fiftieth birthday. Eleven months later, they announced their split. The divorce got uglier when the *Daily Mail* reported Freud had fathered a baby with Liz's friend while they were married. For Rupert, the scandal validated his view that Freud was a deceitful interloper. And in the aftermath, Liz came crawling back to Rupert. "She's terrified of Rupert dying mad at her," a source close to Liz later said.

Then, at the age of eighty-four, Rupert fell in love with the supermodel Jerry Hall. Rupert seemed like the last man Hall would go out with. The 1970s fashion icon was a BBC-watching liberal twenty-five years Rupert's junior. She previously dated rock stars Bryan Ferry and Mick Jagger, her longtime partner with whom she has four children.

In 2013, Hall was in Melbourne playing Mrs. Robinson in the stage version of *The Graduate* when her friend Penny Fowler, Rupert's niece, suggested they meet. Rupert and Hall spent months emailing and talking on the phone before she agreed to a lunch date in New York. When Hall arrived, her hotel room was filled with flowers and chocolates. "He was an old-fashioned gentleman. We laughed together nonstop," she told friends. A couple of nights later, Rupert took her to see *Hamilton* on Broadway. The unlikely pairing—conservative media mogul and liberal supermodel— somehow worked. "They seemed to our surprise very happy and a wonderful fit," recalled Hall's close friend Tom Cashin, who socialized with the pair.

After a few weeks of dating, Rupert and Hall flew on his G650 jet to Texas to meet Hall's Fox News–loving family. Hall left Texas at sixteen to model in Europe, but as she watched her relatives line up to receive Rupert like he was the king of red America, she realized that her family's approval meant a lot. Six months into the relationship, Rupert proposed. "Mick was so unfaithful to you, I'd never be unfaithful," Rupert told Hall, according to a person briefed on the conversation. In March 2016, they wed at London's historic St. Bride's Church off Fleet Street, seven days before Rupert's eighty-fifth birthday. "No more tweets for ten days or ever! Feel like the luckiest AND happiest man in world," Rupert posted after the ceremony.

Lachlan and James flew in for it. In photos, the sons flanked their dad in matching navy suits and white boutonnieres. But behind the formal poses, the brothers' corporate partnership was unraveling. "The wedding was awkward. The three of them were trying to run the company," a person close to James said. The tensions evident at the wedding reflected deeper conflicts that had been brewing since Lachlan's return. Back in New York, the brothers' philosophical differences were driving them toward a reckoning.

RUPERT'S NEW YORK HEADQUARTERS occupied a dozen or so floors of a drab skyscraper in the concrete canyon of Sixth Avenue. Except for *The Wall Street Journal*'s renovated newsroom, most offices had low ceilings, bad lighting, and musty carpets. For James, the tired decor reflected a company stuck in the past when it needed to become digitally focused for the future. Not long after Rupert lured Lachlan back, James spearheaded a bold plan to move the headquarters to an eighty-eight-story tower in Lower Manhattan.

The $4 billion building designed by forty-year-old Danish architect Bjarke Ingels featured a gravity-defying facade of glass blocks cantilevered to one side. When Ingels showed Rupert the renderings, Rupert testily asked, "Why doesn't it fall over?"

Architecture quickly became a proxy battle between the brothers. James wanted the building to embody a company that was open, innovative, and transparent. His aesthetic was "Pacific northwest," warm lumber paired with industrial concrete. Lachlan saw the whole project as a boondoggle. Their father's Australian egalitarianism prized keeping expenses low over aesthetics. A new headquarters would raise Rupert's rent by hundreds of millions of dollars. It annoyed Lachlan that James peacocked around like he was the better businessman when their dad was a legend. James should show more respect.

The dispute brought the succession question to a head. By the winter of 2015, Chase Carey, who was in his early sixties, was tired of being caught between the warring brothers. He told Rupert he wanted to leave after his contract ran out. Investors relied on Carey, a talented executive with a Wyatt Earp handlebar mustache, to be a counterweight to Rupert's freewheeling management. Carey's looming departure required Rupert to make a decision on which son would take over.

On the afternoon of April 22, 2015, Carey and Lachlan invited James to lunch at the Lambs Club, a few blocks from the office. When James arrived, Carey lowered the boom: Rupert decided Lachlan was returning as CEO— and James would report to his older brother. James felt hot anger surge through his body. Time slowed as he processed the betrayal. Sending Liz to fire him in London was an appalling level of cowardice. Having Carey and Lachlan ambush him in public was pathological. It felt like a corporate execution.

James now questioned whether Rupert had ever intended to make him his successor. It was deeply unfair: James had proved himself at Star and BSkyB while Lachlan ran away to Australia and had a string of business failures. Shortly before Rupert recruited Lachlan back, Lachlan lost $100 million investing in the struggling Australian TV network Ten. (Lachlan's turnaround strategy included giving his wife, Sarah, a reality show.) James took the fall for phone hacking even though he had nothing to do with the London tabloids when the hacking occurred. Meanwhile, Rebekah Brooks, who *had* edited both tabloids, got a promotion: Rupert had recently rehired her after her acquittal on four criminal charges. It was the inverted moral logic of Rupert's world that James had dealt with his entire life. James stared back at Lachlan and Carey with resolve. "I'm not going to do that," he said, and walked out.

James flew to Indonesia on a pre-scheduled business trip. Rumors that he quit swirled through the company. James ignored Rupert's and Lachlan's calls and texts. Going dark caused Rupert to blink: when James returned to New York, Rupert told James he would become CEO after all. Lachlan would be chairman, but not James's boss. Rupert had kicked the succession can down the road. Rupert offered James a four-year contract with a salary of $20 million plus bonus, and eventually James signed.

James worked hard to stamp his values on the company. In December 2015, he proudly championed a $725 million takeover of National Geographic's media properties, including the flagship magazine. But James quickly realized his CEO title was a chimera. A few weeks later, Rupert and Lachlan killed the headquarters project that James had been working on for a year. The humiliation seemed designed to infuriate James to the point he would quit. But James had decided he couldn't give in. He and Kathryn were horrified by the rise of Donald Trump. Ailes was turning Fox News into a de facto arm of Trump's racist campaign—James needed to stay so he could stop him.

LIKE MANY AMERICANS, Rupert dismissed Trump's political career as a joke when he descended the golden escalator in June 2015 to declare his candidacy. "Rupert knew he was an idiot," a person close to Rupert said. But that summer Trump rocketed to the top of the GOP field. Rupert was a longtime champion of immigration reform and free trade and loathed

Trump's nativism and know-nothingism. During the Republican primary, Rupert waged a media campaign in the pages of *The Wall Street Journal* and on Fox News to deny Trump the nomination. Rupert told people Ailes was partly responsible for Trump's success. Ailes gave Trump, his longtime friend, a weekly call-in segment on *Fox & Friends* to weigh in on political issues. (Trump used Fox News to mainstream the birther conspiracy theory.) Ailes also had lunch with Trump days before he launched his presidential campaign, and continued to advise him throughout the primaries.

A few days before the first GOP debate on Fox in August 2015, Rupert called Ailes at home. "This has gone on long enough," Rupert said, according to a person briefed on the conversation. Rupert told Ailes he wanted Fox's debate moderators—Megyn Kelly, Bret Baier, and Chris Wallace—to hit Trump on his anti-immigration and protectionist ideas.

On the night of August 6, 2015, in front of twenty-four million people, the Fox moderators executed Rupert's plan. But it backfired spectacularly. Kelly's pointed question regarding Trump's history of misogyny outraged Trump. "I've been very nice to you, though I could probably maybe not be based on the way you have treated me," he said menacingly. Over the next several days, Trump viciously attacked Kelly in the media, including suggesting that her menstrual cycle had influenced her debate question. The Fox audience sided with Trump. Fearing a loss of ratings, Ailes and Kelly capitulated. It was an early sign that Rupert had lost control of the outrage machine Ailes built.

James blamed his dad for empowering Ailes. For nearly twenty years, Fox's profits allowed Ailes to run the network like a ministate. "Leave him alone. He knows what he's doing," Rupert told executives. Ailes had flexed his autonomy by openly belittling James and Lachlan. After Lachlan quit, Ailes boasted that he moved into Lachlan's vacant office, thereby putting himself closer to Rupert than his firstborn son. During phone hacking, Ailes told people James was a "fucking dope." One time, when Ailes spotted James on the security camera smoking a cigarette outside the office, he said to his deputies, "Tell me that mouth hasn't sucked a cock." The executives laughed.

For James and Lachlan, watching Ailes's impunity was another painful reality of being a Rupert child. Ailes's $1 billion profits meant he could do whatever he wanted. Neither of them could act like that.

So on July 6, 2016, when Fox anchor Gretchen Carlson filed an explosive sexual harassment lawsuit against Ailes, James and Lachlan seized an opportunity to finally get rid of Ailes for good.

CHAPTER FOURTEEN

"IF YOU DO THIS DEAL, I'M NEVER SPEAKING TO EITHER OF YOU AGAIN!"

AROUND 10:00 A.M. ON WEDNESDAY, July 6, 2016, James was finishing a hike in Sun Valley when his phone rang. It was Lachlan, calling from the YMCA gym in town where he'd been working out. "Have you seen the lawsuit against Roger?" he asked. James hadn't. Lachlan got him up to speed: that morning, former *Fox & Friends* host Gretchen Carlson sued Ailes for sexual harassment. Fox's PR and legal departments needed direction on how the company should respond. It was an explosive corporate crisis that the rival brothers would have to handle themselves: for the first time, they were attending the Allen & Company conference without their dad, who was honeymooning with Hall in the south of France.

Later that morning, James and Lachlan huddled in their hotel reading the lawsuit. Carlson alleged that Ailes had demoted and later fired her after she complained about his predatory behavior. "I think you and I should have had a sexual relationship a long time ago, and then you'd be good and better and I'd be good and better. Sometimes problems are easier to solve" that way, the suit quoted Ailes telling her. James and Lachlan were disturbed by the specificity of the dialogue in the filing: it suggested Carlson had secretly taped Ailes. It would be devastating if she released the audio.

Rupert was in the air flying back from France, which gave the brothers a brief window to act. They commissioned white-shoe law firm Paul Weiss to begin an internal investigation, and released a terse statement saying the company took the allegations "seriously." For James, the crisis presented an opportunity for redemption: he could demonstrate his business ethics that had been tarred by phone hacking. The brothers emailed their dad news of the lawsuit but waited to tell him about the internal investigation until he landed in Sun Valley. Rupert was vehemently opposed to legal probes of any sort. James and Lachlan wanted to commence one before Rupert could shut it down.

When Rupert landed, he called Ailes. "I have nothing to hide," Ailes assured him. Three days later, on Saturday, July 9, it looked like he very much did. *New York* magazine published interviews with six women who alleged Ailes sexually harassed them over a twenty-five-year period, dating back to the 1960s, when Ailes was a producer on *The Mike Douglas Show*. The accounts painted a disturbing picture of decades-long predatory behavior. A former model said that when she was sixteen, Ailes locked her in his office, pulled down his pants, and demanded a blow job. "I was a kid—I'd never seen a man's privates before," she told the magazine. A former television producer said Ailes told her she would have to have sex with him and his friends if she wanted Ailes to hire her. "I was afraid he was going to pin me down," she remembered.

Ailes was a political street brawler, and the Murdochs knew he would go scorched earth to save his job. The morning after the *New York* exposé, Ailes and his wife, Elizabeth, turned his second-floor Fox office into a war room. "It's all bullshit! We have to get in front of this," he said to executives. "This is not about money. This is about his legacy," said Elizabeth. Ailes told 21st Century Fox general counsel Gerson Zweifach that James was trying to get rid of him in order to help Hillary Clinton defeat Trump. Ailes leaned on Fox anchors to support him in the media. Jeanine

Pirro told a reporter Carlson's claims were "absurd"; Ainsley Earhardt described Ailes as a "family man"; Neil Cavuto wrote an op-ed labeling Ailes's accusers "sick."

Rupert was looking for a reason to protect Ailes—and Fox's $1 billion profit—because Fox represented far more than money. The network had given him something he'd never possessed: the power to shape American politics the way he already did in Australia and Britain. Ailes had built not just a conservative cable news channel but something like a fourth branch of government; a propaganda arm for the GOP; an organization that determined Republican presidential candidates, sold wars, and decided the issues of the day for two million viewers.

Then Megyn Kelly called Lachlan. She told him that, years ago, Ailes made sexually suggestive comments and inappropriately hugged her in his office. This was a revelation. Kelly was in contract negotiations and was considered by the Murdochs to be the future face of the network. Lachlan encouraged Kelly to tell Paul Weiss lawyers about Ailes's harassment.

On Monday, July 11, Paul Weiss lawyers began interviewing Fox employees in a twenty-ninth-floor conference room at the firm's Midtown office. Kelly was only the third or fourth woman to go on the record—but she was by far the most important. After she spoke to lawyers, more than two dozen Fox women came forward to describe their own accounts of Ailes's harassment. When lawyers briefed the Murdochs later that week, James and Lachlan knew they had Ailes cornered. "I think we know where this is going," their dad said.

On Saturday, July 16, James flew to Europe for business. Before leaving, he argued that they had enough to fire Ailes for cause immediately. The clock was ticking. The Republican Convention in Cleveland would start in two days. Fox couldn't afford to be engulfed in scandal for the biggest campaign event of the year. Rupert preferred to ease Ailes out to reduce collateral damage. Breitbart reported that fifty of Fox's biggest personalities were prepared to quit if Ailes was removed, though in reality there was no such pact. That night, Rupert raised the pressure: the *New York Post* front page announced, "The end is near for Roger Ailes." Rupert had Ailes's access to the Fox offices revoked.

On the afternoon of July 21, a few hours before Trump was to accept the nomination in Cleveland, Rupert invited Ailes to his New York penthouse for lunch to hammer out a severance deal. Lachlan joined to savor watching his corporate nemesis be forced out, albeit with a golden parachute: Ailes received $40 million and retained the title of "adviser" in exchange for a multiyear noncompete clause that prevented him from going to a rival network. Ten months later, Ailes died after falling and hitting his head in the bathroom of his Palm Beach mansion.

Rupert took the title of acting CEO of Fox News and assured Ailes he would protect the channel's conservative voice. "I'm here, and I'm in charge," Rupert told Fox staffers later that afternoon with Lachlan at his side.

In September 2016, Fox News paid Carlson a $20 million settlement. But the scandal's blast radius continued to ripple through Rupert's empire. *New York* continued to publish damaging articles that detailed how Ailes's lieutenants had enabled his abuse for years, using company resources to silence victims and spy on employees. James argued Fox needed to purge the Ailes regime and hire CBS News president David Rhodes, who'd started his career at Fox, to run the channel. Rupert and Lachlan opposed a wholesale housecleaning. They weren't going to allow James to push Fox to the political center. The fragile peace that had held since Lachlan returned was about to crack.

FOR MANY AMERICAN FAMILIES during the Trump years, politics became a third rail. And so it was for the Murdochs. Elisabeth and James tilted #resistance, whereas Lachlan was hard-core MAGA. His politics, always conservative, had shifted hard right during his exile. Lachlan was particularly close with former Australian prime minister Tony Abbott, a climate change denier, and Fox News host Tucker Carlson. Rupert was more pragmatic. "Rupert never liked Trump. That's what drove James insane," a person close to James recalled. "James would say to his dad, 'You don't even believe this stuff!'" But Rupert saw one topic that boosted Fox News's ratings more than anything else: Trump.

This created trouble at home. Hall despised Trump—and let Rupert know it. "During dinners we had with Jerry and Rupert, Jerry wouldn't hold back," Cashin, Hall's friend, said. According to a source, Rupert wanted to buy a house in Florida to be closer to Mar-a-Lago, but Hall refused. Hall told friends she was alarmed by Trump's lack of qualifications or respect for the office. At a lunch shortly after the 2016 election, Hall asked Trump to reroute the Dakota Access Pipeline away from Native American reservations that were protesting the project. Trump responded by asking if she wanted to serve in his administration as head of the Bureau of Indian Affairs. "It was horrible. I couldn't wait to get away," she later told friends.

Once Trump was in the White House, Rupert turned Fox News into de facto state TV. It was a continuation of Rupert's time-tested strategy of forging alliances with politicians across the ideological spectrum as long as they advanced his interests. For James, it was a reckoning. He finally seemed to regret his 2009 MacTaggart Lecture. His sister Liz was right: pursuit of profit without values is a recipe for disaster. "I underestimated the ability of a profit motive to make people do terrible things—to make companies do terrible things," James later said.

Trump more than delivered for Rupert. One source with direct knowledge of their conversations said Rupert lobbied Trump to punish Facebook and Google for siphoning his newspapers' advertising revenue. In 2019, Trump's Justice Department launched an antitrust investigation of Google. In 2021, Google settled and struck a lucrative content-sharing deal with News Corp. The source also said Rupert pushed Trump to open up land for fracking to boost the value of Rupert's fossil fuel investments. The Trump administration released nearly thirteen million acres of federally controlled land to fracking companies. Rupert, who sources say became more pro-life in later years, encouraged Trump to appoint judges who would overturn *Roe v. Wade.* "Rupert wanted Trump's Supreme Court justices in so they could make abortion illegal," a source who spoke to Rupert said.

Discontent among the Murdochs simmered for the first months of Trump's term. But after the August 2017 neo-Nazi march in Charlottesville, Virginia, tensions boiled over. James and his wife, Kathryn, a former marketing communications professional turned philanthropist, were aghast that Trump's "very fine people on both sides" comment drew a moral equivalency between tiki-torch-wielding neo-Nazis chanting "Jews will not replace us!" and the counterprotesters standing up to them. James confronted Rupert and Lachlan about Fox News's full-throated defense of Trump's remarks. They rebuffed him. "They were both in denial. They didn't want to see it for what it was," a source briefed on the conversations said. James felt trapped. Finally, Kathryn challenged him. "If you're not going to stand up against Nazis, who are you going to stand up against?" she asked.

James took his criticism public, though in a way that gave him plausible deniability. Days after the march, he donated $1 million to the Anti-Defamation League and sent an email to friends, which promptly leaked to the press, that denounced Trump's refusal to condemn white supremacy. "I can't even believe I have to write this: standing up to Nazis is essential; there are no good Nazis. Or Klansmen, or terrorists," James wrote.

James looked for redemption in London. Shortly before Trump's election, he told his dad they should make another run at Sky. Brexit had driven down the value of the pound, which meant Fox could acquire Sky at a significant discount. Lachlan, while supportive of the deal, argued that James's role in phone hacking made him too radioactive to be the face of it. But James insisted. Acquiring Sky would finally repair James's reputation after the disgrace of phone hacking. In December 2016, Fox bid $14.8 billion to take full control of Sky.

Immediately, members of Parliament mobilized to block it. A new Fox scandal gave them more ammunition. In April 2017, *The New York Times* reported that Fox News had renewed Bill O'Reilly's contract even though network executives knew O'Reilly had settled sexual harassment claims with women totaling $13 million. James fired Fox's number-one-rated host days later. But it wasn't enough to placate critics. In September, an interviewer at the Royal Television Society convention grilled James. "I wonder if the message that comes through is that you presided over this rotten culture at News International and, again, at Fox News, and that people just don't trust you." James's eyes darted back and forth. His brother and dad prevented him from cleaning up Fox News, and now James was having to answer for it.

The Murdoch name had become toxic, like the Sacklers—another billionaire family whose fortune was made by a product, OxyContin, that poisoned society. James wanted out. At that very moment, his dad set in motion a deal that would give the younger son a graceful and lucrative exit strategy.

TWO DAYS BEFORE THE CHARLOTTESVILLE RALLY, Rupert hosted Disney CEO Bob Iger at his Bel Air vineyard, Moraga. Over chicken salad and a couple of glasses of chardonnay, the two moguls discussed the woes confronting their companies. To Rupert's surprise, Iger floated that Disney would be interested in buying Rupert's movie studio and entertainment assets. Rupert would have flatly dismissed the overture in the past. But in the streaming age, legacy Hollywood players like Rupert and Iger lacked the scale to compete with tech giants. The logic of selling 21st Century Fox to Disney made a lot of sense. Plus, Rupert would get to keep Fox News and his beloved newspapers, the source of his political influence. Disney certainly wanted no part of those.

James and Lachlan went to war with each other over the deal. James championed it for business reasons, but also because he and Iger discussed the possibility of James taking a high-level job at Disney after the acquisition. "James thought about what it might be like to have a boss who appreciates you for what you can do instead of a father that just sees you as the child where, no matter what you do, the other son is always better," a person close to James said. Lachlan, meanwhile, felt Rupert and James were rushing into a deal that undervalued Fox's assets. On top of that, the deal seemed like a massive bait and switch. He'd sacrificed his independence in Australia, moved his family across the Pacific, and spent years rebuilding his relationship with his father—all based on the promise that he would inherit a media empire. "Lachlan's whole self-image was that he was going to be the next Rupert," a person close to him said. Now that empire was being sold off, leaving him to run a rump state comprising Fox News, a dying broadcast network; Fox Sports; book publisher HarperCollins; and some newspapers.

As James and Rupert pushed the deal forward in the fall of 2017, Lachlan seemed intent on derailing it. At a dinner with Iger, Lachlan unspooled a rant about illegal immigration that made Iger, an outspoken Democrat who flirted with his own presidential run, very uncomfortable, according to two sources briefed on the dinner. At another dinner in New York, Lachlan exploded at Rupert and James. "He said, 'If you do this deal, I'm never speaking to either of you again!'" recalled a person briefed on the conversation. (Another person close to Lachlan denied this.) Unable to quash it, Lachlan reached a breaking point. According to three sources, he suffered a panic attack about the merger and was briefly treated at an LA-area hospital. (The person close to Lachlan denied this.)

Eleven days before Christmas 2017, Disney and Rupert announced they had reached a $52.4 billion deal. Each Murdoch child received $2 billion. Lachlan would stay on to run Fox News and the family's remaining assets in a new company called Fox Corp. In 2019, Lachlan paid a reported $150 million—the highest price in California history—for the twenty-five-thousand-square-foot Bel Air estate featured in *The Beverly Hillbillies*. James took his walkaway money and launched a media fund called Lupa Systems, investing in liberal-leaning companies like Vice and Tribeca Enterprises. (*Lupa* is Italian for "she-wolf"—as in the one that raised brothers Romulus and Remus, the founders of Rome, before Romulus murdered Remus.) Liz launched a television company called Sister, which produced hits like the Emmy-winning series *Chernobyl*.

The Disney windfall had given each sibling the financial independence to build their own companies—and the freedom to openly oppose their father. No longer dependent on his approval or his money, they could finally tell Rupert what they really thought of his legacy. For the first time in their lives, the children held the power to hurt him as much as he'd hurt them.

For Rupert, the Disney deal was a career triumph. It solved his succession problems. James was out. Lachlan was in. And the price that Disney ultimately paid climbed to $71.3 billion, now seen as a high-water mark of the streaming content boom. The thrill didn't last. In early January 2018, Rupert and Hall were sailing the Caribbean aboard Lachlan's 140-foot, carbon-fiber yacht *Sarissa* when disaster struck.

HALL WAS ASLEEP IN the yacht's stateroom when she bolted awake at the sound of Rupert moaning in agony. She later told friends she found her eighty-six-year-old husband in excruciating pain on the cabin floor. He said he fell down a step trying to get to the bathroom and couldn't get up. Hall alerted the captain. He quickly gave Rupert a shot of a painkiller that allowed Rupert to sleep fitfully while they sailed through the night to the nearest port, Pointe-à-Pitre, on the French island of Grande-Terre, in Guadeloupe. But the emergency kept getting worse. Lachlan's massive boat towered over the pier, and it was perilous to lower Rupert in a stretcher. Once they managed to get Rupert off the boat, they discovered the island's hospital was closed after a recent fire. Rupert had to spend the night on a gurney under a tent in the parking lot until James's private jet landed with a medevac team. By the time Rupert was flown to a UCLA hospital, he was in critical condition. "He kept almost dying," a person close to the family said. Doctors diagnosed Rupert with arrhythmia and a broken back. While examining the X-ray, they saw Rupert had fractured vertebrae before, the person said. Rupert explained it must have been from the time Wendi pushed him into a piano during a fight, after which he spent weeks on the couch.

Rupert's PR team scrambled to spin the sailing accident when reporters started calling. They leaked an email to show he was in command. "I have to work from home for some weeks. In the meantime, you'll be hearing from me by email, phone and text!" it said. But in reality, Rupert was in terrible shape and required Hall to spoon-feed him for months. "Jerry was as sensitive with him as a full-time nurse would have been," her friend Cashin said. Then, in March 2019, Rupert had another fall in his Bel Air home. This time, he tore his Achilles tendon tripping over the box of a chessboard Lachlan had given him for his eighty-seventh birthday. The injury confined Rupert to a wheelchair for months, a source familiar with the incident said. Rupert was in and out of the hospital with pneumonia and seizures. Unlike the politicians Rupert has bullied into submission with his tabloids, human biology is immovable. "There's been a joke in the family for a long time that 40 may be the new 30, but 80 is 80," a source close to Rupert said. On March 11, 2022, he turned ninety-two.

When COVID-19 emerged in early 2020, Rupert's doctors told him he needed to take extreme precautions to protect himself. The pandemic exposed the ultimate contradiction in Rupert's empire-building philosophy. While Fox News hosts railed against lockdowns and pushed dubious treatments like hydroxychloroquine, Rupert followed the science. "He was scared for himself and was very careful," a person who spoke to Rupert at the time recalled. When confronted about the disconnect between his personal behavior and his network's coverage, Rupert would deflect responsibility for his hosts' commentary, though this was at odds with his history of editorial interference. The hypocrisy revealed something essential about Rupert's worldview: he had always been able to separate his personal beliefs from his business interests.

According to sources, Rupert and Hall quarantined in Bel Air without any staff for months. Hall bought robot vacuums to clean the floors, baked sourdough bread, and cooked simple meals of roast chicken, leg of lamb, and vegetarian pasta. During the day, Rupert watched the stock market and took Zoom calls while Hall took online courses in UC Davis's winemaking program. (Hall told friends Rupert wanted her to do it so he could write off $3 million of vineyard expenses as long as she worked five hundred hours a year on winemaking.) At night, she and Rupert played chess, backgammon, gin rummy, and other card games. She usually won, she told friends, except when they played liar's dice. "He's a good liar!" she told them.

Rupert was one of the first people in the world to be vaccinated in December 2020. As the months dragged on, he grew increasingly irate with

Trump's erratic pandemic policies, like the time Trump suggested Americans inject themselves with bleach to kill the virus. "Rupert had a strong view about how things were being mishandled," a former Trump administration official said. Through Fox News, Rupert had more power than anyone in America to pressure Trump to take the pandemic seriously. He did nothing. In fact, he took no responsibility for the COVID misinformation Fox News pumped out day after day. When a friend told Rupert that the channel was literally killing its elderly audience, Rupert replied, "They're dying from old age and other illnesses, but COVID was being blamed," said a source briefed on the conversation. But Rupert wanted to move on from Trump. Having milked him for ratings and profit, he was looking toward a post-Trump future. Shortly before the 2020 election, according to the source, Rupert invited Florida governor Ron DeSantis and his wife, Casey, for lunch at Rupert's vineyard. As they dined outside on steak, Rupert told DeSantis that Fox News would support him for president in 2024.

Rupert was over Trump, but the Fox News audience most certainly wasn't. The disconnect would soon ignite the biggest journalistic scandal in Fox's history and lead to the Murdochs at war with each other in court.

CHAPTER FIFTEEN

FAMILY HARMONY

ON ELECTION NIGHT 2020, Rupert was home in Bel Air following the results on television and working the phones. At 11:20 p.m. Eastern time, Fox News was the first major network to declare Arizona, a crucial battleground state, for Joe Biden, which would all but ensure his election. The Trump voters' official safe space was the first to break the bad news.

The call exploded like a bomb inside the Trump campaign and sent shock waves rippling through Fox News. Trump's son-in-law Jared Kushner called Rupert and implored him to retract the Arizona decision. Rupert later testified he told Kushner, "Well, the numbers are the numbers." The call became a target of Trump's rage. "This is an embarrassment to this country. We were getting ready to win this election. Frankly, we did win this election," Trump declared at an angry early-morning press conference in the East Room of the White House as Biden led Arizona by ten thousand votes.

As Trump cried fraud, Rupert told Fox executives that it was "bullshit and damaging" that Trump refused to concede. Rupert told Lachlan and Fox News CEO Suzanne Scott that the channel's hosts should say Biden won and move on, according to a source briefed on the conversations. Rupert was worried that Fox hosts would take their cues from Trump and repeat his lies on air. "If Trump becomes a sore loser we should watch Sean [Hannity] especially and others don't sound the same. Not there yet but a danger," Rupert emailed Scott.

At one point, Rupert lobbied Trump to concede. "Rupert called Trump to tell him to accept defeat graciously and that he had left a good legacy and that this stolen election stuff would drag everyone down," the source said. Trump refused. "Trump threatened to start his own channel and put Fox out of business," the source said. Murdoch seemed trapped by the people he radicalized, like an aging despot hiding in his palace while the streets filled with insurrectionists. Fox viewers believed Trump's baseless claims that the election was stolen because Trump said so. What's more, many loyal Fox watchers bristled that the network had seemingly had a hand in delivering their president's election night defeat. The irony of a news outlet being punished by its most ardent audience members for committing an act of journalism didn't have much time to settle, because a siege mentality quickly set in.

In the days after the election, Fox hosts and executives panicked as they watched viewers flip to rival channels Newsmax and One America News, whose programs were hyping Trump's stolen election conspiracies. "Do the executives understand how much credibility and trust we've lost with our audience? We're playing with fire . . . An alternative like newsmax could be devastating to us," Tucker Carlson texted his producer the day Fox declared Biden the president-elect. In an email conversation, Scott told Rupert that Fox needed to appease Trump's base immediately. "We need to make sure they know we aren't abandoning them and are still champions for them," she wrote. Murdoch told her he agreed.

What Murdoch did next, or more accurately *didn't* do, formed the core of Dominion Voting Systems' $1.6 billion defamation lawsuit against Fox. According to Dominion's court filings, Rupert protected Fox's ratings by allowing the network's hosts and guests to promote a batshit-crazy theory that algorithms inside Dominion machines secretly switched votes to Biden to steal the election, somehow at the behest of the Venezuelan government.

Meanwhile, Rupert looked for other measures to mollify Trump's audience. On November 20, Murdoch suggested to Scott that Fox should fire its Washington managing editor, Bill Sammon, who was a senior executive on the decision desk that made the Arizona call. "Maybe best to let Bill go right away which would be a big message with Trump people," Rupert said, according to court filings. Sammon retired in January 2021, the same month Fox let go of Chris Stirewalt, another decision desk member. According to court documents, Rupert even discussed buying the rights to Trump's reality show *The Apprentice.*

By mainstreaming Trump's stolen election conspiracy, Rupert and Fox had unleashed dangerous authoritarian forces. Just how dangerous became apparent on January 6, 2021, when a pro-Trump mob rampaged through the Capitol trying to stop Congress from certifying Biden's election. Rupert was horrified as he and Hall watched the attack unfold on television from home. He told Hall that Trump was "trying to kill Mike Pence because he was passing the presidency to Biden," said a source who spoke with Murdoch that day. "Rupert kept calling the White House, Trump, Jared, Sean Hannity, Paul Ryan, Mitch McConnell, trying to get Trump to stop it," said the source.

But then, like a passing storm, Rupert's outrage gave way to a sunnier view of the events. He later told Hall the rioters were just good old boys who got carried away, the source said. Rupert's ability to blithely rationalize the violence on January 6 was a microcosm of how he evaded any responsibility for the immense damage his media empire did to the public square over the past fifty years.

For more than a year after January 6, Murdoch's world disintegrated. The Dominion lawsuit filed in March 2021 intensified, with depositions and document discovery revealing those at the highest levels of Fox News didn't believe Trump's stolen election conspiracies even as the network cravenly promoted his lies for ratings. Lachlan, meanwhile, fled Los Angeles and returned to Sydney. According to two sources, Lachlan's family was ostracized in LA because of Fox's climate change denialism, and in the aftermath of January 6 was facing even more ostracism. As for Rupert, the intensifying legal and personal pressures seemed to be producing erratic decisions, leaving those in his orbit wondering if he had lost the plot.

———

ON THE AFTERNOON OF JUNE 6, 2022, Hall was at her London house nursing a terrible case of food poisoning when she checked her phone. "Jerry, sadly I've decided to call an end to our marriage," Rupert's email began. "We have certainly had some good times, but I have much to do . . . My New York lawyer will be contacting yours immediately." Hall reeled. "Rupert and I never fought," she told people. Yes, there had been disagreements over his antiabortion views and friction with his kids over Hall's rules about masking and testing before they saw Rupert.

Hall's relationship with Rupert's daughters was particularly fraught. Liz didn't like that Hall kept Rupert up past his usual bedtime. During COVID lockdown, Hall had asked Liz and Prue to look at country houses for Hall and Rupert to purchase near London, but instead the daughters bought the listings for themselves.

Hall clashed with Grace too, which wasn't surprising given that Hall had replaced her mom. In the summer of 2021, Hall was upset that Grace organized a father-daughter lunch in Bel Air with Liz and Prue and excluded her. "I was in the kitchen cooking but not allowed to join them outside on the veranda," Hall later texted a friend. In the spring of 2022, Hall was furious when Rupert asked her to leave their $200 million Montana ranch because Grace's therapist called and said Grace was flying in and didn't want Hall around. Hall thought Grace was trying to manipulate Rupert. "Grace wanted to get me out of Montana because she was trying to get Rupert to hire a famous DJ to play at her 21st birthday party at Yale who cost $1.6 million and she thought I would say it was too expensive," Hall texted a friend. On the flight back to LA on Murdoch's private plane, Hall sent him an angry email about Montana. She never anticipated his answer would be to divorce her by email.

That week in London, Hall desperately tried to salvage the relationship. "I thought we were very much in love and happy," she emailed Murdoch. But Murdoch had already moved on, as he'd done many times before. "At this stage, we must leave it to the lawyers to do their best for us individually," he responded coldly. "I am so sad," she emailed him on June 10. "Thank you for making me feel happy and secure for seven years. I will always love you."

Hall and Murdoch finalized their divorce in August 2022. Murdoch's terms were brutal. One part of the settlement was that Hall couldn't give story ideas to the writers on *Succession*, the HBO series loosely inspired by the Murdochs. Hall told friends that Murdoch made her move everything out of the Bel Air estate within thirty days and show receipts to prove items belonged to her. Murdoch's security guards watched as her children helped her pack. When she settled into the Oxfordshire home she received in the divorce, she discovered thirty-two surveillance cameras were still sending footage back to Fox headquarters. Her ex, Mick Jagger, sent his security consultant to disconnect them.

Four months later, Hall got a potential answer for why Murdoch broke off the marriage. Newspapers around the world printed photos of Murdoch vacationing in Barbados with new girlfriend Ann Lesley Smith, a sixty-six-year-old former dental hygienist turned conservative radio host with QAnon-style politics. Smith's life had a series of operatic ups and downs. In her twenties, Smith married John B. Huntington, a descendant of a California railroad fortune. They divorced, she once said, when he became an abusive alcoholic. Smith was suicidal, but then found Jesus in a coffee shop and became a street preacher in Marin County. She married the country music singer and broadcast entrepreneur Chester Smith, who died in 2008. On Facebook, Smith shared a mix of inspirational self-help talk with Christian nationalism and right-wing conspiracy theories. "The voting process may be so corrupted we may live in a de facto dictatorship with oligarchal [sic] control by the party in charge now," one post said. "Rupert has been radicalized by his own echo chamber," said a person close to him, explaining his initial attraction to Smith.

Hall remembered she and Murdoch hosted Smith for dinner at the Carmel ranch about a year earlier. At the time, Smith was dating the ranch manager. Hall didn't think anything of it when Smith gushed to Murdoch that he and Fox News were saving democracy. Or when Smith offered to give Murdoch a teeth cleaning. Or when Murdoch began making trips alone to Carmel, which he explained was because Grace wanted alone time with him there. Looking back, Hall told friends that Murdoch had simply moved on, the way he had ended previous marriages. "When Rupert is done with people that's it! They're gone!" Hall texted a friend. "She was devastated, mad, and humiliated," Cashin said. On the first day of Lent in February 2023, Hall told friends she made an effigy of Murdoch, tied dental floss around its neck, and burned it on the grill.

On March 17, 2023, Rupert proposed to Smith. He gifted her an 11-karat diamond engagement ring said to be worth upward of $2.5 million. The wedding was planned for summer. But quickly Murdoch became increasingly uncomfortable with her extreme evangelical views. Murdoch and Smith hosted Tucker Carlson for dinner in Bel Air. During dinner, Smith pulled out a Bible and started reading passages from the book of Exodus. Smith told Carlson she thought he was a messenger from God. "Rupert just sat there and stared," the source said. A few days after the dinner, Murdoch called off the wedding.

By August 2023, barely five months after calling off his engagement, the ninety-two-year-old mogul had a new girlfriend, the sixty-six-year-old retired scientist Elena Zhukova, whom he would soon marry. They had met through Wendi, who was friends with Zhukova's daughter, the socialite Dasha. Murdoch's pattern of blithely moving on had become almost mechanical.

His increasingly turbulent romantic life with many impulsive decisions alarmed executives. "It's like the King is senile but no one wants to say anything," a source said. According to two sources, Fox settled the Dominion lawsuit for $787 million moments before the trial was set to begin because Fox lawyers didn't want Murdoch to testify in public. "They were hoping and praying to settle for months, but they didn't want to pay up," the second source said. If the trial began, lawyers told Fox execs that Murdoch would be "disgraced on the stand, run out of the boardroom, and his testimony will expose him as a lunatic sliding into senility."

FAMILY HARMONY

———

ON THE AFTERNOON OF JULY 2, 2022, weeks after he divorced Hall by email, Rupert's black Range Rover pulled up to a twelfth-century stone church in the storybook Cotswold village of Westwell. He had traveled to the Oxfordshire countryside to attend Liz's daughter Charlotte's wedding to a hip-hop artist. Invitations instructed the seventy guests to wear "formal theatrical" attire. Murdoch emerged from his SUV looking like Tom Wolfe in a crisp white suit, red suede shoes, and red tie. Then he nearly collapsed.

A day earlier, Murdoch had been in a bed at Cromwell Hospital in London still battling a serious case of COVID, two sources close to him said. Over the course of a week, doctors treated Murdoch's symptoms—labored breathing and fatigue—with supplemental oxygen and antibodies. His recovery was frustratingly slow. At the wedding, Rupert could barely stay on his feet. Lachlan helped guide him through the crowd.

The wedding was the first time the Murdochs had gathered in the same place in more than a year. James and Kathryn decided at the last minute to attend. Liz asked them to come to support her because she was dreading having to see her ex-husband, Freud. When James saw Murdoch, they hugged stiffly. "It was cordial but cold," an attendee said. By this point, James was barely speaking to his dad and brother. The previous year, Murdoch got word to James that it would mean a lot if James attended his ninetieth birthday party, but James didn't go. Their differences over ideology and business strategy were about to turn into a family civil war.

James thought Fox News was a menace to democracy, and released public statements critical of the network. Murdoch and Lachlan were furious—they saw rank hypocrisy from someone who'd walked away with $2 billion and was now spouting liberal pieties to impress elite friends. "If James felt so bad about Fox News, why doesn't he return the money?" a Fox executive said. Murdoch and Lachlan wanted James off the News Corp board. He resigned in July 2020, citing "disagreements over certain editorial content." After the January 6 Capitol riot in 2021, James went further: "Those outlets that propagate lies to their audience have unleashed insidious and uncontrollable forces that will be with us for years."

Lachlan's future would be decided by his siblings, all of whom sat on the board of the trust that controlled the company through a special class of stock. James could join with his two sisters upon Murdoch's death and vote Lachlan out. So shortly after the Disney deal closed in 2019, Murdoch told Lachlan that he should use the billions he made from the sale to buy out his siblings from the trust—just as Murdoch had done with his three sisters in the early 1990s. James, Liz, and Prue were open to a deal, but balked when Lachlan was only willing to pay 50 percent of what their shares were worth. In the summer of 2020, Murdoch pushed Lachlan to see if he could make a deal with James alone. Lachlan raised his offer to 60 percent, but James refused. James knew he had leverage. The longer he held out, the more desperate Murdoch and Lachlan would get. "If they do not get an agreement, they are all fucked," James told his siblings, according to notes of the meeting. Months later, Murdoch offered to buy James out himself at a better price, but James rebuffed him.

Lachlan saw ominous signs that James was plotting a putsch. In the fall of 2022, an Australian journalist published an unauthorized biography of Lachlan that quoted an anonymous source boasting, "Lachlan gets fired the day Rupert dies." Several months later, the *Financial Times* quoted a source close to James saying, "Lachlan will be out, it is as simple as that." Lachlan blamed James for the leaks. "Relies heavily on unnamed sources and quotes from James' people," Lachlan emailed his dad after reading the *FT* article. In early 2023, James organized his sisters against Murdoch and Lachlan's plan to merge News Corp and Fox into a single company to solidify Lachlan's control. "It was a harebrained scheme. They got their ass handed to them by investors," said a person close to James. On January 24, Murdoch officially announced the merger was dead.

The brothers' mutual suspicion devolved into paranoia. Lachlan told his dad that James was leaking stories to the writers of *Succession*. A person close to James said he and Kathryn believed PR operatives aligned with

Murdoch and Lachlan were digging up dirt on them. It was at this point that Lachlan made an ominous decision: if James wouldn't leave the trust voluntarily, then he would make him.

IN THE SUMMER OF 2023, Lachlan asked his closest adviser, a former McKinsey consultant named Siobhan McKenna, to look into how the dispute over the trust might play out. Lachlan was alarmed by what she discovered: after Rupert died, Lachlan's siblings could vote him out of the company. McKenna proposed a radical solution: blow up the trust to strip James of his power. McKenna was Lachlan's closest confidante. She had worked for him since he decamped for Australia in 2005. So he took her advice seriously and told her to hire lawyers to study the options. They called the secret plan Project Family Harmony.

Soon, McKenna reported the lawyers had found a loophole: when Rupert included Chloe and Grace as financial equals in 2006, Murdoch's lawyers inserted language that would allow him to make changes to the children's trusts if he was acting "in good faith" to protect their financial interests. Murdoch could rip up the estate plan to ensure Lachlan's control by claiming in court that it would benefit the children economically. The argument went like this: if James, Liz, and Prue succeeded in turning Fox News liberal, they would destroy the right-wing business model and tank the family fortune.

In September 2023, Lachlan, McKenna, and the lawyers briefed Murdoch on the plan to disenfranchise James, now referred to as the "troublesome beneficiary." Murdoch agreed. He justified the betrayal as political courage. Murdoch's conservative media empire was protecting Western civilization from liberal forces bent on its destruction. James's plot to destroy Fox News was a threat to the "English speaking world," Murdoch said. In this way, Murdoch now saw James less as a son than as the embodiment of the elites he'd been fighting his entire life—and who'd been fighting *him*.

Murdoch's tortured rationale found support in a surprising place: Anna. That winter, Anna told Murdoch he needed to protect Lachlan from James's scheming. As she approached eighty, Anna's politics had become Fox-ified. The mother who had decried Murdoch's succession games now embraced them for ideological reasons. "I'm sure James and Kathryn are very comfortable in their own circle of like minded Woke friends. Fox is playing a huge and important role in calling out the idiocies that surround us," she emailed Murdoch. What Murdoch didn't know was that Anna had been diagnosed with dementia, which raised questions about whether her political transformation was genuine or a symptom of cognitive decline.

Murdoch's lawyers scheduled a special meeting of the trust for a few days after Thanksgiving. The lawyers cautioned that the plan was aggressive and might not survive a legal challenge if the kids sued. It would be much safer if Murdoch could convince his daughters to split with James voluntarily. In November 2023, Murdoch met with Wendi, Chloe, and Grace. He knew exactly which lever to pull: he offered to grant Chloe and Grace full voting rights, which Wendi had fought so hard to give them in 2006. They signed on.

In early December, Murdoch summoned Liz and Prue to his Mayfair flat. Liz sat next to Murdoch on the sofa as he read from a set of talking points and sketched a diagram of the trust on a yellow legal pad. His Australian warble had grown faint in old age, so Liz had to lean in to hear. "These companies are my legacy. I have put everything into them over my life," he said. He was doing this, he explained, to save the English-speaking world from the radical Left. "I love each of my children, and my support of Lachlan is not intended to suggest otherwise. But these companies need a designated leader, and Lachlan is that leader."

Liz later recalled that as Murdoch spoke, she relived childhood memories of sitting with her dad as he drew diagrams of the family business at the dining-room table. But Liz was no longer a child. She was an accomplished fifty-five-year-old businesswoman. Her father had underestimated her entire life. She knew a bad deal when she saw one. "You are completely disenfranchising me and my siblings," she told him, her voice tightening with emotion. "You've blown a hole in the family." Then she left.

Murdoch didn't appreciate her sanctimony. He knew that Liz's lawyer had drawn up a secret memo called Project Bridge that laid out a road map for how the family should prepare for Murdoch's death. *Did Murdoch want to be buried or cremated? Who should issue the statement?* In Murdoch's embattled state, it was evidence that his ungrateful children were plotting for his demise. Historically, Murdoch's anger fueled him. But his nonagenarian body was unable to handle the stress. The morning after his confrontation with Prue and Liz, Murdoch passed out. Doctors rushed to the scene and determined Murdoch had only fainted. Murdoch told his lawyers to convene the trust to formalize Lachlan's takeover.

Liz, who proudly thought of herself as Switzerland, wanted to use her neutrality to broker peace. Before the meeting, Liz called her dad begging him to stop the madness. She had personally organized his ninetieth birthday party in New York. At her daughter Charlotte's wedding, all six children had posed for a photo with Murdoch. Couldn't they figure this out as a family? Murdoch said his relationship with James was "unsalvageable." Liz defended her brother, which Murdoch said was just James's manipulation. "You're being lobbied by James. And you're going to bend to his will," he told her. Liz's desperation hardened to anger. "Do you think I'm a fucking moron?" she snapped.

Liz made one final appeal to Lachlan. "Hey, Liz, I really appreciate your support," he texted back. "Today is about dad's wishes and confirming all of our support for him and for his wishes. It shouldn't be difficult or controversial. Love you, Lachlan."

The special meeting proceeded as planned. Over Zoom, Murdoch informed his children that he changed the rules of the trust to secure Lachlan's leadership. It was war.

CHAPTER SIXTEEN

OBJECTING CHILDREN

FOR SEVENTY YEARS, Rupert Murdoch hid from confrontation. He fired his mentor by letter, divorced a wife by email, and used one child to fire another. But now, in a sterile Nevada courtroom in September 2024, the ninety-three-year-old mogul's money and power couldn't protect him any longer. He would finally face his estranged children under oath.

The trial was also a reckoning for Rupert's children. Discovery had been like an autopsy of a family's slow death, unearthing emails and texts that documented years of emotional pain. Depositions became an arena of psychological abuse. In one, Rupert's lawyer fired humiliating questions at James as Rupert looked on: *Have you ever done anything successful on your own? Why were you too busy to say "Happy birthday" to your father when he turned 90? Does it strike you that, in your account, everything that goes wrong is always somebody else's fault?* At one point, James noticed Rupert tapping on his phone and realized he was scripting the questions for the lawyer to ask. "How fucking twisted is that?" James later recalled.

For years, James had defended his father in public. "The classic characterization of him is as an ogre, someone who is wildly opportunistic and someone who has a checkbook for a heart. It's just not him," he said in 1999. At the *Vanity Fair* Oscar party in 2018, James confronted a journalist who had written critically about the company. "You're just trying to make a buck off my old man!" he said, as Kathryn gently tapped his arm to calm him down. James could defend Rupert no longer.

Rupert crafted narratives in the shadows, but the courtroom would require him to do it in the open. Rupert needed to prove that his decision to give his empire to Lachlan wasn't about politics, misogyny, or primogeniture. It was about money. Preserving Fox News's conservative voice was best for the business. The Nevada probate commissioner would allow Rupert to amend the trust if he acted in good faith to protect his children's financial interests. But James, Liz, and Prue—referred to in Rupert's court filings as the "Objecting Children"—had a crucial advantage: they simply needed to keep the status quo. Their lawyers prepared to argue that Rupert and Lachlan were disenfranchising them to further Rupert's dynastic and political project. If Rupert and Lachlan wanted them out of the trust, then they should pay a fair price for their shares. Anything else was stealing.

Facing the fight of his life, Rupert reached for his most reliable weapon: emotional manipulation. When Prue's birthday arrived weeks before the trial, flowers appeared at her door. More brazenly, Rupert sent documents to James's lawyer with a handwritten note: *Dear James, Still time to talk? Love, Dad. P.S.: Love to see my grandchildren one day.* The message was vintage Rupert: personal appeal wrapped around a business proposition, with a dash of guilt. None of the siblings took the bait. They had learned too much about their dad's methods to fall for his final charm offensive.

For decades, Rupert had weaponized information against business rivals and political enemies. Now his own children were about to turn the tables and weaponize the most damaging information of all: the truth about their father.

THE TRIAL'S OPENING DAY exposed Rupert's corporate Kabuki: Rupert's handpicked trustees, including former attorney general Bill Barr, testified that the trust amendment served the children's financial interests. Barr had researched the issues. But under withering cross-examination, another trustee embarrassingly admitted that he had initially confused Rupert with Alex Murdaugh—the South Carolina attorney who killed his wife and son. His lack of knowledge suggested Rupert had hired him to rubber stamp his change to the trust's governance. The Objecting Children landed a significant blow, which raised the stakes for Day 2: Rupert's testimony.

On the cold and gusty morning of September 17, Rupert arrived at the courthouse in a navy sweater under his dark suit, which he punctuated with a bright yellow tie. Photographs captured his wrinkled face, etched by deep grooves like a complex irrigation system. He climbed the courthouse steps with a pronounced stoop. It was the image of a man under siege.

Rupert's lawyer Adam Streisand had a difficult task ahead. Rupert had a habit of stepping in it, especially when questioned. Years ago, Rupert's PR adviser blanched when Rupert blurted out during an interview that Muslims have an inbreeding problem because they marry their second cousins. Streisand was one of the country's preeminent trust lawyers and well-positioned to shepherd Rupert through the most important testimony of his life. He previously litigated a lawsuit over the estate of William Randolph Hearst.

At first, Rupert stuck to the script. "I just felt sure, very certain that if these things weren't settled, there would be trouble, and the trouble would be damaging," Rupert said, his voice faint but lucid. "If there's uncertainty about the management, the public will feel it, inside the company would feel it." Rupert calmly explained the business rationale for amending the trust. "Everybody would know where they stood, the company would know what it's doing and it would be functionally harmonious," he said.

There was logic to his argument. But James had recruited a legal heavy hitter of his own to dismantle it: Gary Bornstein, the co-head of litigation at Cravath, Swaine & Moore. Under Bornstein's deft cross-examination, Rupert admitted that he changed the trust to protect his conservative legacy as much as the business. It would be a "disaster" for America if James convinced his sisters to depose Lachlan, he said. Bornstein had Rupert cornered. "The solution to that problem of [Liz and Prue] having to make a decision was for you to make the decision for them, correct?" he asked.

"Yes," Rupert replied.

In that single word, he put his self-serving misogyny on full view. When the session ended, Rupert left the courthouse and didn't return for the remainder of the trial. He told the judge he was sick, but James thought otherwise. "It was cowardice," he later said.

AFTER EACH DAY IN COURT, James, Prue, and Liz retired with their spouses to a friend's house in Lake Tahoe, about an hour away. Security was paramount. "They were worried about MAGA lunatics finding out where they were staying," an adviser to the three said. To decompress, they drank wine and reenacted memorable exchanges from the trial, but it was more than just debriefing—it was reconciliation. James and Liz were finally burying years of estrangement engineered by their father's manipulation during the phone hacking scandal. Even Liz and Prue, half-sisters whose relationship had been punctuated by epic screaming fights, found common ground. The mood was cautiously optimistic, though the stakes were too high to truly relax. Gorman, the probate commissioner, kept a poker face during the trial. At night, the siblings Googled him looking for any clues of his potential sympathies. One website said he was on the board of the Reno Jazz Orchestra. Given Rupert's disinterest in art and culture, this was potentially a positive sign. "He can't be that bad," James said.

The trial's third day belonged to the Objecting Children. This was the moment they had waited for their entire lives: the chance to tell their truth under oath and to have a judge rule their father had wronged them. They told a story of hurt and betrayal. Liz testified how "unbelievably close" she had been with her father, but now the relationship was "absent." James broke down crying when he talked about his mistreatment by his father and brother. "There have been a lot of hurtful things over the years," he said. "We worked together very closely for a long time. It's hard." As Lachlan stared back, James thought to himself: *How had it come to this?*

The siblings' emotions calcified during Streisand's pointed cross-examination. Streisand's questions were designed to reinforce the narrative

Rupert's legal team had been pushing since depositions: James, Liz, and Prue were "white, privileged, multi-billionaire trust-fund babies" scheming to advance their left-wing agenda at the cost of destroying their father's companies. Streisand sought to prove this by focusing on a secret meeting the three siblings held in a private room at Claridge's hotel on September 20, 2023. In Streisand's telling, they had gathered in London to plan how they would fire Lachlan upon Rupert's death. "Is it customary for you when you have drinks with your siblings and dinner to book a hotel conference room?" Streisand asked Liz.

Liz admitted it wasn't, but the choice of venue wasn't evidence of a plot: they simply wanted privacy to discuss funeral planning for their father. According to depositions, the meeting had been encouraged by Liz's lawyer Mark Devereux, who conceived Project Bridge to prepare for Rupert's death. Devereux, a self-described *Succession* addict, was deeply troubled when he watched the episode that depicted the fictional mogul Logan Roy's sudden death and the kids' scramble to issue a public statement.

Streisand didn't buy it. He challenged James about the Claridge's summit. "Do you deny saying anything about suggesting that once you do have your agency, that you do something about getting your brother out?" Streisand asked.

"I do deny that," James said.

For much of the afternoon, James contained his trademark aggression. But late in the day, his patience with Streisand's questions expired. "It's garbage," he said. "They're making stuff up or believing things that they are being told to create some sort of boogeyman that is a justification for stealing stuff that they didn't want to buy."

LACHLAN WAS THE LAST TO TESTIFY. The trial had unfolded like a microcosm of his life: he sat silently while others questioned his right to lead. He never asked to be his father's chosen son—it was his birthright, though at low moments it felt like a curse. No matter how much he achieved, critics questioned whether he was fit to stand in his father's shoes.

The legal battle had crystallized Lachlan's anger at his siblings for never recognizing his business record. His several-million-dollar investment in the real estate listing service REA Group was now worth billions. He prudently stayed out of the streaming wars and instead invested modestly in the advertising-supported streamer Tubi. Despite this, his siblings never supported him publicly. In early 2023, Lachlan pleaded with Liz to issue a statement refuting a *Financial Times* article that said James would force him out upon Rupert's death. "This is terrible, and you have to say something," he told her. Liz declined. The betrayal stung. During James's testimony, when Streisand asked if he had ever supported Lachlan, James's answer was brutal: "I don't believe so."

Even Rupert's absence from the courtroom felt like painful déjà vu— just like the times Rupert had left Lachlan to fend for himself against the courtiers who wanted him gone. It was the Rupert way: Dame Elisabeth had thrown Rupert into the water to teach him to swim. "I had to dog-paddle to the side, and I was screaming," Rupert once said. Now Lachlan was drowning alone.

But it was too late to get out of the pool. On the stand, Lachlan struggled. While his siblings gave hours of testimony about Rupert's psychological abuse, Lachlan was the lonely voice describing an attentive father who took him camping and generously made him and his siblings fantastically rich. "He gave the companies to us," he said. The real betrayal, Lachlan said, was his siblings' refusal to knock down the articles that said a coup was coming. "If Liz and Prue and James had come out at any point in this time, publicly, on the record, and said, 'This is false, Lachlan does not get fired the day Rupert dies, we are not a gang of three against him,' that would have stopped the stories," he testified. "It would have been a very simple, straight thing to do, and it would have been a decent thing, too."

It was an emotionally resonant appeal, but a legally ineffective one. Under cross-examination, Lachlan became flustered and evasive, like he was back in the boardroom struggling to debate James. He defended his father's warped philosophy that journalists should feed audiences what they want, even if what they want are lies. The nadir came when Lachlan admitted he had no evidence for his claim that James or his surrogates leaked stories about a coup. The trial had reduced Lachlan to a Fox News host. He was spreading conspiracies just like the network he controlled.

ON SATURDAY, DECEMBER 7, 2024—one year to the day since Rupert launched the legal battle to amend the trust—Commissioner Gorman issued his decision: Rupert lost. In a stinging rebuke, Gorman called Rupert's plan a "carefully crafted charade" to "permanently cement Lachlan Murdoch's executive roles . . . regardless of the impacts such control would have over the companies or the beneficiaries." This wasn't about business, Gorman said, it was about a political legacy. Gorman ruled that Rupert wanted his companies to "continue to be alternative, conservative voices in [the] media after he dies." To achieve this goal, Gorman said Rupert had violated the trust rules by trying to strip James, Liz, and Prue of their voting power to remove Lachlan after Rupert's death. Lachlan fared even worse. Gorman criticized his "lack of candor . . . on the witness stand." It was a humiliating coda. Rupert and Lachlan immediately vowed to appeal.

Gorman's decision was a resounding victory for James, Liz, and Prue. They prevented Rupert from stripping them of their rights to determine the empire's future upon Rupert's death. In 2030, the trust expires, and the siblings are free to sell their shares to the highest bidder. "The effort was an attempt to stack the deck in Lachlan Murdoch's favor after Rupert Murdoch's passing so that his succession would be immutable," Gorman wrote. "The play might have worked; but an evidentiary hearing, like a showdown in a game of poker, is where gamesmanship collides with the facts and at its conclusion, all the bluffs are called and the cards lie face up."

Even Rupert's effort to keep the most intimate details of his family's implosion secret failed: someone leaked three thousand pages of court records to *The New York Times*. In February 2025, the paper published a detailed account of the Nevada trust case.

Many Rupert profiles liken his late career arc to Shakespeare's King

Lear, but the tale of King Midas is more accurate. Like the mythical monarch whose touch turned everything to gold, Rupert built a $17 billion fortune but destroyed everything he loved in the process. His media outlets stoked hatred and division on an industrial scale, and amassing that wealth required him to damage virtually anything he touched: the environment, women's rights, the Republican Party, truth, decency—even his own family.

James and his siblings emerged from the hard-fought legal battle like the besieged Australians at Gallipoli whom Rupert's father sought to save: alive but angry that so much blood had been spilled.

The trust fight had a particularly clarifying effect for James. In early 2024, he began speaking to *Atlantic* journalist McKay Coppins for a lengthy magazine profile. James's choice of whom to open up to was revealing: Coppins had recently published an intimate biography of Mitt Romney. The Utah senator had trusted Coppins with his most private thoughts about watching the Republican Party he loved become something he could no longer recognize. "James thought McKay's book was beautiful," a person close to James said. Like Romney, James was breaking free of a tribe he no longer believed in. The piece had a moment of heartbreaking honesty as James grappled with what his life might have been if he hadn't played his father's succession game. "I used to paint a lot," he told Coppins. "I thought about being an architect. I did film animation in school. I had a story . . . In my head, there were so many—" he said, but never finished the sentence.

About a month after the trial—before Gorman's decision was filed—James and his sisters sent Rupert a letter hoping to reconcile. "Thanksgiving and Christmas are upon us and the three of us wanted to reach out to you personally to say that we miss you and love you," they wrote. "We are asking you with love to find a way to put an end to this destructive judicial path so that we can have a chance to heal as a collaborative and loving family."

Rupert wrote back a couple of days later. He had read the children's trial testimony two times, "only to conclude that I was right": they were unfit to inherit the business. He said he only wanted to speak through lawyers going forward. "Much love, Dad."

It was a brutally cold sign-off, but in many ways true to Rupert's character. Over seventy years, Rupert said he was building a family business. But what he built was a business that destroyed his family.

EPILOGUE

I N THE END, THEY SETTLED. On September 8, 2025—one year after the Nevada court showdown—the Murdochs reached an accord that fulfilled Rupert's wish that Lachlan would inherit the empire. Under the terms of the deal, James, Liz, and Prue forfeited their voting rights to choose a successor, and each received $1.1 billion. A new trust was created that would benefit Lachlan and Rupert's youngest children, Grace and Chloe. The deal proved Rupert's philosophy that money always wins.

Everyone had reasons to settle. For James, Liz, and Prue, Commissioner Gorman's ruling looked less certain once Rupert and Lachlan appealed in January 2025. That uncertainty was made especially clear in May when Nevada appeals court judge Lynne Jones indicated she was sympathetic to Rupert's argument that he amended the trust to protect the business. "Who knows better than Rupert Murdoch the strengths and weaknesses of his family and his children?" she said in court. Trump's election, too, had shifted the culture in Rupert and Lachlan's favor, according to one of their advisers. And Rupert's age also functioned as a ticking clock. At ninety-four, he might not survive the appeals process. Despite all the emotional blood spilled, Liz and Prue wanted closure with their father before he died.

By the time it was over, the common front around the rebellious children had cracked. Liz resented being portrayed in the media as a plotter in James's coup-in-waiting. She never wanted to dethrone Lachlan—she simply objected to Rupert rewriting the rules. This was about principle, not power. But principle had limits. As her adviser explained her decision to settle: "No one wants to be King of the Graveyard. She could fight this, but by the time it ends, so much blood will have been spilled that everyone's dead."

Of all the siblings, James had positioned himself as the moral conscience of the family. He resigned from the News Corp board because of "disagreements over certain editorial content." He told *The Atlantic* that a good company wouldn't lie to "juice ratings." He funded progressive causes and spoke of reforming media. But when the moment came to fight for actual reform of Fox News—when he could have used his position to push for change from within—he took $1.1 billion and walked away. "Prudence, Elisabeth, and James are pleased that the matter is now behind them," James's spokesperson said. His moral awakening, it turned out, had a price tag.

For Lachlan, the battle left him victorious but vulnerable. To buy out his siblings, Lachlan sold News Corp and Fox shares that reduced his control over the companies' boards to 36 percent and 33 percent. That smaller stake means his perch is vulnerable to an activist investor in the future. Fox News remains as dominant as ever. In September 2025, the cable network averaged 2.54 million viewers, more than CNN and MSNBC combined. But Fox's core twenty-five- to fifty-four-year-old demographic shrank 14 percent, as news consumers increasingly get their news online from social media, Tik-Tok, and podcasts. Tabloids, once the engine of the empire's growth, are now, on occasion, a liability. In January 2025, *The Sun*'s parent company issued an "unequivocal apology" to Prince Harry for phone hacking, and paid "substantial damages."

Lachlan is also navigating Rupert's fraught relationship with Trump. In July 2025, Trump sued Rupert for $10 billion after *The Wall Street Journal* reported Trump had contributed a signed drawing of a naked woman as part of a fiftieth-birthday gift for Jeffrey Epstein, later convicted as a sex offender. "Happy Birthday—and may every day be another wonderful secret," Trump wrote to Epstein in 2003, according to the *Journal*. Trump told people that Rupert deceived him. "Rupert assured Trump it wouldn't run," said a person who spoke with Trump at the time. The *Journal* stood by its story, with a representative telling reporters: "We have full confidence in the rigor and accuracy of our reporting, and will vigorously defend against any lawsuit."

In September 2025, despite suing Rupert for $10 billion over the Epstein story, Trump offered him a minority stake in the consortium to acquire Tik-Tok. Rupert accepted—the man who once dictated terms was now taking what Trump offered. After decades building his empire through conquest and control, Rupert was now agreeing to be a minority stakeholder in a Chinese app. The Murdoch empire still mattered. Fox News still moved Republican politics; the newspapers still influenced elites. But power was shifting to platforms Rupert couldn't own and personalities he couldn't control.

Lachlan, Grace, and Chloe inherited an empire that, while still powerful, no longer set the terms of the game. Lachlan got the kingdom; James, Liz, and Prue got their freedom. In early August, a rumor swirled through New York media circles that Rupert was very sick and possibly dying. But later that month, news outlets reported he had dinner with the Greek prime minister at a seaside taverna on the island of Tinos. During a month when billionaires gathered their families on their yachts, Rupert was with his fourth wife while his children were scattered across the globe. He was still in the game, even if he played alone.

ACKNOWLEDGMENTS

I **GOT THE IDEA TO WRITE** this book in the spring of 2023 after *Vanity Fair* published my cover story on the Murdoch succession drama. I want to thank my colleagues at the magazine, especially my editor Matt Lynch, for shepherding the piece that became the foundation for the next two and a half years of work.

I'm grateful to my longtime literary agent, Gail Ross, who has always had my back. Her wise and patient counsel, along with her sophisticated taste, has enabled me to make a living doing what I love most: telling stories about the most consequential figures of our time.

I first met my Simon & Schuster editor, Priscilla Painton, more than twenty years ago when I was a reporter at the *New York Observer* and she was a senior editor at *Time*. When she moved to S&S, I hoped I'd have the chance to write a book for her someday. I'm fortunate this was that book. Priscilla is that rare nonfiction editor who combines the highest journalistic standards with a novelist's ambition to understand the historical and psychological forces that shape a story. She grasped my vision to write this as a family saga rather than a traditional business book. I also want to thank the entire S&S team, especially Johanna Li, who juggled shifting publishing dates and deadlines with grace and humor.

ACKNOWLEDGMENTS

I'm deeply indebted to the many sources who spoke honestly and patiently to help me understand this powerful and secretive family. The depth and scope of this book wouldn't have been possible without the impressive work of my journalistic peers, whose groundbreaking reporting I cite throughout. I particularly want to acknowledge reporters at *Vanity Fair*, *The New Yorker*, *New York* magazine, *The New York Times*, *The Guardian*, *The Wall Street Journal*, *The Financial Times*, and elsewhere whose work informed my own.

I dedicated this book to my wife, Jennifer, whose love and support astound me. I started writing as we welcomed our second child and finished as we moved from New York to London. Without her superhuman patience I wouldn't be writing these words. I also want to thank our extended family, who helped with childcare and meals when I couldn't pull my weight.

Finally, I want to thank my late magazine editor, John Homans. John died in July 2020 at the unfair age of sixty-two. The dozen years I wrote for him at *New York* and *Vanity Fair* shaped me as a writer and, more importantly, as a person. Thank you, John. I miss you.

A NOTE ABOUT SOURCES

THIS BOOK CHRONICLES MORE THAN a century of the Murdoch family's influence on global media and politics, from Sir Keith Murdoch's birth in 1885 through the 2024 Nevada trust battle that may determine the future of the world's last great media dynasty.

The reporting draws on extensive primary and secondary sources gathered over two decades of covering the Murdoch empire, including publishing my 2014 biography of Fox News chief Roger Ailes. For this book, I conducted more than 150 interviews with family members, current and former News Corp executives, political figures, business associates, family friends, and legal sources. These included on-the-record conversations as well as background discussions with sources who requested anonymity due to ongoing business relationships, legal constraints, or family loyalties. Where possible, I have corroborated accounts through multiple sources and contemporaneous documents.

I have been reporting on the Murdoch family since 2004 and have spent time with each family member except Prudence. The family declined to participate formally in this book, though I drew on previous interviews and interactions over the years.

The narrative relies heavily on court documents, particularly from the

A NOTE ABOUT SOURCES

2024 Nevada trust case (court documents obtained and published by *The New York Times*); the phone hacking trials in Britain; and the Dominion Voting Systems lawsuit against Fox News. These legal proceedings produced thousands of pages of depositions, internal emails, text messages, and corporate documents that offer unprecedented insight into the family's private dynamics and business operations.

I also consulted personal diaries and memoirs, particularly those of Harold Evans, Woodrow Wyatt, Andrew Neil, Larry Lamb, Bruce Guthrie, Irwin Stelzer, Les Hinton, and Philip Townsend, which offer intimate glimpses into Rupert Murdoch's thinking and behavior across different eras. Contemporary news accounts, corporate filings, and government documents helped establish timelines and verify details.

For scenes involving private conversations, I relied on accounts from participants, contemporaneous notes, text messages, emails, and detailed reconstructions provided by sources with direct knowledge. In cases where accounts differed, I have noted discrepancies or chosen the version that seemed most credible based on corroborating evidence.

This book aims to be both a family biography and a meditation on power, legacy, and the price of building a media empire. The sourcing reflects that dual purpose—documenting not just what happened, but why it mattered.

NOTES

PROLOGUE

1 ***On the morning of:*** Jim Waterson, "Rupert Murdoch in court battle with three of his children over media empire succession," *Guardian*, September 16, 2024.

1 ***On December 6, 2023:*** Jonathan Mahler and Jim Rutenberg, "'You've Blown a Hole in the Family': Inside the Murdochs' Succession Drama," *New York Times Magazine*, February 13, 2025.

1 ***Murdoch's adult children:*** Mahler and Rutenberg, "'You've Blown a Hole in the Family.'"

1 ***From birth, Murdoch had:*** Andrew Neil, *Full Disclosure* (London: Macmillan, 1996), 180.

1 ***The rivalry played:*** Tim Adams, "James Murdoch: 'I'm Not My Father,'" *Guardian*, November 6, 2011.

2 ***Around 8:00 a.m., the first vehicle:*** Jade Macmillan, "Rupert Murdoch and His Children Arrive at Nevada Court for Secret Hearing That Could Decide Media Empire's Future," ABC News, September 17, 2024; Reuters video footage, "Murdoch family arrives at court as their succession drama plays out in closed court in Reno, Nevada," September 16, 2024.

2 ***The family rebel:*** Gabriel Sherman, "The Raging Septuagenarian," *New York*, February 26, 2010.

2 ***In 2012, James presided:*** Gabriel Sherman, "The King's Dominion," *Vanity Fair*, May 2023.

2 ***Murdoch's second daughter:*** Reuters video footage, "Murdoch family arrives at court"; Gabriel Sherman, "Elisabeth of the Murdochs," *New York*, November 4, 2011.

2 ***Liz thought of:*** Sherman, "The King's Dominion."

2 ***Last came the:*** Reuters video footage, "Murdoch family arrives at court."

3 ***In exile, James's resentments:*** Brian Stelter, "James Murdoch criticizes 'media property owners' who have 'unleashed insidious' forces with election denialism claims," CNN Business, January 15, 2021.

3 *He memorized passages:* McKay Coppins, "Growing Up Murdoch," *Atlantic*, February 14, 2025.

3 *Prue was the only child:* Penelope Debelle, "The day I screamed at my dad Rupert; Murdoch's other daughter speaks for the first time about life with the media magnate," *Sydney Morning Herald*, March 21, 1999.

3 *Then came a gap:* Reuters video footage, "Murdoch family arrives at court."

3 *The arrivals had been:* Mahler and Rutenberg, "'You've Blown a Hole in the Family.'"

3 *Behind Murdoch emerged:* Reuters video footage, "Murdoch family arrives at court."

4 *Commentators described:* Paddy Manning, "This high-stakes meeting could pressure the Murdoch family to relinquish News Corp control," Australian Broadcasting Corporation, October 25, 2024.

4 *In 2005, he quit:* Steve Fishman, "The Boy Who Wouldn't Be King," *New York*, September 9, 2005.

4 *Only after a decade:* Sherman, "The King's Dominion."

4 *When Liz made:* Mahler and Rutenberg, "'You've Blown a Hole in the Family.'"

4 *The courtroom doors shut:* Jim Rutenberg and Jonathan Mahler, "The Secret Battle for the Future of the Murdoch Empire," *New York Times*, July 25, 2024; Mark Robinson, "Nevada Supreme Court to decide if media mogul Rupert Murdoch's family dispute stays secret," *Reno Gazette Journal*, May 6, 2025.

4 *It had been two years:* Author interview with sources close to the family.

CHAPTER ONE

7 *Keith Arthur Murdoch:* R. M. Younger, *Keith Murdoch: The War Correspondent Who Founded an Empire* (HarperCollins, Kindle edition, 2019).

7 *Keith suffered from:* Michael Cannon, "The enigma of Keith Murdoch: A new biography reveals a complex and contentious figure," *Inside Story*, November 18, 2015.

7 *Keith gained fame:* "The Gallipoli Letter, Written by Keith Murdoch 23 September 1915," Australian War Memorial, UNESCO Memory of the World Program, accessed July 8, 2025.

7 *eight-thousand-word account:* Keith Arthur Murdoch, "Gallipoli letter from Keith Arthur Murdoch to Andrew Fisher, 1915," MS 2823 Series 2 Folder 1, National Library of Australia.

7 *"ghastly and costly fiasco":* Cannon, "The enigma of Keith Murdoch."

8 *"It depicted a":* William Shawcross, *Murdoch* (New York: Simon & Schuster, 1992), 21.

8 *"It may not":* Shawcross, *Murdoch*, 22.

8 *For the rest:* Tom DC Roberts, "The Murdochs: How Keith's legacy became Rupert's obsession" *Guardian*, November 17, 2015.

8 *"Napoleon of Fleet Street":* James Walton, "How Lord Northcliffe became the 'Napoleon of Fleet Street,'" *Telegraph*, August 4, 2022.

8 *"A newspaper is":* Shawcross, *Murdoch*, 22.

8 *In 1905, Northcliffe:* "Key moments in the Observer's history—a timeline," *Guardian*, November 7, 2017.

8 *Three years later:* "About Us," *Times* and *Sunday Times*, accessed July 8, 2025.

8 *By 1914, Northcliffe:* J. Lee Thompson, *Fleet Street Colossus* (London: John Murray, 2001), 115.

8   *a rabid anti-Semite:* Shawcross, *Murdoch*, 21.

8   *was increasingly paranoid:* Dominic Sandbrook, "How Lord Northcliffe invented the Daily Mail and became a megalomaniac," *Times*, August 7, 2022.

8   *In 1922, Northcliffe died:* "Northcliffe Dies of Heart Disease at His London Home," *New York Times*, August 15, 1922.

9   *Keith revitalized the:* Thomas Kiernan, *Citizen Murdoch* (New York: Dodd, Mead & Company, 1986), 12.

9   *the* **Herald's** *circulation:* Shawcross, *Murdoch*, 23.

9   *Keith bought rival:* Shawcross, *Murdoch*, 24.

9   *By the late 1920s:* "Cruden Farm," Victorian Heritage Database, Heritage Council Victoria, VHD 197640, accessed July 9, 2024.

9   *"I know you despise":* Walter Marsh, *Young Rupert: The Making of the Murdoch Empire* (Scribe Publications, Kindle edition), 20.

9   *In 1927, Keith noticed:* Younger, *Keith Murdoch*, 188.

9   *Elisabeth gave birth:* Marsh, *Young Rupert*, 40.

9   *By most accounts, Rupert was:* Marsh, *Young Rupert*, 42.

9   *he was knighted:* Julian Clarke, "Keith Murdoch," Australian Media Hall of Fame, accessed July 9, 2024.

10   *"Keith had little patience":* Kiernan, *Citizen Murdoch*, 18.

10   *Rupert discovered:* Marsh, *Young Rupert*, 43.

10   *"The life of":* Shawcross, *Murdoch*, 27.

10   *"I had to dog-paddle":* Neil Chenoweth, *Rupert Murdoch* (Crown, Kindle edition), 37.

10   *"toughen him up":* Chenoweth, *Rupert Murdoch*, 37.

10   *"Maybe they thought":* Shawcross, *Murdoch*, 27.

10   *"He was always":* Shawcross, *Murdoch*, 25.

10   *"my father's nightmares":* Shawcross, *Murdoch*, 25.

10   *When Rupert was ten:* Marsh, *Young Rupert*, 43.

10   *"I felt a loner at school":* Shawcross, *Murdoch*, 29.

10   *He stashed a motorcycle:* Shawcross, *Murdoch*, 29.

10   *"I can remember":* Kiernan, *Citizen Murdoch*, 19.

11   *"Comrade Rupert":* Marsh, *Young Rupert*, 40.

11   *"Nobody took him":* Kiernan, *Citizen Murdoch*, 20.

11   *Rupert graduated:* Marsh, *Young Rupert*, 53.

11   *"My only palpable":* Kiernan, *Citizen Murdoch*, 22.

11   *a bust of Lenin:* Shawcross, *Murdoch*, 32.

11   *"Red Rupe":* Kiernan, *Citizen Murdoch*, 3.

11   *"The Great Thinker":* Chenoweth, *Rupert Murdoch*, 44.

11   *"morning, Comrade":* Steve Hewlett, "Why Britain has reason to be grateful to Rupert Murdoch," *Guardian*, September 27, 2013.

11   *"I was impatient":* Kiernan, *Citizen Murdoch*, 28.

11   *had a car:* Shawcross, *Murdoch*, 32.

11   *Keith threatened to:* Kiernan, *Citizen Murdoch*, 25.

11   *two heart attacks:* Younger, *Keith Murdoch*, 370.

12   *"I can't afford":* Marsh, *Young Rupert*, 21.

12   *In January 1948:* Marsh, *Young Rupert*, 21.

12   *What Keith needed:* Kiernan, *Citizen Murdoch*, 23.

12   *1,800-mile tour:* Marsh, *Young Rupert*, 55.

12 *"He will make":* Marsh, *Young Rupert*, 54.

12 *It was welcome news:* Shawcross, *Murdoch*, 34.

12 *"I think he's got it":* Shawcross, *Murdoch*, 37.

12 *One October night:* Younger, *Keith Murdoch*, 389.

12 *"It was so":* Ali Cromie, "The Murdoch Succession," *Australian Financial Review*, October 17, 1994.

12 *"Some people live":* Larry Lamb, *Sunrise* (London: Pan Macmillan, 1989), 233.

13 *Rupert wanted to:* Kiernan, *Citizen Murdoch*, 38.

13 *the Savoy hotel:* Kiernan, *Citizen Murdoch*, 40.

13 *"the Beaverbrook brothel":* Shawcross, *Murdoch*, 39.

13 *"It made me angry":* Shawcross, *Murdoch*, 42.

13 *On September 8, 1953:* Marsh, *Young Rupert*, 121.

13 *"Hey, Sonny!":* Richard Cooke, "The endless reign of Rupert Murdoch," *Monthly*, July 2018.

14 *Rupert and Rivett ran:* Kiernan, *Citizen Murdoch*, 46–47.

14 *"Expand or perish!":* Kiernan, *Citizen Murdoch*, 50; Shawcross, *Murdoch*, 50.

14 *Rupert's personal life:* Marsh, *Young Rupert*, 140.

14 *"I didn't know who":* David Washington, "Memories of the Murdoch World," *Offset*, November 1985.

14 *A daughter, Prudence:* Chenoweth, *Rupert Murdoch*.

14 *"I was totally":* Shawcross, *Murdoch*, 62.

14 *two rival clans:* Kiernan, *Citizen Murdoch*, 63.

15 *"I was amazed":* Shawcross, *Murdoch*, 51.

15 *Rupert took command:* Shawcross, *Murdoch*, 51.

15 *Editors even made up:* Kiernan, *Citizen Murdoch*, 68, 80.

15 *"In those days":* Kiernan, *Citizen Murdoch*, 81–82.

15 *"He was like a whirlwind":* Shawcross, *Murdoch*, 64.

15 *In 1967, he divorced:* Nadeem Badshah, "The merry wives of Rupert Murdoch: who has the tycoon been wed to before?" *Guardian*, June 22, 2022.

15 *heavy-drinking Adelaide hairdresser:* Michael Wolff, *The Man Who Owns the News: Inside the Secret World of Rupert Murdoch* (Crown, Kindle edition, 2008), 95–96.

16 *"a cocky bastard":* Marsh, *Young Rupert*, 122–23.

16 *After Rivett denied:* Kiernan, *Citizen Murdoch*, 54.

16 *"After much long":* Marsh, *Young Rupert*, 280.

16 *After Rivett's departure:* Chenoweth, *Rupert Murdoch*, 50.

16 *a yacht named* **Ilina***:* "Films that highlight the history of the Sydney Hobart Yacht Race (1)," Cruising Yacht Club of Australia, accessed July 9, 2025.

16 *twenty-four-thousand-acre sheep farm:* Annabelle Dufraigne and Katie Schultz, "Inside the Murdoch Family's Staggering Real Estate Portfolio: As the family that inspired *Succession* dukes it out in court, we take a deep dive into their property holdings," *Architectural Digest*, September 20, 2024.

16 *"I had to admit":* Kiernan, *Citizen Murdoch*, 70.

CHAPTER TWO

17 *Political violence convulsed:* Todd Gitlin, *The Sixties: Years of Hope, Days of Rage* (New York: Bantam, 1993); "Vietnam War U.S. Military Fatal Casualty Statistics," National Archives, accessed July 9, 2024.

17   *One night in mid-October:* Thomas Kiernan, *Citizen Murdoch* (New York: Dodd, Mead & Company, 1986), 89.

17   *the* **News of the World***:* Esther Addley, "The News of the World's sensational history," *Guardian*, July 7, 2011.

17   *"News of the Screws":* "News of the World: An Obituary," BBC, July 8, 2011.

17   *"as British as":* Michael Leapman, "Paper that sells smut with a smirk: The 'News of the World' is celebrating its 150th anniversary," *Independent*, October 1, 1993.

17   *circulation had declined by:* William Shawcross, *Murdoch* (New York: Simon & Schuster, 1992), 69.

17   *Sir William Carr:* Kiernan, *Citizen Murdoch*, 90.

18   *publisher Robert Maxwell:* John Preston, *Fall: The Mysterious Life of Robert Maxwell* (New York: Harper, 2021); Robert Philpot, "From wooden shack to global media magnate: The rise and fall of Robert Maxwell," *Times of Israel*, February 23, 2021.

18   *Catto positioned Rupert:* Kiernan, *Citizen Murdoch*, 94–95.

18   *Rupert and Catto:* Kiernan, *Citizen Murdoch*, 94–95; Michael Leapman, *Barefaced Cheek: Rupert Murdoch* (London: Coronet, 1984).

18   *Carr was usually drunk:* Steve Hewlett, "Why Britain has reason to be grateful to Rupert Murdoch," *Guardian*, September 27, 2013.

18   *"Let Maxwell get it":* Kiernan, *Citizen Murdoch*, 96–97.

18   *Sir William's wife:* Adam Curtis, "Rupert Murdoch: A Portrait of Satan," BBC, April 25, 2012.

19   *Her fears proved:* Kiernan, *Citizen Murdoch*, 101; Shawcross, Murdoch, 75.

19   *"Yes, you hurt":* Kiernan, *Citizen Murdoch*, 103.

19   *Sir William died:* Curtis, "Rupert Murdoch: A Portrait of Satan."

19   *"unbelievable mess":* Shawcross, *Murdoch*, 78.

19   *"A pompous ass":* Kiernan, *Citizen Murdoch*, 104.

19   *Rupert wanted to fire Somerfield:* Kiernan, *Citizen Murdoch*, 105.

19   *"As Editor I am":* Kiernan, *Citizen Murdoch*, 105.

19   *"accept it or quit!":* Kiernan, *Citizen Murdoch*, 104.

19   *circulation remained flat:* Shawcross, *Murdoch*, 74.

20   *Rupert needed a scoop:* Kiernan, *Citizen Murdoch*, 107.

20   *Rupert paid Keeler:* Kiernan, *Citizen Murdoch*, 107.

20   *"cashing in on pornography":* "Memoirs: The Perils of Christine," *Time*, October 10, 1969.

20   *The blowback hit:* Roy Greenslade, *Press Gang: How Newspapers Make Profits from Propaganda* (Basingstoke and Oxford: Macmillan, 2003), 214.

20   *"People can sneer":* Kiernan, *Citizen Murdoch*, 107.

21   *"Keeler—YOUR right":* Simon Farquhar, *A Desperate Business: The Murder of Muriel McKay* (London: History Press, 2022).

21   *The controversy spilled:* Kiernan, *Citizen Murdoch*, 111.

21   *Anna turned to writing:* Kiernan, *Citizen Murdoch*, 160.

21   *In October 1969:* David Frost, *David Frost: an Autobiography. Part One—From Congregations to Audiences* (London: HarperCollins Publishers, 1993), 493–501; Kiernan, *Citizen Murdoch*, 112, 114.

22   *"The son of a bitch":* Kiernan, *Citizen Murdoch*, 108.

23   *"born of the age we live in":* Lamb, *Sunrise*, 4.

23   *The Sun's circulation:* Shawcross, *Murdoch*, 79.

23   *"dull," "trite," "long-winded"*: Kiernan, *Citizen Murdoch*, 122.
23   *"upmarket shit"*: Nathan Robinson, "The Sun Never Sets on Rupert Murdoch's Journalistic Empire," *Current Affairs*, August 2023.
23   *Rupert knew he could*: Les Hinton, *The Bootle Boy: An Untidy Life in News* (London: Scribe, 2018), 300.
23   *Unfortunately, Cudlipp had*: Kiernan, *Citizen Murdoch*, 118.
24   *he hunted for his editor*: Kiernan, *Citizen Murdoch*, 123; Peter Chippindale and Chris Horrie, *Stick It Up Your Punter!* (London: William Heinemann Limited, 1990), 10; Lamb, *Sunrise*, 8, 10.
24   *"When I got The Sun"*: Kiernan, *Citizen Murdoch*, 123.
24   *The first issue*: Chippindale and Horrie, *Stick It Up Your Punter!*, 19.
24   *Rupert invited advertisers*: Kiernan, *Citizen Murdoch*, 124.
25   *riddled with typos*: Chippindale and Horrie, *Stick It Up Your Punter!*, 24, 32.
25   *Later issues ran*: Lamb, *Sunrise*, 83, 140; Chippindale and Horrie, *Stick It Up Your Punter!*, 32.
25   *"Page 3 girls"*: Kiernan, *Citizen Murdoch*, 126.
25   *"Rupert's shit sheet"*: Shawcross, *Murdoch*, 80.
25   *"Dirty Digger"*: Shawcross, *Murdoch*, 76.
25   *MPs called for his prosecution*: Chippindale and Horrie, *Stick It Up Your Punter!*, 48.
25   *"If it's so objectionable"*: Kiernan, *Citizen Murdoch*, 126.
25   *circulation doubled*: "Flirty not dirty at 30," BBC, November 17, 2000, accessed July 10, 2024.
25   *"I answer to no one"*: Kiernan, *Citizen Murdoch*, 126.
25   *The trip was shattered when*: Account of Muriel McKay disappearance drawn from Farquhar, *A Desperate Business*; Lamb, *Sunrise*; Shawcross, *Murdoch*; Chippindale and Horrie, *Stick It Up Your Punter!*.

CHAPTER THREE

27   *In the summer of 1973*: Thomas Kiernan, *Citizen Murdoch* (New York: Dodd, Mead & Company, 1986), 168; "Elizabeth Arden's apartment at 834 Fifth Avenue," photograph, Museum of the City of New York, accessed July 11, 2025; Christopher Gray, "Mr. Murdoch builds his dream house," *New York Times*, December 30, 2007; Laurie Bennett, "Counting the Billionaires at 834 Fifth Avenue," *Forbes*, February 15, 2012.
27   *The Murdochs decorated*: Lois Romano, "EXTRA!! Publisher's Wife Pens Novel," *Washington Post*, October 23, 1985.
27   *He told friends*: Kiernan, *Citizen Murdoch*, 152.
27   *the industry was mired*: B. Drummond Ayres Jr., "Washington Star to shut down after 128 years," *New York Times*, July 24, 1981; Kiernan, *Citizen Murdoch*, 147; William Shawcross, *Murdoch* (New York: Simon & Schuster, 1992), 100.
28   *Around this time*: Kiernan, *Citizen Murdoch*, 147; Griffin Smith Jr., "Weirdo Paper Plagues S.A.," *Texas Monthly*, November 1976.
28   *"You take what"*: William H. Meyers, "Murdoch's Global Power Play," *New York Times*, June 12, 1988.
28   *"The bottom line"*: Kiernan, *Citizen Murdoch*, 156.
28   *The News actually lost*: Kiernan, *Citizen Murdoch*, 150.
28   *The struggles in San Antonio*: Shawcross, *Murdoch*, 87.

28   *In the run-up:* Judy Klemesrud, "Murdoch: Sensationalism first," *New York Times*, November 20, 1976.
29   *Rupert spent $5 million:* Kiernan, *Citizen Murdoch*, 155.
29   *Rupert's fortunes turned:* "The Battle of New York," *Time*, January 17, 1977.
29   *Felker founded* New York: Gail Sheehy, "A fistful of dollars," *Rolling Stone*, July 14, 1977.
29   *"Do you want":* Tom Wolfe, "A City Built of Clay," *New York*, July 3, 2008.
29   *"Clay's real interest":* Kurt Andersen, "Felkerism," *New York*, June 20, 2008.
29   *"[Clay] explained":* Susan Braudy, "King Rupert: The Stealthy," *Huffington Post*, May 24, 2007.
29   *Felker's tutorials:* Michael Wolff, *The Man Who Owns the News: Inside the Secret World of Rupert Murdoch* (Crown, Kindle edition, 2008), 150.
30   *"The way to operate":* Gail Sheehy, "A fistful of dollars," *Rolling Stone*, July 14, 1977.
30   *Felker traveled by:* Tom Wolfe, "A City Built of Clay," *New York*, July 3, 2008.
30   *The seventy-one-year-old:* Gail Sheehy, "The Life of the Most Powerful Woman in New York," *New York*, December 10, 1973; Shawcross, *Murdoch*, 90.
30   *"Everything about his body":* Nan Robertson, "Dorothy Schiff Tells of Relationship with Roosevelt," *New York Times*, May 27, 1976.
30   *In the 1950s:* Shawcross, *Murdoch*, 91.
31   *Felker greased the deal:* Mary Breasted, "Mrs. Schiff Says That She Sold the Post to Avoid Payment of 'Prohibitive,'" *New York Times*, November 21, 1976.
31   *He flattered Schiff:* Shawcross, *Murdoch*, 91; Michael Leapman, *Barefaced Cheek: Rupert Murdoch* (London: Coronet, 1984), 81.
31   *Schiff rejected Rupert's:* Kiernan, *Citizen Murdoch*, 189.
31   *"I sensed she was":* Alexander Cockburn, "Rupert Murdoch Tells All," *Village Voice*, November 29, 1976.
31   *roast beef sandwiches:* Jonathan Mahler, "What Rupert Wrought," *New York*, April 1, 2005.
31   *But weeks passed:* Kiernan, *Citizen Murdoch*, 190.
31   *On November 20, 1976:* Deirdre Carmody, "Dorothy Schiff Agrees to Sell Post to Murdoch, Australian Publisher," *New York Times*, November 20, 1976.
31   *"I may have paid":* Sheehy, "A fistful of dollars."
31   *On the night:* Sheehy, "A fistful of dollars"; Mahler, "What Rupert Wrought."
31   *"You fucking did it!":* Wolff, *The Man Who Owns the News*, 151.
31   *Later that winter:* Leapman, *Barefaced Cheek*, 92.
32   *The fuse was lit:* Sheehy, "A fistful of dollars"; Shawcross, *Murdoch*, 94.
32   *"Rupert Murdoch was":* Kiernan, *Citizen Murdoch*, 190.
32   *Felker confided that:* Sheehy, "A fistful of dollars"; Shawcross, *Murdoch*, 94.
32   *"You've all got houses":* Lucian K. Truscott IV, "Felker's Fall," *New Times*, November 1977.
32   *"You've had a lot":* Sheehy, "A fistful of dollars."
32   *"Clay let on":* Truscott IV, "Felker's Fall."
32   *"I was asking":* Truscott IV, "Felker's Fall."
32   *Without telling Felker:* Kiernan, *Citizen Murdoch*, 192; Truscott IV, "Felker's Fall."
33   *Rupert called Felker:* Sheehy, "A fistful of dollars."
33   *Instead, at a meeting:* Kiernan, *Citizen Murdoch*, 192–94.
33   *True to his word:* Sheehy, "A fistful of dollars."
33   *"We won't work for you":* Sheehy, "A fistful of dollars."

33   *"I can't lose"*: Sheehy, "A fistful of dollars."

33   *On January 7, 1977*: Shawcross, *Murdoch*, 97; Truscott IV, "Felker's Fall."

34   *During a single week:* "The Battle of New York"; David Gelman, "Press Lord Captures Gotham," *Newsweek*, January 17, 1977.

34   *In July,* **Rolling Stone:** Sheehy, "A fistful of dollars."

34   *Rupert appointed himself:* Kiernan, *Citizen Murdoch*, 201–04.

35   *"Australian carpetbagger":* Mahler, "What Rupert Wrought."

35   *"a bad element":* Chet Flippo, "Steve Dunleavy: The Writer They Call Mr. Blood and Guts," *Rolling Stone*, April 19, 1979.

35   *"Something vaguely sickening":* Jack Doyle, "Murdoch's NY Deals," Pop History Dig, accessed July 12, 2025.

35   *"I don't give a damn":* Leapman, *Barefaced Cheek*, 127.

35   *In August 1977:* Glenn Fowler, "Primary Roundup," *New York Times*, August 24, 1977.

35   *"Vote for Cuomo":* Jen Chung, "Ed Koch Held Decades-Long Grudge Against Cuomos Over 'Vote for Cuomo, Not the Homo' Posters," *Gothamist*, February 1, 2013.

35   *"We are dismayed":* Leapman, *Barefaced Cheek*, 130; Kiernan, *Citizen Murdoch*, 209.

35   *"It's my newspaper":* Leapman, *Barefaced Cheek*, 131.

36   *"[Rupert] made the difference":* Jennifer Preston, "Murdoch's Denials of Political Favors Hard to Swallow in New York," *New York Times*, April 27, 2012.

CHAPTER FOUR

37   *"cult of adversarial journalism":* William Shawcross, *Murdoch* (New York: Simon & Schuster, 1992), 155.

37   *"The American press might":* Thomas Kiernan, *Citizen Murdoch* (New York: Dodd, Mead & Company, 1986), 145.

37   *"VOTE TORY THIS TIME":* Larry Lamb, *Sunrise* (London: Pan Macmillan), 154.

38   *Canadian industrialist Ken Thomson:* Leonard Downie Jr., "Sale or Closure Set for London Times," *Washington Post*, October 22, 1980.

38   *£12 million:* Shawcross, *Murdoch*, 128; Harold Evans, *Good Times, Bad Times: The Explosive Inside Story of Rupert Murdoch* (Open Road Media, Kindle edition, 2011).

38   *"This new undertaking":* "Who's Afraid of Rupert Murdoch?" *PBS*, 1995.

38   *"You tell these bloody politicians":* Kiernan, *Citizen Murdoch*, 238.

38   *The government approved:* William Borders, "Murdoch Is Gaining in Bid to Buy Paper," *New York Times*, February 1, 1981.

38   *fiftieth birthday in Australia:* Shawcross, *Murdoch*, 137.

38   *Harold Evans:* Evans, *Good Times, Bad Times.*

39   *On January 17, 1981:* Evans, *Good Times, Bad Times.*

39   *"Nobody could resist":* Shawcross, *Murdoch*, 131.

39   *"No editor or journalist":* Evans, *Good Times, Bad Times.*

39   *Sunday, January 4, 1981:* Harold Evans, "How Thatcher and Murdoch made their secret deal," *Guardian*, April 28, 2015.

39   *"no separate political existence":* Evans, "How Thatcher and Murdoch made their secret deal."

40   *"The Sunday Times was":* Woodrow Wyatt, *The Journals of Woodrow Wyatt, Volume 1* (London: Pan Books, 1998), 372.

40 *Biffen approved:* Evans, *Good Times, Bad Times*; Shawcross, *Murdoch*, 129.
40 *Evans sent off:* Evans, *Good Times, Bad Times*.
40 *"two kinds of politician":* Evans, *Good Times, Bad Times*.
40 *"these commies?":* Evans, *Good Times, Bad Times*.
40 *"You're always getting":* Evans, *Good Times, Bad Times*.
40 *"worth reading!":* Evans, *Good Times, Bad Times*.
40 *"Intellectual bullshit!":* Evans, *Good Times, Bad Times*.
40 *Accountants projected:* Kiernan, *Citizen Murdoch*, 243.
41 *"We are quite literally":* Shawcross, *Murdoch*, 143, 189.
41 *"It was thirty years":* Evans, *Good Times, Bad Times*.
41 *"I want your resignation":* Evans, *Good Times, Bad Times*.
42 *On the night of:* Evans, *Good Times, Bad Times*.
42 *"We're All Falklanders":* Shawcross, *Murdoch*, 150.
42 *Hitler Diaries hoax:* Account of Hitler diary hoax drawn from Robert Harris, *Selling Hitler* (London: Pantheon, 1986); Kiernan, *Citizen Murdoch*, 245–50.
42 *Ed Kosner:* Edward Kosner, *It's News to Me* (New York: DaCapo Press, 2006), 220–22.
42 *For cost-cutting reasons:* Kiernan, *Citizen Murdoch*, 248.
43 *"Fuck Dacre. Publish!":* Michael Wolff, *The Man Who Owns the News: Inside the Secret World of Rupert Murdoch* (Crown, Kindle edition, 2008), 242.
43 *"I don't know why":* Magnus Linklater, "Murdoch's bravado forced through the publication of the Hitler diaries," *Guardian*, April 25, 2012.
43 *"We are in":* Amy Davidson Sorkin, "What Murdoch Learned from the Hitler Diary Forgeries," *New Yorker*, July 14, 2011.
43 *Anna was isolated:* Kiernan, *Citizen Murdoch*, 224.
43 *"They will grow up":* Shawcross, *Murdoch*, 110.
43 *Rupert blithely shredded:* Shawcross, *Murdoch*, 121.
44 *"The guest list was":* Author interview with Anna Murdoch friend.
44 *"He is . . . very impatient":* Wyatt, *The Journals of Woodrow Wyatt, Volume 1*, 243.
44 *"Have I given up":* Anna Maria Murdoch, "Motherhood and Mythology: Summer Thoughts on Sex and Creativity," *Commonweal*, August 31, 1979, 466–69.
44 *"Oh Rupert, don't be":* Kiernan, *Citizen Murdoch*, 225.
44 *"Art, music, hobbies":* Andrew Neil, *Full Disclosure* (London: Macmillan, 1996), 165.
44 *"How can I teach":* Kiernan, *Citizen Murdoch*, 224.
44 *"His Scottish Presbyterian":* Neil, *Full Disclosure*, 181.
44 *"I like people to think":* Philip Townsend, "Murdoch by His Butler," *Punch*, July–August 1998.
44 *"What about the household?":* Lois Romano, "EXTRA!! Publisher's Wife Pens Novel," *Washington Post*, October 23, 1985.
45 *"I wish he would":* Shawcross, *Murdoch*, 187.

CHAPTER FIVE

47 *In October 1985:* "The Forbes 400: Walton Tops List of Richest Americans," Associated Press, October 15, 1985.
47 *Rupert hired . . . Roy Cohn:* Robert Parry, "How Roy Cohn Helped Rupert Murdoch," *Consortium News*, January 28, 2015.

NOTES

48   *The obstacle was regulation:* Neil Chenoweth, *Rupert Murdoch* (Crown, Kindle edition, 2002), 55.

48   *In May 1983:* "Murdoch Delaying Satellite Plans," *New York Times*, November 8, 1983.

48   *"There are really":* Thomas Kiernan, *Citizen Murdoch* (New York: Dodd, Mead & Company, 1986), 272.

48   *Rupert folded Skyband:* William Shawcross, *Murdoch* (New York: Simon & Schuster, 1992), 166.

49   *That August, Rupert flew:* Connie Bruck, *Master of the Game: How Steve Ross Rode the Light Fantastic from Undertaker to Creator of the Largest Media Conglomerate in the World* (Simon & Schuster, Kindle edition, 2013), 202.

49   *Warner Communications reported:* Kiernan, *Citizen Murdoch*, 276.

49   *"Be my guest":* Bruck, *Master of the Game*, 202.

49   *"This guy is living":* Bruck, *Master of the Game*, 202.

49   *By early December:* Kiernan, *Citizen Murdoch*, 276–77.

49   *"If they think":* Kiernan, *Citizen Murdoch*, 284.

49   *News Corp sued:* Shawcross, *Murdoch*, 196.

49   *As for the PR war:* Bruck, *Master of the Game*, 204.

50   *"Rupert issued promises":* Shawcross, *Murdoch*, 196.

50   *"feudal warfare":* Warner Communications, Inc. v. Murdoch, 581 F. Supp. 1482 (D. Del. 1984).

50   *a $40 million profit:* Shawcross, *Murdoch*, 196; Wolfgang Saxon, "Deal Ends Murdoch's Fight to Take Over Warner," *New York Times*, March 18, 1984.

50   *Rupert made a run:* Mark Seal, "The Man Who Ate Hollywood," *Vanity Fair*, November 1, 2005; Alex Ben Block, *Outfoxed: Marvin Davis, Barry Diller, Rupert Murdoch, and the Inside Story of America's Fourth Television Network* (New York: St. Martin's Press, 1990); Shawcross, *Murdoch*, 199.

50   *On March 21, 1985:* Al Delugach, "Murdoch buys 50% of Fox for $250 million," *Los Angeles Times*, March 21, 1985.

50   *His biggest foray:* Joanna Morgan, "New Weir film commemorates Australian assault at Gallipoli," UPI, August 28, 1981.

51   *a show business wunderkind:* Barry Diller, *Who Knew* (New York: Simon & Schuster, 2025), 52.

51   *Diller became Rupert's:* Block, *Outfoxed*, 138.

51   *"You're costing me":* Diller, *Who Knew*, 241.

51   *Diller invited Davis:* Diller, *Who Knew*, 228; Block, *Outfoxed*, 121; Shawcross, *Murdoch*, 206.

51   *Then seventy, Kluge:* Block, *Outfoxed*, 124; Nikki Finke, "The Billionaire's Wife: Patricia Kluge Raises Her Social Profile with a Big L.A. 'Debut,'" *Los Angeles Times*, November 16, 1987.

52   *"There is no dog":* Diller, *Who Knew*, 229.

52   *"I just thought":* Block, *Outfoxed*, 127.

52   *"You're paying a":* Shawcross, *Murdoch*, 207.

52   *Rupert asked:* Block, *Outfoxed*, 133; Shawcross, *Murdoch*, 206.

52   *"What a great adventure!":* Diller, *Who Knew*, 230.

52   *On May 6, 1985:* Elizabeth Tucker and David A. Vise, "Metromedia, Murdoch Agree on TV Sale," *Los Angeles Times*, May 6, 1985.

52   *"You can't rely"*: Shawcross, *Murdoch*, 211.
52   *a coin flip:* Seal, "The Man Who Ate Hollywood."
52   *Rupert bought Davis's:* Al Delugach, "Davis Sells Murdoch His 20th Century Fox Stake for $325 Million," *Los Angeles Times*, September 24, 1985.
53   *Richard Sarazen scribbled:* Block, *Outfoxed*, 128.
53   *Federal law prevented:* "Media Ownership Rules," Congressional Research Service, R43936, accessed July 14, 2025.
53   *"It's not a problem"*: Block, *Outfoxed*, 128.
53   *"I love Australia"*: Ali Cromie, "Inside Story: Murdoch's Succession," *Guardian*, October 29, 1994.
53   *"I was shocked"*: Shawcross, *Murdoch*, 219.
53   *"It was quite"*: Fred Brenchley, "Keating's Dark Plan," *Australian Financial Review*, March 1, 1994.
53   *On the Wednesday:* Kiernan, *Citizen Murdoch*, 301; Shawcross, *Murdoch*, 214.
54   *That Christmas:* Shawcross, *Murdoch*, 228.
54   *Anna would later tell:* Woodrow Wyatt, *The Journals of Woodrow Wyatt, Volume 1* (London: Pan Books, 1998), 265.

CHAPTER SIX

55   *He sailed his:* "1964 Sydney Hobart Yacht Race Film," Rolex Sydney Hobart Yacht Race, accessed July 14, 2025.
55   *Years later, Rupert:* Morning Glory, Yacht Charter, accessed July 14, 2025.
55   *"Why should I"*: Andrew Neil, *Full Disclosure* (London: Macmillan, 1996), 181.
55   *One weekend in:* Neil, *Full Disclosure*, 96.
55   *Rupert had recently:* Richard W. Stevenson, "Village Voice Is Bought by Chairman of Hartz," *New York Times*, June 21, 1985; "Murdoch selling Sun-Times for $145 million," UPI, June 30, 1986.
56   *"in conditions that"*: William Shawcross, *Murdoch* (New York: Simon & Schuster, 1992), 224.
56   *Bruce Matthews, a genial:* Neil, *Full Disclosure*, 106.
56   *Even Rupert would:* Thomas Kiernan, *Citizen Murdoch* (New York: Dodd, Mead & Company, 1986), 314; Shawcross, *Murdoch*, 228; Peter Chippindale and Chris Horrie, *Stick It Up Your Punter!* (London: William Heinemann Limited, 1990), 229.
56   *this was "just a ploy"*: Woodrow Wyatt, *The Journals of Woodrow Wyatt, Volume 1* (London: Pan Books, 1998), 63.
56   *Rupert's accountants projected:* Kiernan, *Citizen Murdoch*, 314; Shawcross, *Murdoch*, 236.
56   *"That's just what"*: "Hello and goodbye to Wapping," SubScribe, accessed July 14, 2025.
56   *"You fuckwit!"*: Neil Chenoweth, *Rupert Murdoch* (Crown, Kindle edition, 2002), 65.
57   *"We Beat Strike Thugs"*: Sun, January 27, 1986.
57   *"I feel like a man"*: "Press: Revolution on Fleet Street," *Time*, March 3, 1986.
57   *"Scab! Scab! Scab!"*: Neil, *Full Disclosure*, 141.
57   *Workers set fires:* Thames News Archives, 1986, accessed July 14, 2025.
57   *"I hate you!"*: Wyatt, *The Journals of Woodrow Wyatt, Volume 1*, 76.
57   *Women Against Murdoch:* Shawcross, *Murdoch*, 235.

NOTES

57   *In the midst:* Wyatt, *The Journals of Woodrow Wyatt, Volume 1*, 100.

57   *As the strike dragged on:* Neil, *Full Disclosure*, 139.

57   *Murdoch had briefed:* Neil, *Full Disclosure*, 137.

57   *"There were suicides":* "Wapping: legacy of Rupert's revolution," *Guardian*, January 14, 2006.

57   *When it was over:* John Huxley, "The Battle of Wapping foisted reform on the newspaper industry," *Sydney Morning Herald*, November 18, 2011.

57   *"a visiting comet":* Les Hinton, *The Bootle Boy: An Untidy Life in News* (London: Scribe, 2018), 258.

57   *Anna woke the children:* Steve Fishman, "The Boy Who Wouldn't Be King," *New York*, September 9, 2005.

57   *"Pop had precious little":* Geraldine Brooks, "Murdoch," *New York Times*, July 19, 1998.

58   *"My dad would be":* *Dynasties*, Australian Broadcasting Corporation, 2001.

58   *"Is Daddy going deaf?":* Shawcross, *Murdoch*, 220.

58   *"tell the boys about sex":* Wyatt, *The Journals of Woodrow Wyatt, Volume 1*, 243.

58   *Elisabeth spent ninth grade:* Ken Auletta, "The Heiress," *New Yorker*, December 12, 2012.

58   *"I had only lasted":* Michael Wolff, Bryan Burrough, James Wolcott, Graydon Carter, and Sarah Ellison, *Rupert Murdoch, The Master Mogul of Fleet Street: 24 Tales from the Pages of* Vanity Fair (Vanity Fair, Kindle edition, 2012).

58   *Elisabeth finished high school:* Sarah Lyall, "Murdoch Blood, Murdoch Empire," *Vanity Fair*, July 1997.

58   *Lachlan also struggled:* Paddy Manning, *The Successor: The High-Stakes Life of Lachlan Murdoch* (Sutherland House Books, Kindle edition, 2022), 23.

58   *Anna moved Lachlan:* Peter Maass, "Power Transfer," *Intercept*, March 30, 2019.

58   *When James was about sixteen:* McKay Coppins, "Growing Up Murdoch," *Atlantic*, February 14, 2025.

58   *"We don't talk about":* Brooks, "Murdoch."

58   *"We were brought up":* Lyall, "Murdoch Blood, Murdoch Empire."

59   *"Rupert's presence brought":* Hinton, *The Bootle Boy*, 358.

59   *Lachlan did a stint:* Manning, *The Successor*, 24.

59   *Elisabeth at the* **New York Post:** Lyall, "Murdoch Blood, Murdoch Empire."

59   *James at* **The Australian:** Mike Safe, "The day James Murdoch took a back seat and was caught napping," Crikey, July 19, 2011.

59   *"Everybody knew who":* John Lippman and S. Karene Witcher, "Read All About It! Press Lord Grooms Kids for Top Jobs!" *Wall Street Journal*, July 3, 1996.

59   **Shame** *and* **The Moor's Last Sigh:** Lyall, "Murdoch Blood, Murdoch Empire."

59   *chin-up contests:* Ian Burrell, "The Other Son Also Rises," *Independent*, March 29, 2014.

59   *game nights that devolved:* Neil, *Full Disclosure*, 180.

59   *Anna published a novel:* Greg Hassall, "Lachlan Murdoch controls his family's media empire, but for how long and at what cost?" Australian Broadcasting Corporation, September 7, 2024.

60   *The deal frenzy:* Shawcross, *Murdoch*, 239.

60   *"a great thrill":* "Murdoch to Purchase Australian News Group," *New York Times*, December 4, 1986.

60   *"His father dying"*: David McKnight and Paulene Turner, "Rupert Murdoch: From Radical to Media King," *Sydney Morning Herald*, December 4, 1986.

60   *The deals came in:* "Murdoch Move in Hong Kong," Reuters, December 6, 1986; Thomas B. Rosenstiel, "Murdoch to buy Harper & Row for $300 million," *Los Angeles Times*, March 31, 1987.

60   *Spanish colonial mansion:* Ruth Ryon, "Rupert Murdoch to Restore Stein Home," *Los Angeles Times*, September 21, 1986.

60   *a Gulfstream jet:* Neil, *Full Disclosure*, 182.

60   *"expansionary lunge"*: Shawcross, *Murdoch*, 265.

61   *In December 1987:* Alan R. Gold, "Kennedy vs. Murdoch: Test of Motives," *New York Times*, January 11, 1988.

61   *"Dracula selling his coffin"*: Alexander Cockburn, *Corruptions of Empire* (Verso, 1988).

61   *On February 8, 1988:* Steven Erlanger, "Murdoch Agrees to Sell The Post to Developer," *New York Times*, February 8, 1988.

61   *"It was a nightmare"*: Shawcross, *Murdoch*, 265.

61   *"We had never"*: Shawcross, *Murdoch*, 257.

61   *Rupert found relief:* "Murdoch Team Takes Over at Triangle Publications," *Los Angeles Times*, November 2, 1988.

61   *"I don't know where"*: Shawcross, *Murdoch*, 274.

61   *"I saw a red smear"*: Hinton, *The Bootle Boy*, 251.

61   *600 percent:* Shawcross, *Murdoch*, 267.

61   *$5.5 billion in debt:* Shawcross, *Murdoch*, 275.

61   *"You can't build"*: Albert Scardino, "How Murdoch Makes It Work," *New York Times*, August 14, 1988.

62   *supported televangelist Pat Robertson:* Neil, *Full Disclosure*, 166.

62   *"Our master is becoming"*: Neil, *Full Disclosure*, 106.

62   *Rupert as "Rambo"*: Neil, *Full Disclosure*, 106.

CHAPTER SEVEN

65   *"All authority comes"*: Andrew Neil, *Full Disclosure* (London: Macmillan, 1996), 160.

65   *"He turns on lovers"*: Neil, *Full Disclosure*, 182.

65   *"I became good at"*: Les Hinton, *The Bootle Boy: An Untidy Life in News* (London: Scribe, 2018), 257.

65   *In the summer of 1988:* William Shawcross, *Murdoch* (New York: Simon & Schuster, 1992), 265.

66   *"any ethical framework"*: Bruce Guthrie, *Man Bites Murdoch: Four Decades in Print, Six Days in Court* (Melbourne: Melbourne University Publishing, Kindle edition, 2011), 101.

66   *"ELTON IN VICE BOYS"*: Peter Chippindale and Chris Horrie, *Stick It Up Your Punter!* (London: William Heinemann Limited, 1990), 313.

66   *"The place simply erupted"*: Guthrie, *Man Bites Murdoch*, 100.

66   *"equivalent of a leper"*: Guthrie, *Man Bites Murdoch*, 103.

66   *"The mythology of Murdoch"*: Hinton, *The Bootle Boy*, 328.

66   *"Murdoch, here"*: Author interviews with former News Corp executives.

66   *"Telephone terrorism"*: Neil, *Full Disclosure*, 176.

NOTES

66 **"Murdoch without a telephone"**: Bruce Dover, *Rupert Murdoch's China Adventures* (Australia: Tuttle, 2008), 115.
67 **"I had to stand"**: Philip Townsend, "How the Sun Came Down on Rupert's Marriage," *Punch*, July 18–31, 1998.
67 **"The most highly regarded"**: Guthrie, *Man Bites Murdoch*, 58.
67 **"Instead, by way"**: Dover, *Rupert Murdoch's China Adventures*, 133.
67 **"I'm beginning to understand"**: Piers Morgan, *The Insider: The Private Diaries of a Scandalous Decade* (Ebury Publishing, Kindle edition, 2012), 62.
67 **"[Rupert] cares little about"**: Guthrie, *Man Bites Murdoch*, 58.
67 **"I'd do anything"**: Ali Cromie, "The Murdoch Succession," *Australian Financial Review*, October 17, 1994.
67 **"Give him some"**: Neil, *Full Disclosure*, 164.
68 **"Your paper is pathetic"**: Chippindale and Horrie, *Stick It Up Your Punter!*, 396.
68 **"Kelvin used to go"**: Neil, *Full Disclosure*, 175.
68 **"Then fuck off"**: Chippindale and Horrie, *Stick It Up Your Punter!*, 105.
68 **the sedative temazepam**: Philip Townsend, "Murdoch by his Butler," *Punch*, July 4–17, 1998.
68 **"angry pills"**: Chippindale and Horrie, *Stick It Up Your Punter!*, 458.
68 **"I had become increasingly"**: Townsend, "Murdoch by his Butler."
68 **The financial earthquake**: Account of Murdoch's debt crisis drawn from Shawcross, *Murdoch*; Roger Cohen, "Rupert Murdoch's Biggest Gamble," *New York Times Magazine*, October 21, 1990; Stephen Fidler, "Murdoch Rescued from the Brink," *Australian Financial Review*, April 16, 1991; Neil Chenoweth, *Rupert Murdoch* (Crown, Kindle edition, 2002).
69 **On September 1**: Anthony Ramirez, "The Media Business: Advertising—Addenda; People," *New York Times*, September 20, 1990.
69 **$600 million credit line**: Shawcross, *Murdoch*, 352.
69 **On October 4**: Chenoweth, *Rupert Murdoch*.
69 **"somewhat terminal"**: Stephen Fidler, "Operation Dolphin Saves Murdoch's Empire from Ruin: News Corp.'s Desperate Restructuring Battle," *Financial Post*, April 8, 1991.
69 **Project Dolphin**: Shawcross, *Murdoch*, 350.
69 **"talked too much"**: Michael Wolff, *The Man Who Owns the News: Inside the Secret World of Rupert Murdoch* (Crown, Kindle edition, 2008), 389.

CHAPTER EIGHT

77 **"The Queen?"**: Philip Townsend, "Murdoch by his Butler," *Punch*, July 4–17, 1998.
77 **Rupert was suspicious**: Peter Chippindale and Chris Horrie, *Stick It Up Your Punter!* (London: William Heinemann Limited, 1990), 89.
77 **"I'm a great believer"**: Neil Chenoweth, *Rupert Murdoch* (Crown, Kindle edition, 2002), 109.
77 **"my retirement plan is"**: Ali Cromie, "The Murdoch Succession," *Australian Financial Review*, October 17, 1994.
77 **he appointed Anna**: Roger Cohen, "Rupert Murdoch's Biggest Gamble," *New York Times Magazine*, October 21, 1990.

77 *"She's there because"*: Nicholas Coleridge, *Paper Tigers: Latest Greatest Newspaper Tycoons and How They Won the World* (Random House, Kindle edition, 2012), 519.

77 *"Lachlan was the"*: Author interview.

78 *In 1987, Lachlan cofounded:* Paddy Manning, *The Successor: The High-Stakes Life of Lachlan Murdoch* (Sutherland House Books, Kindle edition, 2022), 23.

78 *"What the criticism"*: Geraldine Brooks, "Murdoch," *New York Times*, July 19, 1998.

78 *"He was the one who"*: Steve Fishman, "The Boy Who Wouldn't Be King," *New York*, September 9, 2005.

78 *Lachlan trained as:* Manning, *The Successor*, 19.

78 *Rupert invited Lachlan:* Brooks, "Murdoch."

78 *"There was a small minority"*: Author interview.

78 *"He was not a"*: Author interview.

78 *Lachlan majored in:* Maass, "Power Transfer."

79 *"He pushed very hard"*: Maass, "Power Transfer."

79 *Lachlan dedicated his thesis:* Maass, "Power Transfer."

79 *"How would you like"*: Manning, *The Successor*, 36.

79 *In August 1994:* Manning, *The Successor*, 37.

79 *On his first day:* Manning, *The Successor*, 36.

79 *"Son of God"*: Sarah Lyall, "Murdoch Blood, Murdoch Empire," *Vanity Fair*, July 1997.

80 *"That really sort of"*: Ben Potter, "Prince Charming of the press," *Sydney Morning Herald*, January 27, 1996.

80 *After ten months in:* "Murdoch's Son Gets Post," Reuters, December 12, 1995.

80 *Lachlan forced out:* Brooks, "Murdoch."

80 *"Paul Kelly did"*: John Gapper, "Inside Track: A Chip Off the Old Block," *Financial Times*, October 5, 1998.

80 *"I love you, Dad"*: Fishman, "The Boy Who Wouldn't Be King."

80 *being a nepo hire:* Manning, *The Successor*, 66.

80 *Cowley sent Lachlan:* Chenoweth, *Rupert Murdoch*, 307.

80 *"I thought it was"*: Brooks, "Murdoch."

81 *"a movie star"*: Lyall, "Murdoch Blood, Murdoch Empire."

81 *a lime-green Kawasaki:* Emiliya Mychasuk, "Playing Hardball," *Sydney Morning Herald*, April 7, 1995.

81 *$6 million harbor-front home:* Jonathan Chancellor, "Murdoch Jr's $6 million harbour retreat," *Sydney Morning Herald*, August 26, 1995.

81 *"It's not a natural"*: Potter, "Prince Charming of the press."

81 *Lachlan's friendship with:* Manning, *The Successor*, 49.

81 *The gossip grew:* Chenoweth, *Rupert Murdoch*, 309.

81 **The Sun** *once:* Chippindale and Horrie, *Stick It Up Your Punter!*, 217.

81 *a secret plan to launch:* Lachlan Colquhoun, "Murdoch plans a TV scrum-down," *Evening Standard*, November 7, 1994.

81 *Lachlan brokered a:* Damon Kitney, *The Price of Fortune: The Untold Story of Being James Packer* (HarperCollins, Kindle edition, 2018), 67; Manning, *The Successor*, 56.

81 *In December 1995, Rupert promoted:* Jennie Curtin, "League wants News 'fenced'; The Battle for League," *Sydney Morning Herald*, December 15, 1995.

82 *"conquer the world"*: Ben Potter, "Murdoch's son says he's ready for big job," *Age*, January 18, 1996.

82   *began cutting Cowley:* Pamela Williams, "Murdoch and Me," *Australian Financial Review,* September 6, 1997.

82   *"not a great businessman":* Anne Hyland, "Elisabeth should be running Murdoch empire, says Cowley," *Australian Financial Review,* May 31, 2014.

82   *"He was that type":* Gabriel Sherman, "The Raging Septuagenarian," *New York,* February 26, 2010.

83   *"I'm not my father":* McKay Coppins, "Growing Up Murdoch," *Atlantic,* February 14, 2025.

83   *James enrolled at Harvard:* Maureen Dowd, "James Murdoch, Rebellious Scion," *New York Times,* October 10, 2020.

83   *piercing his eyebrow:* Andrew Emery, "When James Murdoch was a hip-hop mogul," *Guardian,* July 11, 2012.

83   *following the Grateful Dead:* Nic Fildes, "Rising Son," *Independent,* December 8, 2007.

83   *"I keep a gun":* Adam Taylor, "James Murdoch Used to Keep a Gun Under His Desk," *Business Insider,* April 24, 2012.

83   *Rupert lured him back:* Fildes, "Rising Son."

83   *"Liz [was] the most":* Gabriel Sherman, "Elisabeth of the Murdochs," *New York,* November 4, 2011.

83   *Growing up, Liz:* Ken Auletta, "The Heiress," *New Yorker,* December 12, 2012.

84   *"Australian television was":* Auletta, "The Heiress," *New Yorker,* December 10, 2012.

84   *Liz moved back:* Auletta, "The Heiress."

84   *Liz was at the time engaged:* Sherman, "Elisabeth of the Murdochs."

84   *"by the way, he's black":* Philip Townsend, "How the Sun Came Down on Rupert's Marriage," *Punch,* July 18–31, 1998.

84   *Liz and Pianim married:* Judith Newman, "Scions in Love," *Vanity Fair,* August 8, 2001.

84   *"If Petronella comes":* Woodrow Wyatt, *The Journals of Woodrow Wyatt, Volume 3* (London: Pan Books, 1998), 271.

84   *Liz and Pianim moved:* Michael Wolff, "The Secrets of His Succession," *Vanity Fair,* October 31, 2008.

85   *"Is this an interview":* Cromie, "The Murdoch Succession."

85   *To cut costs:* Sherman, "Elisabeth of the Murdochs."

85   *"I felt I had to prove":* Auletta, "The Heiress."

85   *"a fucking MBA!":* Auletta, "The Heiress."

85   *In 1996, Liz joined BSkyB:* Sherman, "Elisabeth of the Murdochs."

85   *"I can't extricate myself":* Jonathan Lippman and S. Karene Witcher, "Read All About It! Press Lord Grooms Kids for Top Jobs!" *Wall Street Journal,* July 3, 1996.

86   *"It's not fucking true":* Fishman, "The Boy Who Wouldn't Be King."

86   *Elisabeth demanded Rupert:* Sherman, "Elisabeth of the Murdochs."

86   *"I screamed at him":* Penelope Debelle, "The day I screamed at my dad Rupert," *Sydney Morning Herald,* March 21, 1999.

86   *"They are all taller":* Michael Wolff, *The Man Who Owns the News: Inside the Secret World of Rupert Murdoch* (Crown, Kindle edition, 2008), 357.

87   *"I loved his mind":* Auletta, "The Heiress."

87   *"He was incredibly":* Auletta, "The Heiress."

CHAPTER NINE

89 **"Maybe I should wait":** Andrew Neil, *Full Disclosure* (London: Macmillan, 1996), 181.

89 **"There were vast":** Woodrow Wyatt, *The Journals of Woodrow Wyatt, Volume 3* (London: Pan Books, 1998), 265.

89 **Rupert wasn't happy:** Edward Klein, "Paper Lions," *Vanity Fair*, October 1993.

89 **In 1991, Rupert:** Michael Wolff, *The Man Who Owns the News: Inside the Secret World of Rupert Murdoch* (Crown, Kindle edition, 2008), 318.

90 **Most mornings, Rupert rose:** Nicholas Coleridge, *Paper Tigers: Latest Greatest Newspaper Tycoons and How They Won the World* (Random House, Kindle edition 2012), 510; Ken Auletta, "The Pirate," *New Yorker*, November 5, 1995.

90 **Home Alone *earned*:** Box Office Mojo, accessed July 16, 2025.

90 **"Hollywood ignoramuses":** Steve Fishman, "The Boy Who Wouldn't Be King," *New York*, September 9, 2005.

90 **"He's as smart":** Les Hinton, *The Bootle Boy: An Untidy Life in News* (London: Scribe, 2018), 259.

90 **"This is our town":** Hinton, *The Bootle Boy*, 259.

90 **"a hired hand":** Barry Diller, *Who Knew* (New York: Simon & Schuster, 2025), 228; Alex Ben Block, *Outfoxed: Marvin Davis, Barry Diller, Rupert Murdoch, and the Inside Story of America's Fourth Television Network* (New York: St. Martin's Press, 1990), 121; William Shawcross, *Murdoch* (New York: Simon & Schuster, 1992), 249.

90 **"The movie business":** Klein, "Paper Lions."

90 **his beloved New York Post:** Martin Gottlieb, "Staff Cheers as Murdoch Reclaims Post," *New York Times*, March 30, 1993.

90 **Rupert voted for independent Ross Perot:** Neil, *Full Disclosure*, 166.

91 **"He's a dead duck":** Piers Morgan, *The Insider: The Private Diaries of a Scandalous Decade* (London: Ebury Publishing, Kindle edition, 2012), 122.

91 **A Vanity Fair *writer*:** Klein, "Paper Lions."

91 **Rupert flew to Beijing:** Bruce Dover, *Rupert Murdoch's China Adventures* (Australia: Tuttle, 2008), 14.

91 **"spiritual pollution":** Dover, *Rupert Murdoch's China Adventures*, 105.

91 **"Murdoch didn't bother":** Dover, *Rupert Murdoch's China Adventures*, 20.

91 **Two months later:** Adam Dawtrey, "Murdoch's new News Corp.," *Variety*, September 2, 1993.

91 **Done in a Palladian style:** "Inigo Jones Architecture," Historic Royal Palaces, accessed July 16, 2025.

92 **Addressing the grandees:** Auletta, "The Pirate."

92 **In Beijing, officials reacted:** Dover, *Rupert Murdoch's China Adventures*, 25.

92 **Dover later told:** Dover, *Rupert Murdoch's China Adventures*, 28.

92 **Rupert refused to allow:** Irwin Stelzer, *The Murdoch Method: Observations on Rupert Murdoch's Management of a Media Empire* (Pegasus Books, Kindle edition, 2018), 175.

92 **"She should hold out":** Neil, *Full Disclosure*, 169.

93 **hagiography of Deng Xiaoping:** Dover, *Rupert Murdoch's China Adventures*, 35.

93 **"turgid, barely literate":** Elisabeth Bumiller, "A Long March for Her Father," *Washington Post*, February 13, 1995.

93 **Rupert promoted it:** Auletta, "The Pirate."

93   *"The BBC was driving them nuts"*: Auletta, "The Pirate."

93   *Rupert doubled down:* Dover, *Rupert Murdoch's China Adventures*, 37.

93   *Rupert grew impatient:* Dover, *Rupert Murdoch's China Adventures*, 127.

93   *"Look," . . . "I don't know why"*: Dover, *Rupert Murdoch's China Adventures*, 142.

93   *Phoenix TV:* Fara Warner, "News Corp.'s Satellite TV Venture Makes Strong Inroads in China," *Wall Street Journal*, December 12, 1997.

94   *In late 1997, Rupert's desperation:* Dover, *Rupert Murdoch's China Adventures*, 129; Warren Hoge, "HarperCollins Drops Plans to Publish Book Deemed Too Negative of China," *New York Times*, February 28, 1998.

94   *"boring"*: Sarah Lyall, "Publisher Apologizes to and Will Pay Former Hong Kong Governor," *New York Times*, March 7, 1998.

94   *"most lucid"*: Michael Leapman and Stephen Vines, "The bully boy who's never really changed," *Independent*, March 1, 1998.

94   *"astounded by the"*: Dover, *Rupert Murdoch's China Adventures*, 137.

94   *meeting President Jiang Zemin:* Dover, *Rupert Murdoch's China Adventures*, 146.

94   *"Why is your business strategy"*: Mark Seal, "Seduced and Abandoned," *Vanity Fair*, March 2014.

95   *"We need more people"*: "Dynasty in Distress," *Guardian*, March 27, 1999.

95   *"Her arrival was a"*: Dover, *Rupert Murdoch's China Adventures*, 118.

95   *"Usually the women"*: Fiona Golfar, "The Vogue Interview," *British Vogue*, November 25, 2013.

95   *"Hello, I'm Wendi"*: Seal, "Seduced and Abandoned."

95   *"He turns around"*: Seal, "Seduced and Abandoned."

95   *"She was self-confident"*: Seal, "Seduced and Abandoned."

95   *"All we knew"*: Seal, "Seduced and Abandoned."

96   *Wendi was born:* David Jenkins, "The truth about Wendi Deng," *Tatler*, July 28, 2016.

96   *"We didn't have"*: Golfar, "The Vogue Interview."

96   *She grew tall:* Seal, "Seduced and Abandoned."

96   *"It was not"*: Golfar, "The Vogue Interview."

96   *In 1987, Wendi began:* John Lippman, Leslie Chang, and Robert Frank, "Rupert Murdoch's Wife Wendi Wields Influence at News Corp.," *Wall Street Journal*, October 31, 2000; Seal, "Seduced and Abandoned"; Golfar, "The Vogue Interview."

96   *found "coquettish" photos:* Wolff, *The Man Who Owns the News*, 320.

96   *"She told me I was"*: Lippman, Chang, and Frank, "Rupert Murdoch's Wife Wendi Wields Influence at News Corp."

96   *When asked in:* Golfar, "The Vogue Interview."

97   *Star's CEO assigned her:* Seal, "Seduced and Abandoned."

97   *"He was radiating"*: Dover, *Rupert Murdoch's China Adventures*, 121.

97   *Star employees began:* Dover, *Rupert Murdoch's China Adventures*, 122.

97   *"Look, you may have"*: Seal, "Seduced and Abandoned."

97   *In late 1993, Rupert convinced:* Dover, *Rupert Murdoch's China Adventures*, 32.

97   *"perpetual motion machine"*: Neil, *Full Disclosure*, 435.

98   *Anna unveiled a:* Neil Chenoweth, *Rupert Murdoch* (Crown, Kindle edition, 2002), 305.

98   *"Makes me feel"*: Bruce Dover, "When Wendi Met Rupert," *Sydney Morning Herald*, January 26, 2008.

98   *"I'd probably die"*: Fishman, "The Boy Who Wouldn't Be King."

98   *"Let's divorce"*: Fishman, "The Boy Who Wouldn't Be King."
98   *Anna was blindsided*: David Leser, "Anna and Her Kingdom," *Australian Women's Weekly*, August 2001.
98   *"You've got to"*: William Shawcross, "Murdoch's New Life," *Vanity Fair*, October 1999.
98   *"Even the wife was"*: *Dynasties*, Australian Broadcasting Corporation, 2001.
98   *On April 21, 1998:* "News Corp. Confirms Murdoch, Wife to Separate After 31 Years," *Wall Street Journal*, April 22, 1998.
98   *"It's not an original"*: Leser, "Anna and Her Kingdom."
98   *"a nice Chinese lady"*: *Dynasties*.
99   *"Rupert's Dragon Lady"*: *Punch*, 1999.
99   *"This is war"*: Emily Bell and Mark Honigsbaum, "The Murdoch Divorce," *Guardian*, March 28, 1999.
99   *"extremely hard, ruthless"*: Leser, "Anna and Her Kingdom."
99   *sell the Beverly Hills home:* James Bates, "Watch the Money," *Los Angeles Times*, January 31, 1999.
99   *he booted Anna off:* Fishman, "The Boy Who Wouldn't Be King."
99   *Rupert and Prue flew:* Penelope Debelle, "Father figure Murdoch says goodbye," *Sydney Morning Herald*, November 17, 1998.
99   *attend Lachlan's wedding:* Paddy Manning, *The Successor: The High-Stakes Life of Lachlan Murdoch* (Sutherland House Books, Kindle edition, 2022), 85.
99   *"I was very fond"*: Author interview.
99   *Rupert was angry:* Wolff, *The Man Who Owns the News*, 271.
99   *"Now I have"*: Neil Chenoweth, "Three weddings and a magnate," *Australian Financial Review*, July 3, 1999.
99   *James broke the stalemate:* Author interview.
99   *Rupert would pay her:* Michael Wolff, "The mythical $1.7bn of Rupert Murdoch's second divorce," *Guardian*, June 17, 2013; Chenoweth, *Rupert Murdoch*, 324.
100 *Each child received one vote:* Author interviews; Jonathan Mahler and Jim Rutenberg, "'You've Blown a Hole in the Family': Inside the Murdochs' Succession Drama," *New York Times Magazine*, February 13, 2025.
100 *"We have something"*: Fishman, "The Boy Who Wouldn't Be King."
100 *"He wanted to be"*: Seal, "Seduced and Abandoned."
100 *Late on the afternoon of:* Martin Peers, "Murdoch wedding makes news," *Variety*, June 28, 1999; Chenoweth, *Rupert Murdoch*, 325.
100 *"You will not be"*: Hinton, *The Bootle Boy*, 330.
100 *"He's a kind, gentle"*: Leser, "Anna and Her Kingdom."
100 *Murdoch had promised:* Author interview.
100 *Rupert sold it:* Neil Chenoweth, "Paradise Papers: Rupert Murdoch's Bermuda short," *Australian Financial Review*, November 20, 2017.

CHAPTER TEN

101 *On a March morning:* Michael Wolff, *The Man Who Owns the News: Inside the Secret World of Rupert Murdoch* (Crown, Kindle edition, 2008), 330.
101 *"my retirement plan is"*: Neil Chenoweth, "Son No Longer Shines in Rupert's Court," *Australian Financial Review*, April 1, 2005.

101 *Under Wendi's influence:* Sarah Ellison, *War at the Wall Street Journal* (New York: Houghton Mifflin, 2000), 84; Mark Seal, "Seduced and Abandoned," *Vanity Fair*, March 2014.

101 *executives gossiped about:* Les Hinton, *The Bootle Boy: An Untidy Life in News* (London: Scribe, 2018), 330.

101 *"definitely in love":* Seal, "Seduced and Abandoned."

102 *spent billions on sports:* Murray Chass, "A Family Circle Breaks: Murdoch Owns Dodgers," *New York Times*, March 20, 1998; Alan Cowell, "Murdoch Reported to Have Bid $950 Million for Britain's Richest Soccer Club," *New York Times*, September 8, 1998.

102 *$350 billion merger:* Patrick Barkham, "The AOL Time Warner deal," *Guardian*, January 11, 2000.

102 *the Nasdaq crashed:* Tony Long, "March 10, 2000: Pop Goes the Nasdaq!" *Wired*, March 10, 2010.

102 *"I didn't know what":* Wolff, *The Man Who Owns the News*, 330.

102 *On April 16, 2000:* Jamie Wilson, "Murdoch diagnosed with 'low grade' prostate cancer but keeps on working," *Guardian*, April 16, 2000.

102 *plunged by $10.9 billion:* Steve Fishman, "The Boy Who Wouldn't Be King," *New York*, September 9, 2005.

102 *"impossible to figure":* Wolff, *The Man Who Owns the News*, 367.

103 *In May 2000:* Sarah Ellison, "The Rules of Succession," *Vanity Fair*, November 4, 2011.

103 *"I was not thrilled":* Geraldine Fabrikant and Mark Landler, "Just Which Murdoch Will Become the Next Rupert?" *New York Times*, October 8, 2000.

103 *"Matthew Fraud":* Author interviews.

103 *"very silly girl":* Ellison, "The Rules of Succession."

103 *two months of radiation:* Fabrikant and Landler, "Just Which Murdoch Will Become the Next Rupert?"

103 *That spring, James:* McKay Coppins, "Growing Up Murdoch," *Atlantic*, February 14, 2025.

103 *gambling and shooting:* Neil Chenoweth, *Rupert Murdoch* (Crown, Kindle edition, 2002), 341.

103 *He kept dealmaking:* Geraldine Fabrikant, "News Corp. Said to Agree to Purchase Chris-Craft," *New York Times*, August 12, 2000.

104 *Rupert promoted Lachlan:* Jill Goldsmith, "Son rises again at News Corp.," *Variety*, October 6, 2000.

104 *Rupert exiled James:* Gabriel Sherman, "The Raging Septuagenarian," *New York*, February 26, 2010.

104 *$7 million yacht:* Neil Chenoweth, "Paradise Papers: Rupert Murdoch's Bermuda short," *Australian Financial Review*, November 20, 2017.

104 *"I'm most myself":* Fishman, "The Boy Who Wouldn't Be King."

104 *broke into tears:* Paddy Manning, *The Successor: The High-Stakes Life of Lachlan Murdoch* (Sutherland House Books, Kindle edition, 2022), 88.

104 *Lachlan and Sarah settled:* Gabriel Sherman, "Lachlan's Double Play," *New York Observer*, May 10, 2004.

104 *dropped 5 percent:* "News Corp.'s Shares Plunge," *Los Angeles Times*, October 19, 2000.

105   *Lachlan's biggest challenge:* Gabriel Sherman, *The Loudest Voice in the Room* (New York: Random House, 2014), 285; Fishman, "The Boy Who Wouldn't Be King"; Manning, *The Successor*, 117.

105   *"always banter going":* Sherman, "The Raging Septuagenarian."

105   *"Lachlan thought because":* Author interview.

105   *Rupert recruited Ailes:* Sherman, *The Loudest Voice in the Room*, 172.

105   *By 2001, Fox was:* Sherman, *The Loudest Voice in the Room*, 264.

106   *"We're under attack!":* Sherman, *The Loudest Voice in the Room*, 172.

106   *posing for Annie Leibovitz: Vanity Fair*, October 1999.

106   *"I'm not going to":* Bruce Dover, *Rupert Murdoch's China Adventures* (Australia: Tuttle, 2008), 238.

107   *"Are you going deaf":* Fishman, "The Boy Who Wouldn't Be King."

107   *"She's a bit frustrated":* William Shawcross, "Rupert Murdoch's New Life," *Vanity Fair*, October 1999.

107   *The two began traveling:* John Lippman, Leslie Chang, and Robert Frank, "Rupert Murdoch's Wife Wendi Wields Influence at News Corp.," *Wall Street Journal*, October 31, 2000.

107   *a multiyear renovation:* Sherman, "The Raging Septuagenarian."

107   *According to a former nanny:* John Cook, "It Was Like a Warzone," *Gawker*, July 18, 2012.

107   *"I quit work":* Wolff, *The Man Who Owns the News*, 333.

108   *an indelicate request:* Fishman, "The Boy Who Wouldn't Be King"; Jonathan Mahler and Jim Rutenberg, "'You've Blown a Hole in the Family': Inside the Murdochs' Succession Drama," *New York Times Magazine*, February 13, 2025.

108   *Lachlan and Rupert fought:* Fishman, "The Boy Who Wouldn't Be King."

108   *cable mogul John Malone:* Wolff, *The Man Who Owns the News*, 38.

108   *Disney courted Chernin:* "Contract Stirs New Talk on Disney Job," Reuters, November 26, 2004.

109   *Ailes fanned rumors:* Author interviews.

109   *"Do the show":* Fishman, "The Boy Who Wouldn't Be King."

109   *"Fuck it. I'm out":* Manning, *The Successor*, 131.

109   *his prescient investment:* Manning, *The Successor*, 90.

109   *Rupert was plotting:* Sherman, "The Raging Septuagenarian."

109   *in another life:* Author interview.

109   *"It's easier to be":* Fishman, "The Boy Who Wouldn't Be King."

109   *"It wasn't the most":* Ellison, *War at the Wall Street Journal*, 56.

110   *"I'm resigning":* Fishman, "The Boy Who Wouldn't Be King."

110   *"my own man":* Fishman, "The Boy Who Wouldn't Be King."

CHAPTER ELEVEN

111   *"drinking than journalism":* David Smith, "Daddy's Boy," *Observer*, June 12, 2004.

111   *"forgotten Murdoch":* Ali Cromie, "Splitting heirs; The 'forgotten' Murdoch seems to be making all the right moves," *Sydney Morning Herald*, December 12, 1999.

111   *"Lachlan is very solid":* Author interview.

111   *"After [James] had":* Les Hinton, *The Bootle Boy: An Untidy Life in News* (London: Scribe, 2018), 314.

112　*"We are woefully unprepared"*: Irwin Stelzer, *The Murdoch Method: Observations on Rupert Murdoch's Management of a Media Empire* (Pegasus Books, Kindle edition, 2018), 93.

112　*a media futurist*: Gabriel Sherman, "The Raging Septuagenarian," *New York*, February 26, 2010.

112　*"We're basically agnostic"*: Neil Chenoweth, "The Rising Son," *Australian Financial Review*, June 10, 2000.

112　*"a bullshit job"*: Sarah Ellison, "The Rules of Succession," *Vanity Fair*, November 4, 2011.

112　*disastrous $400 million bid*: Seth Schiesel, "News Corporation Said to Pursue Pointcast," *New York Times*, March 19, 1997.

112　*"The feeling was"*: Sherman, "The Raging Septuagenarian."

112　*"Do you like Chinese food?"*: Michelle Levander, "Making of a Mogul," *Time*, December 17, 2001.

112　*Rupert had recently ousted*: Bruce Dover, *Rupert Murdoch's China Adventures* (Australia: Tuttle, 2008), 149.

113　*On a charter flight*: McKay Coppins, "Growing Up Murdoch," *Atlantic*, February 14, 2025.

113　*a small ceremony*: Coppins, "Growing Up Murdoch."

113　*"be a nightmare"*: Sherman, "The Raging Septuagenarian."

113　*"ruthless like Rupert"*: Author interview.

113　*James gave speeches*: Dan Milmo, "James Murdoch attacks BBC," *Guardian*, January 19, 2001; Bill Carter, "Murdoch Executive Calls Press Coverage of China Too Harsh," *New York Times*, March 26, 2001.

113　*the strategy paid off*: Dan Milmo, "Murdoch's Chinese whispers pay off," *Guardian*, December 19, 2001.

113　*its first profit*: John Lippman, "Star TV Records First Profit on Progress in China, India," *Wall Street Journal*, April 10, 2002.

113　*In the fall of 2003*: Charles Goldsmith, "James Murdoch Is Named Chief Executive of BSkyB," *Wall Street Journal*, November 4, 2003.

113　*The decision was controversial*: Christopher Williams, *The Battle for Sky: The Murdochs, Disney, Comcast and the Future of Entertainment* (Bloomsbury Publishing, Kindle edition, 2019), 42.

113　*In April 2003*: David Teather, "DirecTV Succumbs to Murdoch," *Guardian*, April 10, 2003.

114　*"By the time we did ITV"*: Williams, *The Battle for Sky*, 42.

114　*Darth Vader statue*: Gabriel Sherman, "Elisabeth of the Murdochs," *New York*, November 4, 2011.

114　*"When I'd say"*: Coppins, "Growing Up Murdoch."

114　*"All these grumpy"*: Coppins, "Growing Up Murdoch."

114　*"a decent guy"*: Author interview.

114　*"reclusive James Murdoch"*: Sherman, "The Raging Septuagenarian."

114　*"James played it"*: Sherman, "The Raging Septuagenarian."

115　*"The mountains are"*: Coppins, "Growing Up Murdoch."

115　*Rupert bought MySpace*: Julia Angwin, *Stealing MySpace: The Battle to Control the Most Popular Website in America* (Random House Publishing Group, Kindle edition, 2009).

115　*Stelzer recalled Rupert*: Stelzer, *The Murdoch Method*, 78.

NOTES

115 **Rupert got a tip:** Sarah Ellison, *War at the Wall Street Journal* (New York: Houghton Mifflin, 2000), 63.

116 **Wendi continued to demand:** Michael Wolff, *The Man Who Owns the News: Inside the Secret World of Rupert Murdoch* (Crown, Kindle edition, 2008), 330; Martin Peers, Julia Angwin, and John Lippman, "At News Corp., a Bitter Battle Over Inheritance Splits Family," *Wall Street Journal*, August 1, 2005.

116 **gave Malone serious leverage:** Richard Siklos, "News Corp. to Buy Out Malone's Shares," *New York Times*, December 6, 2006.

116 **On April 9, 2007:** Ellison, *War at the Wall Street Journal*, 85.

116 **"brought in James":** Wolff, *The Man Who Owns the News*, 250.

116 **James flew by private jet:** Ellison, *War at the Wall Street Journal*, 136.

117 **"How could you":** Sherman, "The Raging Septuagenarian," *New York*, February 26, 2010.

117 **Rupert promoted James:** Don Jeffrey and Gillian Wee, "James Murdoch to lead News Corp in Europe, Asia," *Bloomberg*, December 6, 2007.

117 **James and Kathryn socialized:** Sherman, "The Raging Septuagenarian."

117 **"Liz and James talked":** Author interview.

117 **Rupert's friend group expanded:** Wolff, *The Man Who Owns the News*, 335; Mark Seal, "Seduced and Abandoned," *Vanity Fair*, March 2014.

118 **adopting progressive positions:** Mark Sweney, "Murdoch vows to turn News International green," *Guardian*, January 10, 2008; Scott Wong, "Murdoch to Hill: Reform immigration," *Politico*, September 30, 2010.

118 **"I decided to switch":** John Schwartz, "Kathryn Murdoch Steps Out of the Family Shadow to Fight Climate Change," *New York Times*, September 26, 2019.

118 **fundraiser for Hillary Clinton:** Anne Kornblut, "What's in a Murdoch-Clinton Alliance? Something for Both Sides," *New York Times*, May 10, 2006; Gabriel Sherman, *The Loudest Voice in the Room* (New York: Random House, 2014), xv.

118 **James's liberal allies:** Sherman, "The Raging Septuagenarian."

118 **Ailes threatened to:** Sherman, "The Raging Septuagenarian."

118 **"That was the beginning":** Sherman, *The Loudest Voice in the Room*, 324.

119 **"What James figured":** Sherman, "The Raging Septuagenarian."

119 **the $11.5 billion deal:** Williams, *The Battle for Sky*, 89.

119 **James's aggressive leadership:** Richard Branson, "'Murdoch has opened a hornet's nest,'" *Guardian*, March 5, 2007.

120 **"What the fuck":** Hugh Muir and Jane Martinson, "James Murdoch at the Independent: 'like a scene out of Dodge City,'" *Guardian*, April 22, 2010.

120 **"Prue feared that":** Author interview.

120 **"It's what happens":** Author interview.

120 **"The only reliable":** James Robinson, "James Murdoch hits out at BBC and regulators at Edinburgh TV festival," *Guardian*, August 28, 2009.

120 **"Someone had sent":** Williams, *The Battle for Sky*, 90.

120 **"fuck my dad":** Williams, *The Battle for Sky*, 90.

120 **James met Brown's opponent:** Dan Roberts, "George: the private club where Murdoch and Cameron courted," *Guardian*, March 27, 2012; Nick Davies, *Hack Attack: The Inside Story of How the Truth Caught Up with Rupert Murdoch* (Farrar, Straus and Giroux, Kindle edition, 2014), 231.

121 **Over drinks, James:** Davies, *Hack Attack*, 232.

NOTES

121   *"totally inexperienced"*: Tom Watson and Martin Hickman, *Dial M for Murdoch: News Corporation and the Corruption of Britain* (Penguin Publishing Group, Kindle edition, 2012), 62.

121   *Cameron aggressively courted:* "David Cameron took free flights to meet Rupert Murdoch," *Guardian*, October 24, 2008.

121   *"Gordon has a"*: John Cassidy, "Murdoch's Game," *New Yorker*, October 8, 2006.

121   *"Labour's Lost It"*: Will Woodward, "The Sun comes out for Conservatives, declaring 'Labour's lost it,'" *Guardian*, September 29, 2009.

121   *"It was a low blow"*: Hinton, *The Bootle Boy*, 417.

121   *"Your company has"*: Hinton, *The Bootle Boy*, 418.

CHAPTER TWELVE

125   *"Operation Rubicon"*: Nick Davies, *Hack Attack: The Inside Story of How the Truth Caught Up with Rupert Murdoch* (Farrar, Straus and Giroux, Kindle edition, 2014), 315.

125   *"James wanted BSkyB"*: Author interview.

125   *his Boeing 737:* Gabriel Sherman, "The Raging Septuagenarian," *New York*, February 26, 2010.

126   *"I'm just sick"*: Julia Day, "Murdoch seeks to calm investor fears," *Guardian*, November 16, 2005.

126   *"Don't let him"*: Paddy Manning, *The Successor: The High-Stakes Life of Lachlan Murdoch* (Sutherland House Books, Kindle edition, 2022), 136.

126   *Lachlan launched:* Manning, *The Successor*, 135.

126   *In 2009, Liz had:* Mark Sweney, "Elisabeth Murdoch rejects seat on News Corp board," *Guardian*, February 25, 2009.

126   *Her company Shine:* Emma Keller, "Elisabeth Murdoch profile in The New Yorker reveals a daughter's PR acumen," *Guardian*, December 3, 2012.

126   *acquired Reveille:* Leigh Holmwood, "Shine buys Ugly Betty producer Reveille," *Guardian*, February 14, 2008.

126   *James warned her:* McKay Coppins, "Growing Up Murdoch," *Atlantic*, February 14, 2025.

126   *do family therapy:* Sarah Ellison, "Murdoch Clan Met with Family Therapist to Discuss News Corp.'s Future," *Vanity Fair*, November 2, 2011.

127   *vent their grievances:* Author interview.

127   *"a car crash"*: Coppins, "Growing Up Murdoch."

127   *an ultimatum:* Sarah Ellison, "The Rules of Succession," *Vanity Fair*, November 4, 2011.

127   *News Corp bought Shine:* Tim Adler, "News Corp Buys Shine For $673M," Deadline, February 21, 2011.

127   *"He disinvited her"*: Author interview.

127   *Liz and Freud threw:* Details of party drawn from Ken Auletta, "The Heiress," *New Yorker*, December 12, 2012; Simon Walters and Glen Owen, "Chipping Norton Set's final hurrah," *Daily Mail*, July 17, 2011.

128   *phone of Milly Dowler:* Nick Davies and Amelia Hill, "Missing Milly Dowler's voicemail was hacked by News of the World," *Guardian*, July 4, 2011.

128   *a British judge sentenced:* Chris Tryhorn, "Clive Goodman sentenced to four months," *Guardian*, January 26, 2007.

128   *Andy Coulson resigned:* Stephen Brook, "News of the World editor quits," *Guardian*, January 26, 2007.

128   *Cameron hired Coulson:* Davies, *Hack Attack*, 183.

128   **New York Times** *investigation:* Don Van Natta Jr., Jo Becker, and Graham Bowley, "Tabloid Hack Attack on Royals, and Beyond," *New York Times Magazine*, September 1, 2010.

128   *Cameron to finally dump:* "Andy Coulson quits Downing Street communications role," BBC, January 21, 2011.

129   *James was linked:* Tim Arango, "Editor Says a Murdoch Paid to Settle on Phone Tap," *New York Times*, July 21, 2009.

129   *"You cannot just sit":* Coppins, "Growing Up Murdoch."

129   *shut down* **News of the World:** Sarah Ellison, "Murdoch and the Vicious Circle," *Vanity Fair*, October 2011.

129   *Coulson was arrested:* John F. Burns and Alan Cowell, "Former Aide to Cameron Is Arrested in Tabloid Scandal," *New York Times*, July 7, 2011.

129   *blamed James for:* Coppins, "Growing Up Murdoch."

129   *"He was slumped":* Les Hinton, *The Bootle Boy: An Untidy Life in News* (London: Scribe, 2018), 391.

130   *"getting annoyed":* Sam Jones, Ed Pilkington, and Andrew Gumbel, "Phone hacking: Murdoch goes on defensive over 'total lies' by MPs," *Guardian*, July 15, 2011.

130   *"Dude, our old man":* Coppins, "Growing Up Murdoch."

130   *like a "candy store":* Mark Sweney, "Rupert Murdoch's News Corp sued over 'nepotism' in buying his daughter's firm," *Guardian*, March 17, 2011.

130   *She blamed James:* Ellison, "The Rules of Succession."

130   *Liz went to Wapping:* Gabriel Sherman, "Elisabeth of the Murdochs," *New York*, November 4, 2011.

131   *"I was chatting with Dad":* Coppins, "Growing Up Murdoch."

131   *Rupert met the Dowlers:* Tom Watson and Martin Hickman, *Dial M for Murdoch: News Corporation and the Corruption of Britain* (Penguin Publishing Group, Kindle edition, 2012), 230.

131   *"worst day of":* Ellison, "Murdoch and the Vicious Circle."

131   *"Rupert was shaken":* Mimi Turner, "Rupert Murdoch 'Very Humbled' as He Apologizes Personally to the Family of Murdered Schoolgirl Milly Dowler," *Hollywood Reporter*, July 15, 2011.

131   *"smoking gun" emails:* James Kirkup, "'Smoking gun' emails fuel claims of a cover-up," *Sydney Morning Herald*, July 12, 2011.

131   *"an industrial scale":* "Brown in ferocious Commons attack on News International," BBC, July 14, 2011.

131   *News Corp abandoned:* Michael J. de la Merced, "News Corp Drops Bid for BSkyB," *New York Times*, July 13, 2011.

131   *Lachlan arrived from:* Ellison, "Murdoch and the Vicious Circle."

131   *The scandal went global:* Hinton, *The Bootle Boy*, 420.

132   *he told James:* Ellison, "The Rules of Succession."

132   *Brooks resigned:* James Martinson and Nicholas Watt, "Rupert Murdoch's bloody Friday as Rebekah Brooks and Les Hinton quit," *Guardian*, July 15, 2011.

132   *police arrested Brooks:* "Rebekah Brooks arrested by hacking police," BBC, July 18, 2011.

132   *Kathryn, later said:* Coppins, "Growing Up Murdoch."

132   *The Murdochs did:* Ellison, "The Rules of Succession."

132   *Freud and Liz skipped:* Sherman, "Elisabeth of the Murdochs."

132   *"most humble day":* Reid J. Epstein, "Murdoch's 'most humble day,'" *Politico*, July 19, 2011.

132   *More than ninety:* Hinton, *The Bootle Boy*, 431.

132   *was found dead:* Amelia Hill, James Robinson, and Caroline Davies, "News of the World phone-hacking whistleblower found dead," *Guardian*, July 18, 2011.

132   *soap opera elements:* Lisa O'Carroll, "Andy Coulson: affair with Rebekah Brooks was 'wrong,'" *Guardian*, April 14, 2014.

133   *News Corp paid out:* Mark Sweney, "News Corp bonuses cut following phone-hacking scandal," *Guardian*, September 5, 2012.

133   *Coulson was sentenced:* Lisa O'Carroll, "Andy Coulson jailed for 18 months for conspiracy to hack phones," *Guardian*, July 4, 2014; Dylan Byers, "Rebekah Brooks acquitted in hacking case," *Politico*, June 24, 2014.

133   *"not fit and proper":* "Rupert Murdoch 'not a fit person' to lead News Corp—MPs," BBC, May 1, 2012.

133   *"Murdoch Principles":* Coppins, "Growing Up Murdoch."

133   *This assertion was undermined:* Sarah Lyall and Ravi Somaiya, "Hacking Cases Focus on Memo to a Murdoch," *New York Times*, February 11, 2012.

133   *James and Kathryn blamed Liz:* Sherman, "Elisabeth of the Murdochs."

134   *Liz and Freud told people:* Sherman, "Elisabeth of the Murdochs."

134   *Liz spent the next year:* Auletta, "The Heiress"; "Elisabeth Murdoch: speech in full," *Telegraph*, August 23, 2012.

135   *"I thought it was":* Patricia Sellers, "The Fortune interview: Rupert Murdoch," *Fortune*, April 10, 2014.

135   *"the best speech given":* Sarah Dingle, Australian Broadcasting Corporation, August 24, 2012.

135   *died at 103:* Lisa O'Carroll, "Rupert Murdoch's mother Dame Elisabeth dies aged 103," *Guardian*, December 5, 2012.

135   *"She just wanted":* Mark Duell, "'My mother's love gave me more than I can ever hope to repay': Rupert Murdoch pays emotional tribute to his beloved mother Elisabeth, 103, at memorial service," *Daily Mail*, December 18, 2012.

CHAPTER THIRTEEN

137   *excised the malignancy:* Amy Chozick and Michael J. de la Merced, "At News Corp., a Plan to Sever Publishing Arm," *New York Times*, June 26, 2012.

137   *"It was emotional":* Patricia Sellers, "The Fortune interview: Rupert Murdoch," *Fortune*, April 10, 2014.

137   *"Nothing characterizes her":* Amy Chozick, "Declaration of Independence," *New York Times*, June 15, 2012.

137   *they slept separately:* John Cook, "It Was Like a Warzone," *Gawker*, July 18, 2012.

137   *announced on* **Charlie Rose:** Air date July 20, 2006.

137   *she called . . . screaming:* Author interview.

138   *Wendi demanded that:* Author interview.

138 *sleep in the garage:* Author interview.

138 *MySpace's failed expansion:* Mark Seal, "Seduced and Abandoned," *Vanity Fair*, March 2014.

138 **produced Snow Flower and the Secret Fan:** Elisa Lipsky Karasz, "Wendi Murdoch and Florence Sloan: The Producers," *Harper's Bazaar*, July 6, 2011.

138 *grossed just $11 million:* Box Office Mojo, accessed July 17, 2025.

138 *"You could feel":* Seal, "Seduced and Abandoned."

138 *"Who wouldn't fall":* "Rupert Murdoch on Wendi Deng: my 'very tough' wife," *Irish Independent*, July 21, 2011.

138 *"It would start with":* Seal, "Seduced and Abandoned."

138 *Wendi shoved:* Seal, "Seduced and Abandoned."

138 *Rupert broke vertebrae:* Gabriel Sherman, "Inside Rupert Murdoch's Succession Drama," *Vanity Fair*, May 2023.

139 *a "war zone":* Cook, "It Was Like a Warzone."

139 *James heard from:* Jonathan Mahler and Jim Rutenberg, "Rupert Murdoch's Empire of Influence," *New York Times*, April 3, 2019.

139 *Ailes told executives:* Gabriel Sherman, *The Loudest Voice in the Room* (New York: Random House, 2014), 389.

139 *"paved with betrayal":* John Cook, "Fox News's Favorite Investigator Was Paid to Smear Murdoch's Wife," *Gawker*, January 24, 2014.

139 *"Everybody was talking":* Sellers, "The Fortune interview: Rupert Murdoch."

139 *"Of course she's cheating":* Sarah Ellison, "Inside the Final Days of Roger Ailes's Reign at Fox News," *Vanity Fair*, September 22, 2016.

139 *The conversation with Lachlan:* Seal, "Seduced and Abandoned."

139 *In 2010, Rupert made Blair:* Henry Porter, "Tony Blair is godfather to Murdoch's daughter? Now it all makes sense," *Guardian*, September 5, 2011.

140 *But Wendi's own words:* Seal, "Seduced and Abandoned."

140 *Rupert, feeling betrayed:* Tim Fish, "Media Mogul Rupert Murdoch Buys Moraga Vineyards," *Wine Spectator*, May 13, 2013.

140 *Rupert filed for divorce:* Amy Chozick, "After 14 Years, Murdoch Files for Divorce from Third Wife," *New York Times*, June 13, 2013.

140 *Within a day:* Kim Masters, "Wendi Murdoch Blindsided by Divorce Filing (Analysis)," *Hollywood Reporter*, June 14, 2013.

140 *Both Wendi and Blair:* Seal, "Seduced and Abandoned."

140 *Lachlan and James stayed:* Seal, "Seduced and Abandoned."

140 *"He was always":* Sellers, "The Fortune interview: Rupert Murdoch."

140 *"I'm not thinking":* Gabriel Sherman, "How Rupert Murdoch Brought His Prodigal Son Back into the Fold," *New York*, March 27, 2014.

140 *Rupert corralled his sons:* Paddy Manning, *The Successor: The High-Stakes Life of Lachlan Murdoch* (Sutherland House Books, Kindle edition, 2022), 212.

141 *Then, a health crisis:* Sellers, "The Fortune interview: Rupert Murdoch."

141 *On March 11, 2014:* Manning, *The Successor*, 218.

141 *"Rupert has a":* Sherman, "How Rupert Murdoch Brought His Prodigal Son Back into the Fold."

142 *takeover offer for Time Warner:* Andrew Ross Sorkin and Michael J. de la Merced, "Murdoch Puts Time Warner on His Wish List," *New York Times*, July 16, 2014.

142 **Rupert withdrew his bid:** Michael J. de la Merced and Jonathan Mahler, "After Pushback, Murdoch Abandons Fox's Pursuit of Time Warner," *New York Times*, August 5, 2014.

142 **Liz divorced Freud:** Mark Sweney, "Matthew Freud and Elisabeth Murdoch to divorce," *Guardian*, October 6, 2014.

142 **she sent Ailes an apology:** Gabriel Sherman, "The Raging Septuagenarian," *New York*, February 26, 2010.

142 **A final straw:** Simon Walters, "Murdoch's son-in-law bans him from his 50th birthday party after mogul's claims about ex-wife Wendi and Blair," *Daily Mail*, December 14, 2013.

142 **The divorce got uglier:** Nick Craven and Amanda Perthen, "PR guru Matthew Freud hid secret love child from his wife Elisabeth Murdoch for TWO YEARS after affair with one of her friends," *Daily Mail*, December 19, 2015.

142 **"She's terrified of":** Sherman, "Inside Rupert Murdoch's Succession Drama."

142 **Rupert fell in love:** Account of Hall's courtship drawn from Sherman, "Inside Rupert Murdoch's Succession Drama."

143 **Rupert's New York headquarters:** Author visits to the building.

144 **The $4 billion:** Andrew Rice, "Revealed: The Inside Story of the Last WTC Tower's Design," *Wired*, June 9, 2015.

144 **It annoyed Lachlan:** Manning, *The Successor*, 225.

144 **Carey and Lachlan invited James:** McKay Coppins, "Growing Up Murdoch," *Atlantic*, February 14, 2025; author interviews.

144 **Lachlan lost $100 million:** Annie Davies, "Channel Ten: some of Australia's best known billionaires face massive losses," *Guardian*, October 10, 2017; Aaron Patrick and Max Mason, "Lachlan Murdoch's Ten decision will shape the television industry," *Australian Financial Review*, April 30, 2017.

145 **Lachlan's turnaround strategy:** Michael Idato, "Lachlan Murdoch's messy legacy at Ten," *Sydney Morning Herald*, March 27, 2014.

145 **Meanwhile, Rebekah Brooks:** Ravi Somaiya, "News Corp. Set to Rehire Rebekah Brooks, Acquitted Executive," *New York Times*, March 1, 2015.

145 **"I'm not going to":** Coppins, "Growing Up Murdoch"; author interviews.

145 **James flew to Indonesia:** Author interviews.

145 **a four-year contract:** Georg Szalai, "Fox Details Terms of James, Lachlan Murdoch's Four-Year Contracts," *Hollywood Reporter*, July 17, 2015.

145 **In December 2015:** Emily Steel, "National Geographic and Fox Form a Commercial Media Company," *New York Times*, September 9, 2015.

145 **Rupert and Lachlan killed:** Rick Rojas, "News Corp. and 21st Century Fox Won't Move to World Trade Center," *New York Times*, January 15, 2016.

145 **Like many Americans:** Trump-Murdoch relationship drawn from Sherman, "Inside Rupert Murdoch's Succession Drama"; Gabriel Sherman, "The Revenge of Roger's Angels," *New York*, September 2016.

146 **"I've been very nice":** Irin Carmon, "Megyn Kelly grills Donald Trump about sexism," MSNBC, August 6, 2015.

146 **"Leave him alone":** Sarah Ellison, "Roger, Over and Out," *Vanity Fair*, November 2016.

146 **After Lachlan quit:** Sherman, *The Loudest Voice in the Room*, 326.

146 **a "'fucking dope'":** Sherman, *The Loudest Voice in the Room*, xvi.

146   *"Tell me that mouth"*: Sherman, "The Revenge of Roger's Angels."

147   *So on July 6, 2016*: Michael M. Grynbaum and John Koblin, "Gretchen Carlson of Fox News Files Harassment Suit Against Roger Ailes," *New York Times*, July 6, 2016.

CHAPTER FOURTEEN

149   *Around 10:00 a.m. on*: Sarah Ellison, "Roger, Over and Out," *Vanity Fair*, November 2016.

149   *"I think you and I"*: Michael M. Grynbaum and John Koblin, "Gretchen Carlson of Fox News Files Harassment Suit Against Roger Ailes," *New York Times*, July 6, 2016.

150   *Rupert was in the air*: Gabriel Sherman, "The Revenge of Roger's Angels," *New York*, September 2016.

150   *The brothers emailed*: Ellison, "Roger, Over and Out."

150   *Three days later*: Gabriel Sherman, "6 More Women Allege That Roger Ailes Sexually Harassed Them," *New York*, July 9, 2016.

150   *"It's all bullshit!"*: Sherman, "The Revenge of Roger's Angels."

150   *Jeanine Pirro told*: Brian Flood, "Fox News' Jeanine Pirro Rips Gretchen Carlson's 'Absurd' Lawsuit," *TheWrap*, July 7, 2016.

151   *"a family man"*: Christina Dugan Ramirez, "Fox News' Elisabeth Hasselbeck and Ainsley Earhardt Come to Roger Ailes' Defense amid Sexual Harassment Claims," *People*, July 12, 2016.

151   *Then Megyn Kelly called*: Author interviews; Brian Stelter, *Hoax: Donald Trump, Fox News, and the Dangerous Distortion of Truth* (New York: Simon & Schuster, 2021), 68.

151   *On Monday, July 11*: Ellison, "Roger, Over and Out"; Gabriel Sherman, "Can the Murdochs Contain the Damage from the Ailes Investigation?" *New York*, July 13, 2016.

151   *"I think we know"*: Ellison, "Roger, Over and Out."

151   *James flew to Europe*: Sherman, "The Revenge of Roger's Angels."

152   *Rupert invited Ailes*: Sherman, "The Revenge of Roger's Angels."

152   *Ailes died after*: Clyde Haberman, "Roger Ailes, Who Built Fox News into an Empire, Dies at 77," *New York Times*, May 18, 2017.

152   *Rupert took the title*: Sherman, "The Revenge of Roger's Angels."

152   *Fox News paid Carlson*: Ellison, "Roger, Over and Out."

152   *James argued Fox needed*: Sherman, "The Revenge of Roger's Angels."

152   *Rupert and Lachlan opposed*: Gabriel Sherman, "Inside Rupert Murdoch's Succession Drama," *Vanity Fair*, May 2023.

152   *Lachlan was particularly*: Paddy Manning, *The Successor: The High-Stakes Life of Lachlan Murdoch* (Sutherland House Books, Kindle edition, 2022), 166; author interviews.

152   *"Rupert never liked Trump"*: Author interview.

153   *Hall despised Trump*: Sherman, "Inside Rupert Murdoch's Succession Drama."

153   *"I underestimated the"*: McKay Coppins, "Growing Up Murdoch," *Atlantic*, February 14, 2025.

153   *Trump more than*: Sherman, "Inside Rupert Murdoch's Succession Drama."

154   *neo-Nazi march*: Sherman, "Inside Rupert Murdoch's Succession Drama"; Coppins, "Growing Up Murdoch."

154   **sent an email:** David Smith, "'No good Nazis': James Murdoch criticises Trump over Charlottesville," *Guardian*, August 17, 2019.

154   **another run at Sky:** Christopher Williams, *The Battle for Sky: The Murdochs, Disney, Comcast and the Future of Entertainment* (Bloomsbury Publishing, Kindle edition, 2019), 171–72.

154   **Fox bid $14.8 billion:** Chad Bray, "21st Century Fox Reaches $14.8 Billion Deal for Remainder of Sky," *New York Times*, December 15, 2016.

154   **mobilized to block:** James Martinson, "Ed Miliband slams Sky bid: 'Murdoch has learned nothing,'" *Guardian*, December 20, 2016.

155   **"don't trust you":** "Why should Fox take over Sky? James Murdoch makes the case," Royal Television Society, accessed July 17, 2025.

155   **Two days before:** Ben Fritz and Amol Sharma, "How the Disney deal was done," *Australian*, December 16, 2017.

155   **James and Lachlan went:** Account of dispute over Disney deal drawn from Sherman, "Inside Rupert Murdoch's Succession Drama."

156   **Disney and Rupert announced:** Brooks Barnes, "Disney Makes $52.4 Billion Deal for 21st Century Fox in Big Bet on Streaming," *New York Times*, December 14, 2017.

156   **Each Murdoch child:** Natasha Bach, "Rupert Murdoch's Children Are in Line for a $2 Billion Payday—Each—When the Family Media Empire Breaks Up," *Fortune*, October 17, 2018.

156   **In 2019, Lachlan paid:** "Lachlan Murdoch's $150m Beverly Hillbillies mansion buy breaks record," Associated Press, December 2019.

156   **James took his:** Coppins, "Growing Up Murdoch."

156   **Liz launched a:** Pamela McClintock, "Elisabeth Murdoch, Stacey Snider Launch Content Venture with Jane Featherstone," *Hollywood Reporter*, October 1, 2019.

157   **Hall was asleep:** Sherman, "Inside Rupert Murdoch's Succession Drama."

157   **Rupert's PR team scrambled:** Gabriel Sherman, "Sources: Rupert Murdoch Was Hospitalized with a Serious Back Injury," *Vanity Fair*, January 17, 2018.

158   **When COVID-19 emerged:** Sherman, "Inside Rupert Murdoch's Succession Drama."

158   **Rupert and Hall quarantined:** Sherman, "Inside Rupert Murdoch's Succession Drama."

158   **Rupert was one of:** Sherman, "Inside Rupert Murdoch's Succession Drama."

CHAPTER FIFTEEN

161   **On election night 2020:** Gabriel Sherman, "Inside Rupert Murdoch's Succession Drama," *Vanity Fair*, May 2023.

161   **Jared Kushner called Rupert:** Martin Pengelly, "Murdoch told Kushner on election night that Arizona result was 'not even close,'" *Guardian*, July 28, 2022.

161   **"Frankly, we did win":** Christina Wilke, "Trump tries to claim victory even as ballots are being counted in several states," NBC News, November 4, 2020.

161   **"bullshit and damaging":** Steve Benen, "Newly exposed internal messages create a nightmare for Fox News," MSNBC, February 17, 2023.

161   **Rupert told Lachlan:** Sherman, "Inside Rupert Murdoch's Succession Drama."

162   **"Rupert called Trump":** Sherman, "Inside Rupert Murdoch's Succession Drama."

162   **"Do the executives understand":** "Defamation suit produced trove of Tucker Carlson messages," Associated Press, April 24, 2023.

162   *According to Dominion's:* Paul Fahri and Elahe Izadi, "Fox News sued by Dominion in $1.6 billion defamation case that could set new guardrails for broadcasters," *Washington Post*, March 26, 2021.

163   *"Maybe best to let":* Peter Baker, "Inside the Panic at Fox News After the 2020 Election," *New York Times*, March 4, 2023.

163   *Sammon retired in:* Jordan Williams, "Fox News's DC managing editor Bill Sammon to retire," The Hill, January 18, 2021; Margaret Sullivan, "Chris Stirewalt lost his job at Fox News. But he knows he was right," *Washington Post*, June 13, 2022.

163   *He told Hall:* Sherman, "Inside Rupert Murdoch's Succession Drama."

163   *like a passing storm:* Sherman, "Inside Rupert Murdoch's Succession Drama."

163   *Lachlan, meanwhile, fled:* Sherman, "Inside Rupert Murdoch's Succession Drama"; Paddy Manning, *The Successor: The High-Stakes Life of Lachlan Murdoch* (Sutherland House Books, Kindle edition, 2022), 349.

164   *"Jerry, sadly I've decided":* Email viewed by author.

164   *"Rupert and I never":* Sherman, "Inside Rupert Murdoch's Succession Drama"; Manning, *The Successor*, 349.

164   *Hall's relationship with Rupert's daughters:* Author interviews.

164   *Liz didn't like that:* Wolff, *The Fall: The End of Fox News and the Murdoch Dynasty* (New York: Henry Holt and Co., 2023), 153.

164   *During COVID lockdown:* Author interviews.

164   *"I was in the kitchen":* Text viewed by author.

164   *$200 million Montana ranch:* Luke O'Neil, "Rupert Murdoch buys $200m Montana cattle ranch from Koch family," *Guardian*, December 10, 2021.

164   *"Grace wanted to get":* Text viewed by author.

164   *On the flight back:* Author interviews.

164   *That week in London:* Emails viewed by author.

165   *Hall and Murdoch finalized:* Sherman, "Inside Rupert Murdoch's Succession Drama."

165   *Four months later:* Sherman, "Inside Rupert Murdoch's Succession Drama."

166   *Rupert proposed to Smith:* Sherman, "Inside Rupert Murdoch's Succession Drama."

166   *"Rupert just sat there":* Gabriel Sherman, "Tucker Carlson's Prayer Talk May Have Led to Fox News Ouster: 'That Stuff Freaks Rupert Out,'" *Vanity Fair*, April 25, 2023.

166   *By August 2023:* Jim Rutenberg, "Yep, He Did It Again," *New York Times*, March 7, 2024.

166   *"It's like the King":* Sherman, "Tucker Carlson's Prayer Talk May Have Led to Fox News Ouster: 'That Stuff Freaks Rupert Out.'"

167   *Rupert's black Range Rover:* Sherman, "Inside Rupert Murdoch's Succession Drama."

167   *Liz asked them to:* Author interviews.

167   *"If James felt so bad":* Author interview.

167   *He resigned in:* Michael M. Grynbaum and Edmund Lee, "James Murdoch Resigns from News Corp, Ending Role in Family Empire," *New York Times*, July 31, 2020.

167   *"Those outlets that":* Mattha Busby, "James Murdoch says US media 'lies' unleashed 'insidious forces,'" *Guardian*, January 16, 2021.

168   *Lachlan's future would be:* Alex Barker, "The Murdoch family trust: how the scions could battle for control," *Financial Times*, January 9, 2023.

168   *buy out his siblings:* Jonathan Mahler and Jim Rutenberg, "'You've Blown a Hole in the Family': Inside the Murdochs' Succession Drama," *New York Times Magazine*, February 13, 2025.

168   *"Lachlan gets fired"*: Manning, *The Successor*, 327.
168   *Lachlan blamed James:* Mahler and Rutenberg, "'You've Blown a Hole in the Family.'"
168   *"It was a harebrained"*: Author interview.
168   *The brothers' mutual suspicion:* Mahler and Rutenberg, "'You've Blown a Hole in the Family'"; Sherman, "Inside Rupert Murdoch's Succession Drama."
169   *a former McKinsey consultant:* McKay Coppins, "Growing Up Murdoch," *Atlantic*, February 14, 2025; Mahler and Rutenberg, "'You've Blown a Hole in the Family.'"
170   *"I'm sure James and Kathryn"*: Mahler and Rutenberg, "'You've Blown a Hole in the Family,'" *New York Times*, February 13, 2025.
171   *She had personally organized:* Wolff, *The Fall*, 110.

CHAPTER SIXTEEN

173   *"How fucking twisted"*: McKay Coppins, "Growing Up Murdoch," *Atlantic*, February 14, 2025.
173   *"The classic characterization"*: James Bates, "Watch the Money," *Los Angeles Times*, January 31, 1999.
174   *"You're just trying"*: Author interview.
174   *When Prue's birthday arrived:* Jonathan Mahler and Jim Rutenberg, "'You've Blown a Hole in the Family': Inside the Murdochs' Succession Drama," *New York Times Magazine*, February 13, 2025.
174   *More brazenly, Rupert:* Coppins, "Growing Up Murdoch."
174   *The trial's opening day:* Account of the trial drawn from Mahler and Rutenberg, "'You've Blown a Hole in the Family.'"
175   *On the cold and gusty:* Scott Sonner and Alex Veiga, "Army of lawyers flanks Murdoch family as court battle gets underway," *Australian Financial Review*, September 17, 2024.
175   *Rupert's PR adviser blanched:* Michael Wolff, *The Man Who Owns the News: Inside the Secret World of Rupert Murdoch* (Crown, Kindle edition, 2008), 271.
175   *Streisand was one of:* "Top Litigators in Los Angeles," *Los Angeles Business Journal*, August 22, 2018.
176   *"It was cowardice"*: Coppins, "Growing Up Murdoch."
176   *"There's no good hotels"*: Coppins, "Growing Up Murdoch."
179   *Gorman issued his decision:* Jonathan Mahler and Jim Rutenberg, "Rupert Murdoch Fails in Bid to Change Family Trust," *New York Times*, December 9, 2024.
180   *In early 2024:* Coppins, "Growing Up Murdoch."
180   *"James thought McKay's book"*: Author interview.

INDEX

INDEX

INDEX